THE HIST

The History of Ishmael

PART I

Ian Smale

KINGSWAY PUBLICATIONS
EASTBOURNE

First published 1988
Reprinted 1991

Front cover photo: David Thatcher

British Library Cataloguing in Publication Data

Smale, Ian
The history of Ishmael.
Pt. 1
1. Christian life—1960–
I. Title
248.4 BV4501.2

ISBN 0–86065–617–9

Printed in Great Britain for
KINGSWAY PUBLICATIONS LTD
1 St Anne's Road, Eastbourne, E Sussex BN21 3UN by
Clays Ltd, St. Ives plc.
Typeset by Watermark, Crostwight, Norfolk

To Joseph, Daniel and Suzy.
This book is your roots. Learn from my successes
and failures and go on to achieve more
for the kingdom of God than I have.
Remember, commit yourselves to God
care for your families,
cherish the church,
and be concerned for the lost.

All my love, Dad.

Contents

Acknowledgements

Special thanks to Irene for spending many devoted hours poring over this manuscript, typing in and correcting the one or two mistakes I made while writing it....

To Mary Harman for her wonderful donation of a computer, without which I would never have managed to get this book into print.

Also to Joseph for his patience in teaching us how to use it.

Thanks to Mike Morris , David and Heather Thatcher, and Mum and Dad for reading it through and the many other thousands of people who have been a tremendous influence in my life but due to lack of space are not mentioned in this book.

Foreword

> Therefore, since we are surrounded by a great cloud of witnesses, let us throw off everything that hinders and the sin that so easily entangles, and let us run with perseverance the race marked out for us. Let us fix our eyes on Jesus, the author and perfecter of our faith, who for the joy set before him endured the cross, scorning its shame, and sat down at the right hand of the throne of God.
>
> *Hebrews 12:1–2*

To have known, loved, served, cared for, trusted and shared the past sixteen years of my life with Ishmael as his wife, mother of his three children, help-meet, critic, confidante and best friend, it has been beyond all my expectations of what God can do through a man and in a marriage. They have been years of recurring excitement, devastation, elation, adventure, tears, joy, hard work and abundant blessings. In fact, how do you live with a hurricane and survive?

We have been through so much together that probably the ordinary, normal person would find hard to believe. Through it all I have clung firmly to my unshakable belief that we are in this together for God.

To me Ishmael, or Ian as I affectionately call him, has been the most loving, caring, patient, wise, impetuous, hilarious, gentle but strong, godly husband I could ever wish for. I have seen him broken before the Lord, battered by the enemy, but always a tower of strength in his faith in his Lord to come back up again fighting. He is spurred on by his inexhaustible ideas and aspirations to reclaim people for God by whatever means and gifts he has chosen to precipitate upon him. This has proved to be the strength of our relationship, inseparable in our love for God and for each other.

Most people would perhaps think because of his itinerant role that his ministry is one of glamour, travelling the world. Many fail to see the cost of leaving a wife and children behind. To Ishmael this has been the most costly sacrifice of all. We believe firmly in the biblical principle laid down in 1 Timothy 5 verse 8, 'If you cannot take care of your own family, you are worse than the heathen.' I have known him travel hundreds of miles through the night and still get up at the crack of dawn to see the children and hear their news. He is a workaholic, believing too much sleep is a waste of time. I have known him survive on just a couple of hours. He is the only person I know that can pack forty-eight hours into twenty-four and make it seem like five minutes.

Our children respect, honour and love him dearly; he is a continual bundle of energy and fun to them and often an embarrassment in the right sense of the word. They have shared our laughter and tears. He is honest and loyal to his friends whom I honour; they have been instrumental in discipling us, and knowing them has enriched our lives. Reading between the lines many will be able to identify with the experiences in this book. Those in leadership particularly will know that to cope with success is often harder than failure. But be encouraged.

When we started out on this adventure together, I knew my calling from God. 'Serve me with all your heart, take care of this man, support him, love him, honour and obey him, be a comfort to him, be aware of his needs, minister to him and be strong.' Throughout these pages, the desire of Ishmael's heart and mine is that we all fulfil our calling for and through our Lord Jesus, for our children and for the generation to come. To God be all the praise and glory.

IRENE SMALE

1

Wakey, Wakey

Wakey, wakey, wake up my soul
Wakey, wakey, wake up my harp and lyre
And I will wake up the sun.

The date was August 10th 1949 and the location was a nursing home called St Brendon's, which was very close to Clifton Suspension Bridge – and Bristol zoo. Dorothy Irene Smale was lying down taking it easy in the maternity ward just minutes away from giving birth to her second child. John, the devoted father-to-be, felt having babies was very much a woman's job so he continued his work down at the Port of Bristol Authority – no doubt prematurely celebrating the new arrival, as it was one of his jobs as the Dues Inspector to test the rum. Meanwhile, back at the nursing home, the excitement was building up. You see, in the old days it was the custom that the family doctor was the privileged person to attend and oversee the birth, but as fate would have it, our doctor was not feeling well. Yes, he'd gone to see a doctor. Neither Dorothy nor her offspring were very amused when the news reached them that the birth was going to be delayed for six hours (this was a new arrival in Maternity, not a late arrival at Paddington) and that she was to be given special injections to stop the contractions. But after nine months of togetherness, who was going to argue about a few more hours?

In the fullness of time the great event happened. Both our family doctor and I clocked in at about the same time, both of us looking rather red and embarrassed. But that didn't last for long. With shouts of 'You've got a bouncing baby boy' coming from one corner, and me all set to pursue my recording career with my first screams from the other, our delayed arrivals seemed of little importance as everyone's attention seemed now to have homed in on me. I was just lying there, no doubt loving every minute of being the main attraction.

Mind you, I wasn't the only local attraction. Taking place in Bristol at exactly this time was the hanging of an acid bath murderer just a couple of miles down the road in Horfield Prison. So, sadly for me, he stole the front page coverage in the local newspaper the following day. Needless to say, I sacked my press agent after that.

My first few days were quite traumatic as a suitable name had to be found for me. For some reason my parents decided I wasn't to be called John after my father, nor had they had any heavenly message like 'Call this child Ishmael'. Eventually all agreed that I looked a bit of an Ian Stuart, so with this handle I was christened.

Then came the time to start growing up, which was greatly helped by the presence of my black-and-white cat, Lucky, and my older sister, Heather. I wouldn't say that my parents were superstitious, but my greatest comfort in times of need was 'Lucky Heather'. My big sister and I were inseparable, and we are still very close today.

I never liked school. I always thought that infants' school was a waste of time as all I seemed to do was play with building-blocks and marbles. That would have been all right if I was to have a future in building bowling alleys.

Mind you, school was not all bad – it did bring out the romantic side in me. I well remember how, at the ripe old age of six, I kissed my first girl. Her name was Mary, and I must confess that the main reason I liked her was because her dad owned a record shop. Of course in those days they were all those massive 78s, but recorded music meant a lot to me even all those years ago and set me dreaming of being a future Bing Crosby (he was the Freddy Mercury of the day). One of the first records I invested in was 'Tubby the Tuba', which was quite prophetic of both my future ministry and shape.

At this stage of my development I never did anything wrong or right, as I had imaginary friends who would achieve these for me. When things went right it was Africa and her baby Apricot who did it, and when wrong, it was none other than that arch-villain Manquin Hoo. I never particularly wanted to receive credit or correction – it was much easier just to pass the buck.

I had a lot of time for my Grandma, as she loved cuddling me. I was also very fond of my Uncle Eric, Aunty Joan, and my only male cousin, David. Whenever we went to their house we were guaranteed to have fun, and they always made it clear that they were as pleased to see us as they were the grown-ups. Uncle Eric would drive us all over the place in his massive Ford Consul, and he would never grumble about all the singing and shouting coming from the noisy bunch in the back seat. The highlight of our visits to Uncle Eric was when he would walk over to his cupboard after lunch and bring out a large tin crammed full of every variety of chocolate bar. From that day to this I became totally addicted to those irresistible brown chunks of sheer ecstasy. Self-control was going to have to come at a later date.

Throughout my childhood I really only had one ambition – I wanted to be a cowboy. I would spend many happy hours playing by myself and, because I have been gifted with a very vivid imagination, I didn't just play at being a cowboy, I actually *was* a cowboy. You would rarely see me without my hat on, making clicking noises with my teeth, and pretending to ride a horse. I'm convinced that is why even now my ears stick out and I am bow-legged. It always amazed me that the cowboys always beat the Indians. Of course nowadays we would say it is racist, but in those days I just felt sorry for the Indians. It was strange that my heroes such as the Lone Ranger, Bronco Layne and various other hombres with names more associated with horses than with humans never seemed to get dirty let alone wounded or shot. In saying this then it would come as no surprise to you that I imitated my heroes in every way, except knocking back the whiskey. I also had this very secure feeling that, with my trusty gun strapped by my side, I was invincible. Well, that's what I'd been taught, hadn't I?

One hot, dry Saturday afternoon, Heather and I decided we'd mosey on down to the OK allotment, which just happened to join onto our back garden. As Heather walked and I rode my imaginary white stallion, Trigger, we happened to spy this mean little kid half hiding behind his fence in his back garden. Mark was a trifle strange to put it mildly, and today was no exception. While most sensible kids would play with their toy cars, soldiers or cowboy outfits, Mark would always find some odd bit of rubbish which fascinated him for hours, like some latter-day conservationist. Today he was examining the unusual phenomenon of half a house brick.

Having pulled my trusty steed to a halt, it took me no time at all to enter into an intelligent conversation with him. The subject, being of my own choosing, was, 'I bet you wouldn't dare throw that brick at my head' to which he kept replying that he would. I, of course, had no fear as I knew that we cowboys were a protected species, so I kept on taunting him till he politely did as I asked. I never knew such a dumb little kid could be such a good shot. I just stood there amazed – I didn't even fall off my horse. I felt no tears welling up; all I remember was touching the top of my head and feeling all this wet stuff pouring out, and watching Heather who was crying and screaming. As I staggered back to our garden I even made a joke about it, that's how certain I was that I could never be hurt. For as I said before, these things don't happen to cowboys, do they?

Needless to say, a cracked skull didn't do any permanent damage (this point is not open to debate). Nowadays I find that by having my hair fairly long, I don't have to answer the question, 'How did you get that dent in your head, or has it always been that funny shape?'

Apart from the head case incident, I didn't suffer much in those early days. Mind you, I did have one recurring ailment that kept plaguing me, and it always happenened when I was trying to do something that required extreme concentration and manual exertion. (Nowadays that would be the equivalent of me trying to put an MFI chest of drawers together.) My first symptom was a nasty touch of the hot-and-bothereds, and this would be rapidly followed by an outbreak of huge water blisters all over my body. I hated the look of these, and I also hated pain, but they had to go, as I found it rather embarrassing that my appearance was not dissimilar to that of the underside of an octopus's arm. I discovered an instant cure to my problem, however, which involved covering the offending protrusion with a handkerchief and whacking it with a twelve inch ruler. I was very much for the short sharp treatment – a rubbing-salt-in-mouth-ulcers sort of person. You may not find my medical expertise recommended by doctors, but there again I never discovered my singing voice by listening to opera.

Now I must confess my spiritual progress was nowhere near as advanced as my romantic, musical or even medical attainments. My dad and Heather enjoyed going along to the local high Anglican church, whereas Mum and I, being rather more non-conformist, were already being prepared for the house-church movement as we preferred to stay at home. I was taught that the Sabbath was not so much the day of rest, but more the day of dress, and I couldn't stand it. Each Sunday morning, rain or shine, arctic conditions or heat wave, there at the bottom of my bed waiting for me to clamber into it was my grey suit. Now, this was no ordinary attire, but a special religious garment that, like sack-cloth in the Bible, was only to be worn for discomfort and to remind me of what day we were celebrating. It was 100% itch-guaranteed, and the double-seated trousers constantly made it look like I had sat in something that I shouldn't have. To put it another way, it was up to scratch and it kept me humble.

My family was not gifted with great intellectual ability, but there was a fair amount of talent floating about among my relatives. My Uncle Allan was a design consultant for

Wills tobacco, and was one of the creators of a little character known as Woodbine Willy who grew to be as popular and addictive as the product he was selling (that was Willy by the way, not my Uncle Allan). But Uncle Allan had a much more exciting future lined up for him than just being a baccy boffin. It began when he was approached by a missionary society to design a Christian exhibition called 'The Way'. Uncle had to do masses of research because C.T. Studd, Gladys Aylwood and the many other Christian heroes who were to be represented had very little to do with tobacco or Woodbine Willy. Fortunately his daughter, Moira, was a great help to him as she had just become a Christian. So what with her whispering in one ear, Uncle Allan having to read the Bible himself to get his facts right, plus the Holy Spirit speaking to his heart, it's not surprising that he soon became a committed Christian, followed shortly by the rest of his family and even some of his Woodbine work-mates.

My mum and dad didn't know what to make of this strange experience that their relatives were going through, and what made them even more confused was when this little group of hot gospellers all felt God was telling them to sell up, leave Wills and Bristol, and move to a big house called Sea Court, which could be found with great difficulty in a coastal village called Goring in Sussex. Before we could say Arrivederci they had all deserted us and gone, lock, stock, but no barrel!

My parents would not have appreciated the fact, but the prayer hotline from Sussex to Bristol was kept very busy over the next few months. It wasn't long before we were invited to spend a holiday by the sea with our newly committed Christian cousins in their cosily cramped Christian community (try saying that with a mouthful of peanuts), and of course we accepted the invitation for various reasons. My mother accepted because she loved a good debate. The subject made no difference to her, she would argue with the best of them. Who could be better than her brother, poor Uncle Allan, with his new-found faith? I've inherited a lot from Mum.

Dad, on the other hand, was completely different. He didn't like confrontation at all, much preferring the quiet life. His main hobby was gardening, and his allotment proved to be a perfect sanctuary to hide away from the important issues that Mum was in earnest to discuss. As well as cooking and eating he was quite good at carpentry too, and this is what attracted him to our south coast vacation, as they were designing and constructing yet another exhibition where his skills would be invaluable. He also knew that by being adequately armed with hammer, nails and 'blu tac' he was guaranteed to make so much noise that he wouldn't have to talk to anyone. As for Heather and me, we just wanted to be by the seaside.

On arrival it wasn't just a few pilgrims that welcomed us but a newly established company called the Christian Publicity Organisation (CPO). With all my previous experience of the wild west, I could see that these were no bunch of cowboys but a team of professionals who knew what they were up to. However, our first day in sunny Sussex was totally predictable: we kids enjoyed playing with our cousins on the beach, Dad was using hammer and nails out in the garden, and Mum and Uncle Allan were going hammer and tongs in the lounge.

On our first evening, which happened to be a Saturday, we were told there was going to be a meeting in the house. This threw poor old Dad who was under the impression that it was wrong for anything religious to take place unless it was on Sundays. Anyway, as we sat in the lounge all sorts of strange people joined us – Baptists, Brethren, Methodists. But the strangest sight was an old boy who arrived with a large suit-case. As we watched he opened up his case and brought out a squeeze-box. I'd only heard of sailors using these, so when he was introduced as a missionary I automatically assumed that he was some sort of seafarer.

We were all seated in a big circle, which made me think of ring-a-ring-o'-roses, and as folks introduced themselves they each gave a little speech about their life history and how ultimately they had become Christians. Mum and Dad gave this bit a miss, but they were quite surprised that all these mini-preachers seemed so cheerful as they were always under the impression that religion and happiness were as opposite as a pig and a parson. Then the musical missionary got up to do his bit. We knew a few hymns, but this chap just played short little tunes which he called choruses (I wondered who'd pinched the verses). To our amazement, while he played ring-a-ring-o'roses actually took off: people sang, jumped around and even clapped their hands – *during* the song instead of at the end of it. Everyone really looked like they were enjoying themselves. What a strange meeting, what a strange holiday, what a strange year 1957 was going to be.

The rest of the holiday week continued as it had started, except by now the Holy Spirit was clearly speaking to Mum and Dad, so much so that Dad was biting his nails instead of hammering them, and Mum was getting hammered as Uncle Allan was trying to nail her down. You see, Mum had felt that Christianity was only for people who had problems – and she didn't have any, and Dad felt that he already was a Christian because he went to church each Sunday. But now, after having the words 'repentance' and 'being born again' explained to them, they both realised that unless they did something about what they had heard they had more chance of meeting the man on the moon than of going to heaven.

It was quietly one evening, before going to bed, that Mum and Dad prayed to God, confessing that they hadn't matched up to what he wanted them to be, and asking him to come and live in their lives, because from that time onwards they just wanted to live for him.

Now, this prayer had a special significance for Dad. When he was a tank commander in Italy in 1943, he was blown up by a land-mine. Lying on the battlefield very seriously injured with twenty-seven major wounds, he had prayed that if God would take him back to England and allow him to walk and work again he would do whatever God wanted him to. And now, fourteen year's later, God was reminding him of that promise and was asking him if he would really be willing to leave home, a good secure job, bewildered parents and relations, and disturb Heather's education as she was just about to take her eleven-plus examination. But that wasn't all. The cream on the cake was, would he be obedient enough not only to move down and live with these people but also, just as the early church had done in Acts chapter 2, would he be happy about giving them all his money, furniture and personal treasures? Dad was always a man of his word, and he said yes.

When home time came and we were being driven to the station, Uncle Allan sensed that my parents' lives had been stirred up. He told them to just go back and forget all about it, knowing full well, I'm sure, that they never could.

Dad was very quiet all the way home as he pondered over all these new things that he had experienced, not realising that his life would never be the same again. When we arrived at our front gate he looked up and saw that his father had installed a brand new ITV aerial in our house while we had been away. As Dad saw it he knew that we would not be here to see it working.

Life changed rapidly from that time onwards. We would have the Bible read to us regularly, we would pray together as a family, and we would even have to say a prayer before we were allowed to start eating our meals. Mum and Dad joined the local Baptist church, and I joined the Sunday school. While they enjoyed learning more about God, I enjoyed aggravating all the little girls and getting picture stickers which entitled me to a free Bible once my book was full. A sort of Christian Green Shield stamps incentive.

Dad was now certain that we should be moving to Sussex, and even Mum agreed to submit to his guidance. The local minister wasn't quite so convinced as it was beyond his understanding why following God meant moving to Sussex. My grandmother also took the news pretty badly, feeling devastated at the prospect of losing yet another member of her family to the South Coast Bible drain.

Even Uncle Allan wanted them to check their guidance as he wasn't sure how they could fit four more people plus a cat into Sea Court without changing its name to Paddington Station.

The fact that everyone was trying to put us off going was just the confirmation Dad needed that it was time to be up and off, even if it did mean dossing down in a stable once we arrived. Mum was duly convinced a little later on. At a time when no one was buying houses, someone saw a little 'For sale' notice that she had scribbled in the front window and immediately bought our house. Even Heather and I were so sure that we should be moving, and were so caught up in this whole new lifestyle, that we too drew out all our money from our Post Office savings accounts and, without any pressure, were looking forward to handing over all our worldly wealth as well.

On bonfire night, while people were enjoying blowing up Guy Fawkes for the umpteenth year, the Smale family dropped a bombshell on all around them. They packed up their bags, cowboy suits, records, and other vital necessities (even Lucky the cat, who bearing in mind where we were going, was a cert for a name change), said farewell to the security that good old Bristol had once offered, and set off south on what was to be the start of a new and exciting adventure.

2

Do Not Store Up Treasures on Earth

Do not store up treasures on earth
Where the moth can destroy
Where the rust can decay
Where the thief can break in
And steal things away.
But store up for yourselves treasures in heaven
Where your treasure is that's where your heart is.

It was strange leaving our three-bedroomed terraced house to arrive at our new home which, to a little lad like myself, resembled a great mansion similar to the one I had been taught that Jesus was preparing for me 'way beyond the blue'. Our first task was to unpack a very bad-tempered Lucky from the tuck hamper we had used to transport him in. He showed his usual total lack of interest as he was introduced to his new surroundings. On reflection our Lucky seemed more like a wild cat than a domestic one, he would growl instead of purr, and when anyone showed him any sort of affection his immediate response was to take a swipe at them. All these symptoms pointed to the fact that he was suffering from an acute case of rejection, but no one particularly felt led or brave enough to pluck up the courage to get close to him to give him the ministry that he so obviously required.

Next on the agenda was our introduction to our new extended family. Having heard how Jesus had reproduced a few loaves and fishes, I now saw how my relations were also being multiplied at just about the same rate. I knew of course my Uncle Allan, Aunty Margaret, and my cousins Moira and Lyn, but then came Uncle John, Aunty Jean, and their little two-year-old daughter, Hilary, Uncle Brian, and Uncle Tom Cobbley and all. I had no recollection of the latter half of my list as actually being part of our family tree, but it was confirmed to me that they were when they welcomed my Mum and Dad by calling them 'brother' and 'sister'. I've always had trouble working out family relationships ever since.

Once inside we were shown to our quarters. To say it was cosy would be a vast understatement. All that was available was one tiny room hardly big enough to swing our aforementioned cat, Lucky, around in, and another room which Lucky could have just about managed to swing us around in. The plan was that Mum and Dad would have the bigger room, and Heather and I would take it in turns to intrude on their privacy and share with them. The alternative was the luxury of sleeping in our own detached cupboard.

Still, who cares about being somewhat cramped? I've always been an outdoor person, and the garden was superb. I knew it would take me years to explore it fully, and even after all that time I couldn't be sure that I would have discovered all the secret hideouts and got rid of all the lurking Injuns.

I was also introduced to a rather snobby, aggressive game which involved covering the grass with metal hoops and sticking a miniature totem pole in the middle. The players then got hold of a couple of enormous wooden hammers and started bashing overgrown cricket balls of different colours as hard as they could through the hoops or, failing that, whacking their opponent's ball as far into the flower beds as was humanly possible. This gentle art was called croquet, but I preferred to pronounce it crockett (after my hero, Davy, of course). As life was so claustrophobic, this game proved to be a fantastic tonic for getting rid of pent-up pressures, when shouting, screaming, swearing and fist fights would not really have been appropriate, bearing in mind what our little community stood for.

Weekdays always commenced by rising early. We all had our household chores which had to be done before breakfast (I'm sure this idea came from the old hymn 'There's a work for Jesus none but you can do'). Then came the bit I loathed the most, affectionately known as 'family prayers'. It was as if someone had been programmed so that, the moment the last piece of toast had been ravaged from the toast-rack and the last gulp of tea had been audibly sounded, he stood up, ceremoniously marched over to the wall, and with great reverence took down, wait for it, the Keswick Block. Now for the uninitiated, the Keswick Block was a small pad stuck onto a red cardboard backing. Each morning someone would tear a sheet off the pad and uncover a verse of Scripture which would bless us for the day. Alongside the Scripture verse was a short word of explanation.

Now, all the grown-ups around the table may have benefited from this, but it was certainly not written with us kids in mind. To start with, the scripture was taken from the Authorised Version and I never was a 'Thee's and Thou's' sort of person, and the explanation seemed like an ongoing competition to see which expositor knew the most long words. Sadly, it didn't end there. No, this was just the beginning. There followed what seemed an eternity of discussion, sometimes over a point raised, and at other times over a point that maybe should have been raised. This went on till either the subject or those around the table had become exhausted. Needless to say, it was usually the former of the two that tended to dry up first. Finally, family prayers concluded with what was called 'a time of open prayer'. Iwas convinced that all this meant was that people knew how to open in prayer, but certainly didn't know when to finish.

On the financial side of things, although no one was forced to pool their belongings, we as a family were happy to give what little we had. At first we considered investing it in another property which may have given us all a bit more breathing space. But God made it very clear to us that he wanted a Christian newspaper printed that would be the same size as the *Daily Mirror* and as readable, but instead of presenting bad news, it was to be a good-news paper. Its main aim was to put across the good news of Jesus in a way that Mr Average could not only understand, but hopefully also enjoy reading. After much prayer and planning, the then revolutionary evangelistic newspaper *Challenge* was born.

While such important developments were taking place, even I had to learn that life was more than just playing games. I still had the dreaded school to help me waste away my daylight hours. A new school would be difficult, not because I found it hard to make friends, but because I had the terrible handicap of the surname 'Smale'. I could never understand why people simply couldn't call me by the name I was christened with. Why did they have to vary it to give everyone else a laugh but leave me feeling thoroughly embarrassed? These variations ranged from 'smelly' to 'smiler' and from 'snail' to 'smell'. There was many a day when I wished that God would change my name to Smith. This handicap had one advantage though: I couldn't help feeling sorry for anyone else who was having a tough time, and it would often come as second nature to me to befriend the kid in the class whom no one liked or people made fun of.

As much as my parents agreed with my theology on this point, they were understandably a little worried about some of the weirdos I was mixing with and the bad habits a very impressionable child from a Christian community might pick up. One such friend that I had acquired from my 'help the underdog campaign' was a policeman's son who could not go into a sweet shop without bringing out pocketfuls of plunder. My job was to feel guilty for both of us, extract the stolen items, and go back and give it to the somewhat amazed shopkeeper. The problem was that the shopkeepers were now keeping their eyes on me as much as the villains because of my unusual honesty.

Back in the big house major adjustments were taking place as everyone was desperately trying to learn more about God, while at the same time, whether they wanted to or not, having to learn more about each other as well. I was also amazed to discover that some of these young Christians, who had given up everything to follow God, were still enjoying a crafty cigarette. It obviously took a little while for habits of a lifetime to die.

In the evenings all sorts of side-shows were arranged for us kids, as the idea was not just to deal with the spiritual side of one's personality, but also to deal with the part, which sounds more like something from a fibre diet, called the 'whole man'. I remember a very posh lady coming in to speak to us on how to sing properly. Now, I'm afraid that one of my weaknesses is that if I get the giggles nothing can stop me. This happened to be one of those evenings. It was coming up to Christmas, and the lady told us all to listen as she taught us how to sing 'In the bleak mid-winter'. Well, when she started wailing with what on reflection must have been a trained operatic voice, I felt a fit of giggles coming on, and although I did manage to keep my lips closed I could not stop myself shaking. Determined not to be interrupted she glared at me and tried to continue, but by now I was in such a state of shakes that I found it impossible to keep my lips held closely together which allowed a sound to seep through which can only really be described as a rather rude noise.

This made her stop rather abruptly, and turning to me she informed me that it was my turn to perform. With great difficulty I managed to manoeuvre my mouth into the right position to get my first note out, and with all the concentration I could manage I began to sing 'In the bleak mid-winter'. But try as hard as I could, I kept getting my Ms and Ws mixed up, and it kept coming out as 'In the bleak wid-minter'. This was all too much for me, and I just collapsed on the floor in uncontrollable laughter. This was the last straw for the poor lady who got up and walked out, never to be seen by me again. Here beginneth and endeth my only voice training lesson. I didn't feel that my voice had improved much, but I felt my giggling abilities were now near perfection.

On the subject of music, anything apart from Christian

songs and the odd classical piece was considered worldly. There were no televisions and only one radio, but as there was always so much going on, no one seemed to show withdrawal symptoms at not getting their daily shot of canned entertainment. However, there were at least two unsanctified folk who broke the rules. One was my now teenage cousin Moira, and the other was yours truly.

Now, Moira had managed to secure from somewhere both a portable record-player and a boyfriend called Rodney, and together they somehow smuggled in the 'fab', new and 'rave' (everything was 'fab' or 'rave' in this era), which happened to be the seven-inch, forty-five RPM record. In came those flexible frisbys with strange names like Parlophone, Decca, Mercury and Columbia at the top, and even stranger names like Tommy Steele, Terry Dene, Buddy Holly, Elvis Presley, Cliff Richard and even a character called Wee Willy Harris written underneath. To make way for the new, out went poor old Tubby who had blown his last tuba. Even Davy Crockett had crossed his final frontier. These had now become 'square'. By that I mean they were still round but ... oh, you know what I mean.

Moira continued her rebellion by sneaking in some magazines containing photos of these rock n' rollers, cutting them out and sticking them in a scrapbook which she then lent to me. I spent hours gazing in wonder and amazement at my new-found heroes, all the time trying to picture myself in denim drainpipes, drapes, creepers and with a quiff and long sideburns. From that time on, the days of the once all-important cowboy outfit were numbered.

None of the adults made a big fuss about our cultural compromises. They knew it was all part of growing up, and besides there were far more important things to consider. I don't know if you realise this, but every young Christian goes through a period of eschatological escapism. (Older Christians may become similiarly detached from real life by watching James Bond type films.) Now, we all know that the 'doctrine of the things to come' is very important, but with young Christians for a short period of time it tends to become all important. I remember one evening when the adults were going through this phase. They had spent a long time considering the second coming of the Lord Jesus, how he would come and, once all the prophecies had come to pass, when he would come. After a study like this everyone naturally gets hyper-excited.

As they all went to bed, it was Uncle Brian's turn to stoke up the solid fuel boiler for the night, but to his horror he discovered that the fire looked as if it had gone out. He peered in through the top door and all he saw was blackness, but he didn't realise that the blackness was not dying embers but the cuttings from Uncle Allan's hair. Thinking that the fire needed slight rejuvenation, he rushed out to the garage, found a tin of paraffin, and without thinking twice chucked the whole lot onto the smouldering, hair-covered fuel. It will come as no surprise to anyone with any type of scientific or industrial background that what resulted was an enormous bang followed by a strange crashing sound which was amplified all over the house, if not all over the world. But that was when things really took off. Only seconds later the scene of the catastrophe was packed with praising, pyjama-clad people, prancing excitedly around the kitchen table with their hands high in the air, positively convinced that the thunderous sound that they had all heard was the last trumpet preparing the way for the Lord Jesus' return to earth.

Uncle Brian, however, had sadly missed out on all the celebrating as he was in the front garden examining what had once been the tall chimney-stack but was now scattered all over the driveway. The feeling of elation being shared by those in the kitchen soon changed, and they came down to earth with an almost bigger bang than they had heard earlier, as their eyes suddenly focused on the ceiling which was covered in black hair. Poor Lucky, what a way to go – by premature cremation, barbequed in the prime of his life. He was such a nice cat.

Uncle Brian returned into the house and in no time at

all he had told everyone the whole story, thus letting the cat out of the bag. Uncle Allan's hair was scraped off the ceiling and a 'resurrected' Lucky put in an appearance with an expression on his face which simply said, you won't get rid of me that easily. I don't know what disappointed everyone most, that fact that it wasn't the second coming or the fact that it wasn't Lucky on the ceiling.

Sunday was a very long day, only fractionally better than Bristol because I didn't have to wear my itchy suit, but it would have been considered a sin to wear jeans. To balance out this minor revolutionary change in the Sabbath fashion scene was a minimum attendance of three church meetings on Sunday. In the morning we attended our local Evangelical Free church. I was always ushered out into the Sunday school during the singing of the second hymn. I was quite a self-conscious, shy person, so I never enjoyed the big, second-hymn procession as I always thought everyone was looking at me.

Once in our shabby little back hall however, I came into my own. I was not academically thick, but I was academically lazy, I never felt the need to work hard at subjects that I had no interest in, and in exams I never particularly felt the need to show others how brilliant I was or, as in most subjects, wasn't. But here in this hall everything changed because the one thing that I was interested in was hearing stories from the Bible. As the teachers would talk about Jesus, King David, the Acts of the Apostles and Samson – in fact, any story with plenty of action in it – I would soak it up like ink on blotting paper.

In the afternoon I went to the Congregational church Sunday school. This had two main attractions. The first was that I was not only able to learn more Bible stories, but we also had Bible tests, and because I had this insatiable interest in the subject, my ego was boosted when I got good results. Secondly, on the bank outside the hall there was long grass and a pile of old sacks and bits of wood. Straight after the meeting, the minister's son and I would rush out, lift up the rubbish, and catch lizards, slow worms, and all sorts of other little slimy creatures and take them home as pets, which would always thrill my mum.

In the evening it was either back to the Evangelical Free, or travelling round with Dad and others watching them take meetings in all sorts of places. What made this so good was that even though I was still shy, I loved it when they let me pray, do a reading, or choose a hymn, in fact anything that gave me a chance to stand up front and contribute. As yet, although people had taught me about how to become a Christian, it had not really appealed to me. That was until someone told me about being 'born again' and actually getting a second birthday. Now, I found that very appealing as I loved my birthday and all the excitement that surrounded it.

My biggest worry, though, was that I would forget which day my second birthday was on, so to make it easy I decided that I would become a Christian on August the tenth, which of course was the same date as my first birthday, so then I would have twice the fun and also never forget the date. Whether or not this was Spirit-led or just downright unbiblical I will leave you to work out, but I looked forward to the tenth, which just so happened to be on a Sunday. As I said I would, I committed myself to the Lord Jesus there in the Evangelical Free church Sunday school. And I knew that I was now a Christian and would have no fear in telling all my friends exactly what had happened.

One of the things that convinced me that Jesus was alive and powerful was the miracles I was seeing. Contrary to public opinion the community was not rich, in fact there were times when we were broke. When it started it was agreed that each adult would receive two pounds a week and each child one, so apart from the family allowance provided by the government, this had to pay for the individual's clothes, food, and pocket money. This lasted for about a week and then the funds dried up. We then realised that God didn't want us to have our own little separate food supplies. He really wanted us to live as a community.

From that time on God always provided. We once

found an enormous piece of meat left anonymously on our doorstep, and at another time a local church gave us all the left-overs from their harvest festival, thus keeping us in fresh vegetables for weeks. We never went without.

It must be made clear at this point that laziness would never have been tolerated. We lived on the premise that if you don't work you don't eat, and even though much time was spent in prayer and Bible study, this was outside normal working hours. Both the men and women were busy either printing, cooking, designing, gardening, photographing, washing, cleaning or collating numerous booklets, leaflets and newspapers both for our own use and the church at large. Of course, there were always a few minutes to spare, so we filled this time up by delivering *Challenge* to every house in our area. If there were any more minutes left over we'd get involved with all sorts of other projects that were happening on a national level. What proved to be of great importance here was our involvement with the MPs Sir Cyril Black and John Henderson, and encouraging other MPs in the House of Commons' Christian Fellowship. A priority for any final second left (or more to the point, any energy left) was to troop off to the local recreation ground and test out each other's grace and good sportsmanship with a game of football.

Talking about recreational activities, it may be worth mentioning my romantic involvements. At this stage of my life they were by no means a major event. It seemed as if I was the only available lad, except for Uncle Brian, surrounded by the fairer sex, and that all the new recruits to the community seemed to have been blessed with daughters rather than sons, so the choice was like trying to find a rosy apple in an over-ripe orchard.

The more people heard of CPO, the more people wanted to join us. We realised that Sea Court had a limited lifespan purely because space was running out. We had to keep reminding ourselves that God was making us into saints not sardines. Around this time a young man called Uncle Philip Vogel and his fiancée, Hilary, were so impressed by what they saw that once they had got married they moved into a caravan a few miles away just to be part of us.

At this point Uncle Allan, while praying, was given a picture of the new house that we were to move into, and he spent the whole night writing down every last detail, even down to how many outbuildings it had. Cash as usual was very tight, but this would never get in the way of pursuing God's will. Uncle Allan contacted all the local estate agents, and in no time at all his desk, which was once covered with *Challenge,* was now covered in details of houses for sale. As he ploughed through them nothing seemed to hit him in the eye as being the right one. He was wondering what the next step should be when there was a knock at the door. When he opened it, there stood a rather smartly dressed, posh-speaking, gentleman. He introduced himself as ex-naval Sea Commander Derek Sangster, and he wanted to find out exactly what these lively land-lubbers' lifestyles were all about.

Uncle Allan explained all about our history, and he couldn't really avoid mentioning the dream house as his desk-top spoke for itself. While he was called away to answer the phone, Derek decided to pass the time quietly by perusing the pile of property papers. Suddenly this old sea-dog got as excited as if he'd found some buried treasure, because there in the pile he had uncovered the details of a large house called 'The Old Rectory', standing in twelve acres of ground and situated in a small village about eight miles away called Clapham. As he thrust this incredible discovery into Uncle Allan's hands, the latter was amazed both at the fact that his vision and The Old Rectory were one and the same, and that it should take somebody that he had never met before to come and reveal it to him. Before he could say 'bosun's locker', the excited seaman had pulled my shell-shocked Uncle into his car and driven off to explore the big house.

Within a twinkling of an eye, both knew that this was the house that God had chosen. Before Uncle Allan had time to wonder where the thousands of pounds to buy it were to come from, this stranger sitting next to him just got out his cheque book and wrote a cheque for the full amount, explaining that this was a gift from God.

We were only at Sea Court for less than a year, and I had not only enjoyed it, but had also learned a great deal simply from being there. But now our little group of pilgrims was on the move again, this time to a huge old house where I was going to be blessed with lots more uncles and aunties, brothers and sisters, and even four cows and a dog. The most important thing for me, though, was that this was going to be the first time that I had lived where I would see haystacks instead of houses, tractors instead of cars, trees instead of lampposts, and breathe in fresh air rather than carbon monoxide. Would my body and mind be able to cope with such major readjustments, and was I really the Wurzel type? Well, I would soon find out!

3

The Facts of Life

Every member needs a body,
Every body needs a head,
Every member needs a vision,
Without new blood it is dead.
On a limb a wandering member
Will find life will soon depart.
The strongest will cannot survive
Disconnected from the heart.

The Old Rectory really had to be seen to be believed – it was sheer luxury and elegance, the best that God could have provided. The house itself was full of character. It stood as proud as a palace with its walls regally bathed in a beautiful blue flower which came from the creeper Wisteria. Inside the house there were eleven bedrooms, three bathrooms, two kitchens, two lounges, one very large dining room, a library, a cloakroom, and even a dairy. Once outside you were confronted with numerous outbuildings and cowstalls, three heated greenhouses, three paddocks, two lawns, a tennis court, a potting shed, a rockery, a fish pond, a fruit garden, a vegetable garden, a walled kitchen garden, an orchard, and a partridge in a pear tree. No wonder it took all night for Uncle Allan to receive the original vision of the house – it would take him that long to write it all down!

This house was good news for me as I was now able to have my own bedroom. It was the strangest room that I had ever seen, because by the window some steps led up to what best resembled a three-sided pulpit, the top of which was covered with thick slate. I thought that either some mad scientist had used it to concoct weird experiments, or else the old vicar who must have lived here many years ago used it to practise what he was preaching, and needed the slate to chalk up his score for his performance and presentation.

The first major change that took place was that the newspaper *Challenge* stayed in Goring with some of the folk, while the big four – Uncle Allan, Uncle John, Uncle Brian and Dad whose hearts were behind the printing company of CPO – now moved into The Rectory. Because these were both looked upon as commercial ventures, it was decided to select a name that would serve as an umbrella for the whole work, and from that time on we were known as the 'Turn to Christ Organisation'. We even had car stickers and little badges to prove it.

On arrival we were introduced to a lady called Miss Jones. (I still wonder what her Christian name was. I don't think it was Indiana.) She was different from any other woman that I had seen, mainly because she was the first person from the female gender that I had seen with muscles like a blacksmith – she could easily have been related to Arnold Schwarzenegger.

Talking about film stars, just time for a quick conundrum. What has sixteen legs, is totally spoilt and overfed, has four udders, and goes by the names Daphne, Daffodil, Buttercup and Freesia? No, it's not Miss Jones, but it is her four best friends which happened to be cows. Along with these playmates she also had three generations of loyal cats who followed her every move, and when we inherited The Rectory, whether we wanted them or not, we also inherited Miss Jones and her mangy menagerie.

Actually, Miss Jones was a dear old soul. She stayed with us for six months during which time she tried to train up my greener-than-broccoli-but-very-eager-to-learn father, whose qualifications for being her successor were that nobody else wanted the job, and that he enjoyed eating potato crisps. His new responsibilities meant a new position, so as well as being a director of Turn to Christ, he had now taken on the role of estate manager. Now, although that position sounds rather grand, Dad was never given a deerstalker hat, a pipe, and a Range Rover to drive around in, but he was equipped with the Christian equivalent which was a pair of wellies and a plastic mac.

I enjoyed helping Dad, and as he was learning, so I was learning from watching him. Even before Miss Jones had gone he decided that the four pet cows were an economic disaster. This came to his attention when he realised that the more food he pushed in one end didn't necessarily guarantee that more milk was going to come out of the other. In fact, if manure had been worth as much as milk, we would have been millionaires in no time. So sense prevailed over sentiment, and the four old girls came unstuck and probably finished their days as part of a tube of Bostik.

I'm sure Dad won't mind me saying this, but he had always been one for the birds, so he bought in two hundred poultry and twenty-five geese which he really took under his wing, and in the end he spent more time in the chicken-run than he did with the human race. Dad got very attached to the largest gander who was affectionately known as Charlie. He was one of the most vicious animals you could ever meet. Whenever he saw anyone approaching, he would put his head down and run straight towards them hissing as loudly as he could. Dad, who had obviously been studying the life of David in the Bible, thought that just as David killed lions and bears with his bare hands, so he could master this belligerent bird. It didn't take him long to work out a special party piece for any audience who had the time to waste watching. He would enter the chicken-run, as a matador would enter a bull-ring, and as Charlie would open his beak and charge towards him hissing, so Dad would clench his teeth and with the fearless cry of 'come on Charlie' grab hold of the poor bird's neck and put on a show which could best be entitled, 'Man and Gander Wrestling in the Mud.'

Now, before you bird-lovers complain about cruelty to man-eating Charlies, I need to explain that he enjoyed these romps as much as Dad, but unlike Dad he didn't play by the Queensbury rules. One day, as there was no audience present, Dad had chosen not to wrestle with Charlie, but he still had to go into the run to repair the six-foot high fence. As he was bending down facing the fence, he didn't consider his rather vulnerable position as behind him stalked the far from gregarious gander who had spotted the large, unsuspecting and tempting target confronting him. Then it happened – the charge of the flight brigade. With wings flapping, tail wagging, and beak gaggling, Charlie not only managed to hit the bull's-eye but also clamped his jaws shut on a certain part of Dad's anatomy which I don't think he would want me to mention. While enjoying a tetanus jab in the local hospital, Dad decided that maybe it was not such a good idea to be overfriendly with our fine feathered friends.

Once the cows had been moved on to greener pastures, a building project commenced which converted all the cowstalls into studios, carpentry buildings and even a laundry. New uncles and aunties were moving in at a rate of knots, and thanks to the healthy country air and lack of late night entertainment, all the young married couples were proving to be unusually prolific as well.

As I was now ten, I had long since grown out of my cowboy outfit, but I still enjoyed dressing up. This was one of the main reasons why I 'felt led' to go to the local Anglican church and join the choir. Mr Baker was the choir-master and organist, and he was very strict. Many a time I remember him turning round from his mighty wind-driven wurlitzer in the middle of the service and thumping me in the back for chatting up all the pretty little choirgirls during the sermon. In fact, these pretty little choirgirls were the only reason I kept going. I didn't like the smell of old churches, I didn't like chanting old psalms, I didn't like singing old hymns, and I didn't particularly like miserable old choir-masters either.

I never got paid for my vocal endeavours. All I got was

a sweet at the end of the choir practice on Thursday nights – that's if I hadn't been asked to leave before the end for being a distraction and a disruptive influence on my fellow choristers. Once I had been asked to clear off, however, I liked to remind those inside that I hadn't gone home. I found the best way of doing this was by throwing metal dustbin lids onto the roof. I thought that the noise they made as they clattered down the slates and crashed onto the tarmac below would help the choristers as they fumbled around trying to find the right key for the next hymn.

Although I was becoming slightly rebellious, I wasn't really a bad kid. I still went to a Baptist church on occasions, where I fell in love with Bunyan's *Pilgrim's Progress*. I joined the Anglicans by becoming a Pathfinder on Sunday afternoons, and if the odd Bible study seemed a bit stuffy, I always found that a fight with the vicar's son, Brian, had the desired effect of livening things up. The vicar, despite a maniacal laugh, was a good man. I spent many happy hours with him being prepared for confirmation and my big break with the bishop, who was the first person to lay hands on me without intent to injure. Talking about happy hours, it always fascinated me that he was able to knock back the remainder of the Communion wine from the chalice each Sunday morning and manage to walk home in a straight line.

There was not a great abundance of cash at The Rectory, as Uncle Allan's motto seemed to be, if we've got it, then let's give it all away. The adults, however, were given pocket money of five shillings a week. This they were at liberty to blow on extravagant and riotous living, such as a bar of chocolate, a tin of talcum powder, or even a bus trip to the nearest large town, Worthing. The only trouble was that by the time that they had tithed their precious five bob, they wouldn't have enough money for the return fare, so it was advisable to save up for a couple of weeks before embarking on such a luxury as that.

You don't need a lot of money to have fun though, and one pleasure I really enjoyed was playing football. I was good enough to be in the school team, and I actually won three bronze medals for my skills. Even though I was fairly short, due to having stumpy legs that resembled upturned beer bottles, I was quite an aggressive player, usually playing in defence. I hoped that my future might be in football until I brought down the school's leading striker with a flying tackle and almost broke his leg. After that it was decided to drop me from the team as this was not the sort of play that was encouraged at primary school level. From that time on I had to be content playing against the big men I lived with as they, like me, loved a bit of the rough stuff.

As the fame of the community spread, many different characters came to visit us. These included Arthur Wallis, who had just typed out a study on the church and wanted Uncle Allan to read it, Roy Hession, and even a very young George Verwer, who I believe had a bit of trouble with the fact that we were living in such apparent luxury, but was heartened that we shared his vision of a big ship that would travel the world proclaiming the good news of Jesus. There was also a recently converted tramp called Peter Newman.

As well as these men of God I've just mentioned, who went on to break fresh ground in their different spheres, we also had other interesting personalities who didn't to my knowledge go on to achieve quite such great heights. One of these was a Glaswegian called Jock. Now to give Jock his due, he tried his hardest to live up to the high reputation and standards that Turn to Christ was portraying, but he just couldn't seem to make it. Just as we did at Sea Court, we all took part in daily chores. Jock decided to show his talents with the painting and decorating contingent, which was all very well until people realised that he didn't have the ability to stop after painting one wall. The trouble was that Jock splashed so much paint on the adjoining walls that he felt it was his duty to paint those too. So all the freshly decorated walls were being repainted with whatever colour Jock happened to have in his hand at the time. The other thing that tended to upset the purest painter was that Jock had a great knack of putting his foot in it – the paint pot that is. Instead of painting the walls, a lot of time was taken up in scraping the floors.

The Community opened its arms to all sorts of people. We were not interested in their past as long as they were keen to go on with God. One gentleman – I'll call him Rob – happened to have a record that was longer than Daly Thompson's decathlon. Now, the folk in the community had a great love for Rob. Even though they knew about his past, they felt they must trust him. After a while of living with us, they couldn't understand how he could keep on affording to go to Worthing, and keep buying new clothes. No one could judge him because he could have had more faith than anyone else, and by praying over his five shillings he could have multiplied them. A while later though, a humble washerwoman found the secret of Rob's success and new-found fortunes. As she was about to wash his trousers she noticed a wad of tickets in his pocket, and on closer examination she discovered they were tickets from a pawnbroker. It seemed as if Rob had only half of the community spirit in that he could not quite cope with only being allowed five shillings a week. But he could cope with sharing everyone else's possessions, so he shared much of the silver lying about the house with the local pawnbroker, and then pocketed the cash to subsidise his standard of living.

You might think that with such revolutionary teaching and radical lifestyle Turn to Christ was a charismatic group in the fullest sense of the word. However, all that people knew about the Holy Spirit was what they had been taught from their respective denominations. So when it came to the subject of baptism in the Holy Spirit, it was very much one man's theological viewpoint against no man's actual experience.

Now, Uncle Philip Vogel was not happy about this. At a meeting in the house when someone had talked on the subject, Uncle Philip, who had never been the sort of person to hide his feelings, declared in front of everybody that he was not going to leave the room until he'd actually been baptised in the Holy Spirit. Due to the variety of upbringing among the people, emotions and reactions started to run a bit haywire. Some were afraid, another left the room and went up to her bedroom because she thought it was evil, and the remainder either waited and watched or wondered what to do, just walking around out of the heat in the hallway.

Then it was as though the Holy Spirit came down just as he had in the early church. Uncle Philip burst out speaking in tongues; those in the room with him lay prostrate on the floor unable to move; those in the hallway were literally thrown to the ground; some felt they saw the walls shake, and even the lady who thought it was evil and was in her bedroom received the fresh outpouring that God was giving them. From that time onwards things were never to be the same, although some still had problems working out the theology behind the new experience.

All in the garden was not rosy however. Turn to Christ was run by a directorship which included Uncle Allan, Uncle John, Uncle Brian and Dad, but there was a little bit of unrest that Uncle Allan seemed to get the final say in everything. Relationships were not improved when New Trinity College, a boarding school in Herstmonceux, East Sussex, contacted the directors. The principal was a Christian, but unlike most private schools New Trinity College mostly contained children who had been neglected and dumped there by their parents. The college needed financial help as it had got into debt, and the sum of two hundred pounds was mentioned. The directors all agreed that this should be sent, but that Dad, who had yet another hat as the Turn to Christ bookkeeper, should go and investigate the college's financial position.

When Dad arrived at the college he discovered to his horror that not only was there no food for the children but that a nought had been mislaid and in fact the debt was two thousand pounds and not two hundred. On his return Dad shared the news with the other directors. The gulf widened as Uncle Allan and he thought that the community should give them the money and also have input into the college as a new venture, while Uncle John and Uncle Brian thought it was more advantageous to invest the money in developing the ministry of CPO. Again, Uncle Allan had his way.

I didn't realise that all these new developments would affect me, because the adults were very discreet and we were kept in the dark about a lot of things. However, soon after the agreement to give the money to the college, Dad heard the Lord tell him that he was to send me over to the college, confirming it with the story of Abraham and Isaac. Dad cried many tears at the thought of sending me away to live, but he knew that he had to do what God had said for both our sakes. When he told me the news that instead of starting at the secondary modern school that I was all prepared and kitted out for, I was to move away to boarding school, I found it hard to believe that God should want such a thing to happen.

I vividly remember saying goodbye to my mum and sister Heather, and being taken over to this miserable, old, ramshackle building that, although it was only the other side of Sussex, seemed like it was the other side of the world. It was strange to be introduced to a lot of children whom I had never met before, and being shown to a dormitory which I was to share with three other lads whom I didn't know. What made things worse was that I was the creep who had been sent in to spy, whose father was one of the new directors of some strange Christian organisation who had come in to spoil what they were enjoying.

I lay in bed that first night feeling very lonely and quite afraid. Even though I knew my Dad was downstairs staying the night, he seemed a million miles away. We had always been a very close family, and this feeling of isolation was one I'd never experienced before. As I was lying there I could hear the older teenagers outside shouting and laughing, and then I nearly jumped out of my skin as somebody sent a stone smashing through our bedroom window.

On impulse I leaped out of bed and ran towards the

stairs with the other lads in my dormitory, only to be confronted by one of the new teachers, Mr Duke. After telling us that we were not allowed out of our bedrooms, whatever had happened, he told us to go and wait in our bedroom and he would be back to deal with us later. He then found my Dad and simply asked his permission to cane me. Dad had to say yes, but again I know he spent a lot of that night in tears. Mr Duke then took us to his room one at a time and whacked us. I was the last, and I painfully remember getting four of the best. I just couldn't hold back my tears. All my emotions were surfacing at once and the physical pain that had been inflicted on me was the least of the causes. I suffered more from thoughts like, I've never been beaten before, I've let my Dad down, I'm a Christian, and I've let Jesus down by being wicked, I'm supposed to be an example to those other kids in my room, I've failed them. Every step back to my bedroom seemed to bring more tears, but I had no pride. I didn't care if my new room mates discovered that they were sharing their room with a cry-baby.

On entering the room I couldn't have been more surprised, for there sitting on my bed were the other three in tears as well. Within seconds, though our tears were drying up, we all told our tales, talking at great length about our courage in facing Mr Duke. They were all amazed to find out that I had received more lashings than them. Suddenly I wasn't the odd boy out, I was now the hero.

From that time on I really enjoyed my boarding-school days, even though they only lasted a few months. God answered all my prayers, even sending my mother over to me to work as the house mistress. I loved the evenings as we used to play wide games, and in the middle of the many acres of grounds stood a huge redwood tree which everyone would try and climb, except those like me who couldn't stand heights.

One answer to prayer I particularly remember happened just before a meal time when I'd somehow managed to lock myself in the toilet. There was no way that I could get the door opened. I knew the staff were pretty strict on being on time for meals, and I didn't feel I needed to get the cane again and hence become a super hero, so I opened the window and jumped two storeys onto the grass below. As I landed, I thought I heard my legs crack – but fortunately it was only a branch that I had landed on. I walked into the dining room shaking, and as white as a sheet, but at least I didn't get into trouble for being late.

It was at New Trinity that my interest in fishing began. We would go to a small pond just a few hundred yards away, and whatever bait we used we always caught some fish. We usually managed to fall into the pond as well, but even that didn't stop the fish from biting.

As I mentioned earlier, my days in private school only lasted a few months. The building was decaying more quickly than a mouthful of rotting teeth, so rather than just throw the pupils out on the streets, as some of their parents still could not be found, we were all herded back to The Old Rectory, which was also deteriorating rapidly due to the growing unresolved internal issues. The school was renamed Bethel School, but it was really a stop-gap till all the pupils had been relocated with their parents. I then started travelling seven miles to the nearest secondary modern school in Littlehampton. I can't say my one year's private school tuition had done a lot for me academically. The entrance exam for the school in Littlehampton revealed that I was very much 'D' stream material.

My spiritual state was far from healthy. Boarding school and all the changes had taken their toll, and now I just wanted to be like other kids rather than be a Christian. I wanted to do things that ordinary people did and went to all sorts of extremes to try and become normal. I tried smoking, but because I couldn't get hold of any tobacco I tried puffing away at basket cane, straw, even pieces of wood. In the end I started smoking cigarettes that my friends gave me, but my mum found me out. I felt so guilty and evil because of the wicked sin that I had committed that I went to my bedroom and spent the whole evening crying my heart out, wondering if Mum or God would ever forgive me.

I did find that travelling away from The Rectory each day was now proving to be a blessing, as the love which had been its foundation had now disappeared due to a diverging ministry and the leadership struggle. Whereas in the past it had been left to Uncle Allan to choose other directors, this was now looked upon as undemocratic. So votes were taken to elect new leaders, and while Uncle Allan just scraped in my Dad was voted out.

All was not doom and gloom though, because even in these hard months God blessed me with two things which would be great assets to me in future years. The first was the birth of my brother, Timothy John, twelve years after I had been born. Everyone in the last few years had called each other brother, which was proving to have meant very little, but now for the first time I had a real one. At about the same time, after watching me win a friendly fight with one of the school kids, Uncle Philip Vogel nicknamed me 'Ishmael', a name which was said in jest but remained in my memory banks for years.

As time continued, the heart and soul went out of the community. Some prophesied the word 'Ichabod' over it, saying that 'the glory of the Lord had departed'. Uncle Allan couldn't cope with all that was happening and did more and more work in London, until inevitably he and his family moved out altogether, taking the now meaningless name 'Turn to Christ' with them.

The Smale family was now the odd one out. We couldn't move because we had nowhere to go and not enough money to buy anything anyway. We were the last of the old order – not CPO any longer, as all the remaining residents were, and not Turn to Christ either, although still being loyal to Uncle Allan. Dad spent weeks in London assisting Uncle Allan who was hoping to purchase another large house and start all over again. Yet in spite of all the frustrations and tensions that the adults were experiencing, we children were always treated well.

As the once beautiful grounds now looked sad and neglected, so did Dad. Uncle Allan's vision of just a few years ago had collapsed, leaving many broken people crushed by its failure. On reflection there was no one person to blame. In fact, it's still hard to see where and when things went wrong, but at the end of the day there were no winners, we were all losers. *Challenge* and CPO continued, but moved down to Worthing. The Old Rectory was sold, and the house was divided up and went onto the market as separate apartments. I would have loved to have seen the community continue and prosper as it did in those early days. I would have loved my children to have had a taste of what it is like when God's people live in perfect harmony together.

Anyway, God had far from finished with us as a family. A couple called Reg and Hazel (at last I was able to drop the Uncles and Aunties), who owned a rather dilapidated house right next to the railway track in Littlehampton, kindly offered to take us in. Our new home was slightly different from what we had been accustomed to, but no one is proud when they are desperate. I was learning that God's way is not merely climbing up one ladder, getting richer, fatter and more prosperous. Sometimes it means changing ladders while only halfway up and continuing on one that seems a lot more risky and dangerous. But that builds up your faith and brings a greater realisation that following in the steps of the Master is never easy or predictable but often exciting. And I, for one, was soon to discover just that.

4

We Are One, We Are Family Together

We Are One, we are family together,
'Cause we've one Father caring for us all.
We are one, we are related to each other,
Lord help me to love my family much more.

It was in January 1963 that we actually moved into Railway Cuttings. Reg, who had been so kind as to offer us somewhere to live, was a very unusual man to put it mildly. His appearance resembled a strange mixture of Rambo, David Bellamy and Samantha Fox, the former due to his muscular body (even more impressive than Miss Jones'), and the latter to the fact that whatever the weather he always wore shorts and was nearly always topless.

But despite his rugged exterior, our Reg had a heart of gold. His occupation was 'odd-job man extraordinaire', master of the half-finished bodge-up, as we were to discover on our arrival at our new home, which was a partially converted signal-box.

Our family was to share the upstairs rooms. These included a living-room which had a large hole in one wall where a fireplace had just been removed, plus a boiler in the corner for the time when central heating would eventually be installed. Then there were two bedrooms, one of which Mum shared with Heather and baby Tim, and the other which I shared with Dad. There was also a passageway which was to be transformed into a kitchen. The bathroom and toilet were downstairs and only accessible by walking through Reg and Hazel's kitchen. The toilet had no lock on the door and the bathroom had no door to lock, so we all became proficient whistlers. The garden was a rockery surrounded by iron sculptures, in other words, heaped high in brick rubble with the odd bath, drain-pipe, and toilet cistern bringing with it its own air of sophistication.

But even after saying all these unflattering truths, Reg and Hazel were kind enough to open up their home to us, for which we were truly thankful, and I enjoyed many happy hours going round with Reg, not so much to learn the tricks of his trade, rather to get my muscles to look like his.

As we were one of the last to leave the Old Rectory, all the best possessions had long since been removed to various parts of the country, and our sole inheritance was a very nice three-piece suite. Sadly, there was no way that we could get it upstairs, and it ended up being an ideal place for Reg to store his bags of cement.

CPO had kindly given Dad a gift of seven hundred pounds to help him make a new start, so we were able to buy such necessities as sheets, blankets, and cooking and eating utensils. Although life was very basic, we all came back down to earth, got our heads together, and started enjoying our new-found freedom. Mum would keep saying to us, 'Let's pretend that we are missionaries in Africa living in a mud hut.' Now I'm really glad that our house-proud mother remained so positive, and although she was a great encouragement to us, you had to have a very good imagination, and top quality mud, to be able to stand up to a busy main road ten foot from your lounge, and a train rattling past your bedroom every few minutes.

Dad, with all his self-taught farming experience, secured a job with Crispa Cress. By working all hours of the day and night he not only soon became a supervisor, but also brought home a fair amount of cash and cress.

I was now making a lot of friends at my new school, but some of them were not a very good influence on me, and I was just the sort of kid who wanted to be influenced. I couldn't shake off the desire to be the same as them, and

I would try to copy many of the things they said and did, but I never seemed to get as much out of doing these things as they did. Having just achieved teenage years, a lot of them kept on about drinking alcohol, which not only had I never tasted, but I couldn't even remember ever seeing. Among Reg's unique collection of unusable items in our back-garden were a lot of old bottles which he presumably used to store meths, white spirit, diesel and other such poisonous substances. I saw this as my chance to taste some of this much desired booze, so while nobody was watching I took off the tops of any bottles that had just a small amount of liquid in them and took a swig. Boy, did it taste rough.

Bicycles were also the in thing. So long as it had cowhorn handlebars and big tyres, the bike itself could be as old as the hills and still remain trendy. So even with our low income I could still be one of the boys.

While living at Railway Cuttings we only had two really embarrassing visitations. The first was from one of the bigwigs of the Unevangelised Fields Mission. He was obviously not overimpressed with our avant-garde, bareboarded, wallpaper-peeling property. The second was from my Grandad who wasn't hard up for a few bob and wasn't at all happy with his son living in this sort of squalor. He put his money where his mouth was and offered to buy us a house. The new house went under the grand name of 'Rose Cottage'. It was on the same road that we were living in then, but about one mile nearer Littlehampton and, thankfully, one mile further away from the railway line.

Our ever-helpful handyman, Reg, offered to move us. As he backed his open-top trailer against the side of the house wall, he convinced us that the best way to handle the operation was for us to pass all our worldly possessions carefully down to him through the second-storey lounge window, and for him to catch them and load them up. This all sounded quite feasible until we discovered that Reg could not even catch a cold if someone sneezed straight into his face. This was when the Lord finally convinced us that there was no point in laying up treasures on earth where moth could corrupt – or Reg could destroy.

Possessions were unimportant to us as we travelled that mile and arrived at yet another dwelling place. At last we were back in a little home of our own again. All right, so the front door did open straight onto the pavement and every four-legged creature could leave us a little blessing as they passed by. But as we entered that house with our battered belongings, we felt a sense of relief and security that we hadn't known for quite a few years, and we praised God for it.

My school was also much nearer now, so two of my best friends, one called Alan Hoare, who was nicknamed Alfie, and the other Brian Greaves, who was nicknamed Jim, used to come and call for me on their bikes and we would pedal off to school together. I have already mentioned that I was not a model student. I was in the 'D' stream, with only the 'E' stream below, which was reserved for the mega-slow and the ultra-thick. I saw no point in aiming to get higher up the educational league table as it was a well-known fact that the brighter you were the harder your work became and the more homework you were given. I could see no advantages but plenty of disadvantages in displaying your intelligence to others.

My impressions of some of the major subjects were not inspiring. Mental arithmetic would live up to its name and drive me insane, and the only sort of 'taking away' I would have enjoyed is if they had taken away this depressing subject altogether. Science – I only ever went to two of these lessons in my life, and I couldn't even discover how to light my Bunsen burner. At this stage they gave me a free transfer to the metalwork department. Metalwork: I had a chuckle at a tool which was known as a Bastard File, though of course with my upbringing I was actually too embarrassed to ever call it by that name; also I couldn't understand why we kept making things like pokers, when we all had gas fires. But above all that I hated the oily greasy smell and getting my hands and clothes messed up, a snob from the word go. Art and craft meant having to draw some manky old pot of flowers, or someone sitting on a chair, and it bored me to tears, if you wanted to reproduce the object dying in front of you, for goodness' sake buy a camera and do the job properly. And craft was very similar, fancy giving big boys a lump of clay and expecting them to do something more creative with it than flicking it around the room at the people you least liked, which was invariably the teacher. Religious knowledge, praise the Lord that I was already a Christian, had I not have been, after a couple of hours in this lesson, I'd have found it easier to become a Martian than a missionary. The only subject I really enjoyed was English. Admittedly, I couldn't speak it very well, and I even had trouble spelling it, but I loved writing and telling stories.

At first glance, it may have looked like I was unambitious and completely talentless, but that couldn't be further from the truth. My teachers noticed that I had unusual gifting and, wishing to give me every encouragement to further my rare abilities, I was put in charge of the school milk. Each morning dozens of crates were delivered from the local dairy, and the first half of my job was to stack them up and count out the right number of bottles for each class. Once this taxing task had been completed, the other half of my commitment was to count the empties as they were returned. All my school reports were totally predictable saying things like, 'Must try harder,' and, 'Could do better,' but now I had a bonus postscript on the end which said, 'But he would make a good milkman.'

The biggest yawn of all, though, was assembly each morning. Somehow the school had been landed with hundreds of smartly bound congregational hymn books, and though neither teacher nor pupil had any desire to enter into morning worship, each day we would religiously plod through some little-known lament. Hardly had the last word of our song of praise been mimed (mind you it had been a lovely piano instrumental) than the Headmaster would leap to his feet and, flowing in full reverence for the occasion, blow his top over some misdemeanour committed by one of the worshipping little angels standing on the floor in front of him. This would, of course, be followed by a daily dose of the Lord's Prayer.

While all this charade was going on, I was much more interested in looking at the lads around me, as fashion was something that I had never been involved in. Starting from the head, Brylcreem was making its mark – in more ways than one. The hairstyle consisted of a defined parting with the hair swept back to produce the D.A. at the back; the neck was shaved to show off a straight line above the collar known as the Boston Cut. Then came the pullover, which had to be at least ten sizes too big, which balanced off the drainpipe jeans which had to be at least ten sizes too tight. White socks could just about be squeezed underneath the jeans and tucked into very pointed winkle-pickers which had a two- or three-inch cuban heel. Of course, my Mum would never allow me to have any of these clothes, and most definitely not the shoes, which didn't help my insecurity problem as by default I was now the smallest person in the class.

Music and girls started to play an even more prominent role in my life. Most weekends, my friend Jim and I would walk around the streets of Littlehampton eyeing up the 'crumpet'. Jim would carry an old transistor under his arm blaring out the latest pop music, while it was my job to wolf-whistle at the passing girls, which was no easy feat as I had to try and whistle more loudly than Jim's stupid radio. Needless to say these romantic advances were not totally successful, in fact after an hour or two we would both end up whistling the pop tunes and forgetting about the girls.

I still had a passion to do something musically, but the only problem was that I couldn't play any instruments and I was far from confident enough to stand out the front and be the lead vocalist. Having made friends with two of my classmates, Stuart and Trevor, and discovered that they were quite talented musically, we decided to form a band in which I would be the drummer. My other friend, Alfie, was chosen as the singer, not so much for his singing but more for his sense of humour and that he didn't seem to mind us blaming him for everything that went wrong.

Thanks to the wonders of hire purchase, Stuart, Trevor and Alfie went out and bought a bass guitar, a lead guitar, an amplifier, a public address system and a microphone. Thanks to the wonders of Christian parents, I wasn't allowed to buy things on hire purchase. But somehow I got a tall marching drum which I used as my bass drum, an old snare drum which to say that it came out of the ark would have been an insult to Noah, and a tiny cymbal which was less melodic than the noise the old dustbin lid made as it clattered down the roof in my old choir practice days. But it was a start.

We found the best venue to practise was the Girl Guides' hall, first because it was free, and second because it invariably came fully equipped with Girl Guides. Our band had two names, one was 'The Handsome Beasts', and the other was 'Kaos'. The trouble was that one name was highly appropriate while the other was totally untrue (I'll leave you to work out which was which). We modelled ourselves on 'The Animals' but looked more like the monkeys. I wouldn't say that we had an enormous following: If we had done a tour of telephone boxes up and down the country, we still couldn't have guaranteed to fill even one of them.

We did do the odd gig though, and that always seemed to be in Littlehampton's equivalent of the Hammersmith Odeon – yes, right first time, the infamous Guides' hall. The sheer visual impact of our concerts left much to be desired. To start off, Alfie was rarely seen because we often forgot to tell him when the gigs were on. Alfie himself had the most amazing talent for buying new clothes that never seemed to fit him. In fact, I've heard rumour that if he stood outside any Oxfam shops, they would ask him kindly to move along as he was giving them a bad name. So with no Alfie, I did most of the singing while hiding behind my drum.

The observant fan would also notice that without Alfie we only had one thirty-watt amplifier and rather a lot of things that needed to go through it. Due to the amplifier only having two inputs, the bass guitar, sometimes two other guitars, plus a couple of mikes all had to be carefully soldered onto two jackplugs, and everything had to come out of this one small speaker. Could anything be more embarrassing for this up-and-coming group of potential superstars? Well, yes. As I never had a loud crash cymbal I would get someone wearing short trousers to sit next to the kit. When I needed a cymbal noise I would whack him on the leg with my drum-stick and he would respond appropriately with a loud scream which, though it didn't sound quite the same, certainly gave our show that live feel.

Having become good friends with the Girl Guides, I thought it wouldn't be a bad idea to join the Boy Scouts. After all, Scouts and Guides go together like cholesterol and cream, and they always seem to be meeting up together for the odd march or parade. As I never looked my best in green, I decided to join the Sea Scouts as they wore much more attractive blue uniforms. We met in a little hut near the River Arun, and apart from playing strange games like British Bulldog, we would learn how to tie knots, give the kiss of life, and explain the difference between a toggle and a woggle.

I loved going on the camps. I remember one particular camp at Brockenhurst in the New Forest where we set up our tents by a picturesque stream. That night we all decided to go into Southampton to the cinema, oblivious to the fact that while we were crunching popcorn and being entertained by some film located in the sweltering heat of the Sahara desert, it was belting down with rain outside. When we eventually emerged from the smoke-ridden fleapit that we, being good Scouts (clean in thought, word and deed), had helped to create, we rushed back to the forest to find that the banks of the stream had burst and all our tents and possessions had floated off never to be seen again. Fortunately, the church came to our rescue and we spent the night in a creepy old parish church. Even if you were only slightly afraid when you tried to get to sleep, it was guaranteed that you would be petrified by morning.

Another time we camped at a lovely site up the River Arun which required quite an exciting canoe row to get there. It was at this camp that I was first introduced to brown ale, and I must admit I enjoyed the flavour. It certainly tasted a lot better than the liquid I had previously thought to be alcohol back in Reg's back garden.

I was never what you would call a successful Scout, although I did manage to get my Backwoodsman's Badge even though I didn't really understand what the word meant. I was as good at scouting as Baden-Powell would have been at playing computer games. The founder would not have been proud of me – after all these years I had not got my first-class badge, and I wouldn't have known how to sew it on if I had. My biggest humiliation was that after all the many hours of teaching I had received, I still didn't know the difference between a toggle and a woggle.

Dad had not been feeling so well while working at the cress centre of the universe, so after a short stint of book-keeping for a Christian heating engineer, who had to sack him within a short while because he couldn't afford to have his books kept, got a job with the Missionary Optical Service. Now leaving to one side all the old jokes about making a spectacle of oneself, this work was much appreciated by the short sighted Africans. Millions of old spectacles would be sent to them, with even the odd bonus of a set of false teeth. These would be sorted and cleaned and the good lenses put into the good frames. Dad would tour the country to get his optical illusions and at times I would go with him to keep him company. It came to pass, though, that the missionary optical HQ moved to the West Country, and when Dad was asked if he wanted to move down and join them, praise the Lord he said no.

Dad was also suffering from recurring headaches. After intensive tests it was discovered that he had a half-inch ball bearing, left over from the war, lodged in his brain. After a time at Atkinson Morley Hospital, it was decided that it was much too dangerous to operate, but the condition was very serious and would affect him for the rest of his life. Once Dad realised the severity of his problem, he knew that there was only one thing to do, and that was, as James chapter 5 says, to call together the elders of the church and ask them to pray for him. This he did, and he has had no trouble ever since. After this episode, Dad took a job as a gas man.

My church life continued, though not with the same zeal as previous years. However, I didn't want to limit my new found drumming skills to the secular market; whether God wanted them or not, I wanted to inflict them on him as well. Back at Rose Cottage I found the chance to do this when our family invited the youth group round for a rousing singsong. While someone tickled the ivories and the saints sang sweetly, I'd beat the living daylights out of my drums.

Now you may not believe this, but in my mid-teen years I was very much an introvert. I will never forget the day when we had a school prize giving and, to my horror, I discovered that I had actually won a prize for my literary skills. The Headmaster was standing on the stage and going through the list of names and I knew that mine was getting closer and closer. Then came that word that I was dreading to hear, 'Smale'. I had to get up from the back of the hall, walk all the way to the front, clamber up on stage and, without fumbling, shake hands with the Head and receive my special trophy, which happened to be the book *Treasure Island*. They must have got this title in a job lot, at a special deal, because even the maths prizes were *Treasure Island*. As I made my way those few yards, which seemed like miles, my nerves had made me develop an embarrassing twitch with my head, and by the time I finally reached the stage, my head was wobbling so much that there must have been some fears that it might actually fall off of my shoulders. The masters on the platform must have seen my predicament, for the strange thing was that they had now started doing it as well. I've often tried to imagine what the platform party must have looked like with a load of men and a boy creating a new craze (later to be known as headbanging).

At the age of fifteen the time was coming when, if I didn't want to stay on at school to take exams (perish the thought), I was allowed to leave. The only trouble was, after all the career talks that I had sat through nothing seemed to leap out and smack me in the eye. As well as my major responsibility with the milk, I had also been entrusted with helping to look after the school garden, and in the end they thought I was so keen that they gave me my own piece of allotment. Just the thought of gardening left me cold, and being outside most of the year I usually was. But I carried on and did it because, let's face it, anything was better than having to sit inside and do lessons.

Dad suggested that maybe I should work for the local council in a clerical capacity, and one of the church elders who already worked there would put in a word for me. But after a very short interview we could all see that there would be more chance of the Queen joining a Trade Union than me joining local government.

My thoughts turned to a nice cushy outdoor job – farming. Dad rang round all the local Christian farmers, who either said that they had no vacancies or suggested that I went and worked for them for no wages, the argument being that then I could work for the Lord and also get some experience in farming. What a rip off! William Wilberforce come back.

Eventually a farm was found that was looking for someone just like me. It had no Christian connections and being situated in a town called Petworth, which was about twenty miles away from Littlehampton, would mean me having to leave home and move away. So at the ripe old age of fifteen and a half, I packed up the few belongings I had, jumped into Dad's car, and said goodbye to Mum, Heather and little Tim. As I waved from the car window thoughts went flashing through my head. I'm going to be a man, grown-up, able to fend for myself, even able to grow a beard. But all these aspirations were a little further away than twenty miles, maybe twenty years would have been more accurate.

5

He Has Showed You, O Man, What Is Good

He has showed you, O man, what is good.
And what does the Lord require of you?
To act justly and to love mercy
And to walk humbly with your God.

It was in the summer of 1965 that I arrived at Kilsham Farm, Petworth, and it wasn't until I had said goodbye to Dad that I realised I wasn't quite the mature adult that I had tried to kid myself I was. I was introduced to the farmer, Bill Bradshaw, and his wife Joan. I soon got to know two of their children: Peter, who was a couple of years older than me and was away studying at agricultural college, and Dorothy, who was a little younger than me and was still at school. The family was completed by Fanny Adams the cat and Bob the black mongrel dog. Poor Bob had a bit of a dog's life as his main talent was barking at everything, but more usually than not at nothing, and without exception each of the Bradshaw family had learned to reply to his outbursts by screaming the delicate phrase, 'Shut up, Bob!' This was either done in solo or unison.

It had been made very clear to the Bradshaws that I was a Christian, which to my mind was not going to make life any easier to bear. On that first evening, and many subsequent ones, I would sit alone in my bedroom, too frightened to go downstairs. My bedroom consisted of a very bouncy single bed, a dark-stained oak cupboard and wardrobe, a chair and a bedside table with a lamp on it.

The view out of my window was of a large back garden, which was more like a jungle than a cultivated area, and then no houses, just freshly harvested fields with the odd decaying straw bale as far as the eye could see. In years gone by I had dreamed of becoming a missionary and living in one of the most sparsely inhabited lands in the world, and now I was beginning to believe that my dream had come true. While hiding in that room, however, I did find things to do. I had my drum-sticks so I was able to tap very quietly so no one would hear me on various objects like the window-sill and cupboard. There was also a large pile of copies of *Farmer's Weekly* which I would thumb through trying in vain to acquaint myself with various machines and animals which I had not only never seen but also never heard of. It was during that first night on the farm that I wondered what on earth I was doing there.

I slept very badly that night as I kept checking my alarm clock. I was awake very early, making sure I managed to nip into the bathroom without seeing anyone. Then I got dresssed and sat on my bed until I heard Mrs Bradshaw's dulcet tones scream out and inform the rest of the family, if not the rest of the neighbourhood, that breakfast was ready. I crept downstairs and joined the family sitting around a large unpolished wooden table. After saying good morning and lying about how well I had slept, I was offered some fried eggs. After saying a polite yes please, I wished that I hadn't, as I was presented with a couple of broken yellow-and-white objects fighting for their lives so as not to drown in a sea of fat. They bore no resemblance to the way my Mum would fry eggs back home.

It was the unearthly hour of 7.30 a.m. when the farmer and I donned our wellies and PVC macs. Bill shouted to Bob, and one man and his dog and I set off, not exactly to mow the meadow but more to be shown what a meadow actually looked like. Before we reached any fields though, Bill decided that I should be introduced to some of the farm animals. After being shown a calf, a cow and a bull, I was shown the other farm workers. On our way to meet the workers I was trying to sound agriculturally intelligent and asked Bill what else he had on his farm. He explained to me that the farm was mainly arable and that hundreds of acres were mainly down to wheat and barley, but he also grew oats, potatoes and mangolds. I'd never heard of the last item in his list and assumed he said marigolds. He continued by telling me that he had a milking herd, a beef unit, sheep and chickens, cockerels and turkeys. I didn't really appreciate the way that he looked at me as he mentioned the word 'turkey'.

Even in those first few minutes I could tell that Bill was not a happy man and I found myself being frightened by him. Later I discovered that the money for the farm had been put up by his wife, so poor old Bill was probably suffering from an acute inferiority complex and had a chip on his shoulder that was larger than one of his dutch barns.

As we entered the farmyard I was introduced to old George who also seemed quite grumpy, had no teeth, and didn't particularly seem impressed by meeting me. Then there was George the cowman who was about fifty, seemed quite cheerful, but likewise was unimpressed by meeting me. Finally there was old George's son, Jim, who was about thirty, looked skinny, but was without doubt, both the strongest and the hardest worker on the farm; with the possible exception of the farmer's wife. As I met Jim I learned two things, one was that I think he liked me and the other was some Anglo-Saxon words that hopefully described how much he liked me.

Farmer Bradshaw then pointed to some wooden buildings and told me to go and see if the chickens had enough water and meal. My first lone assignment and it sounded chickenfeed, if you'll excuse the pun. The chickens lived in six very large and very smelly deep-litter houses, and as I burst open the door of the first one and stepped inside, the houseful of hens went positively bananas. They screeched and squalked with such volume that it got me dreaming about our band and how one day we might have to cope with millions of hysterical, screaming, female fans. I soon came down to earth with a bang though, because amid the mayhem they started flapping and flying in every direction possible. I ran towards the nearest food hopper, trying to avoid the low-flying fowls, but by now not only had a dust storm started, but the aroma of the ammonia had seeped through the two foot high dung mounds that I was staggering over. It was all too much for me. Even with my limited scientific past, I knew I needed oxygen. I ran back towards the door, fell out of it taking a couple of very surprised chickens with me (who couldn't believe their luck that they had now become free range), slammed the door shut, and coughed, spluttered and very nearly had a second showing of the eggs I had eaten for breakfast.

Wondering what all the commotion was about, a horrified farmer's wife came rushing over to me, more worried about her flea-infested breakfast-providers than her new employee. She then gave me the first sermon I had ever heard on how to enter a chicken house. From that time on, the only time I've ever liked chickens is when I've seen them tandooried.

I was then sent back to the cowsheds to clean out what the cows had left behind in return for parting company with their hard-earned milk. I couldn't understand it. They were only in the building for such a short time, yet they left their mark over floors, walls and even the ceiling. Old George joined me, backed the dung-spreader up to the door, and proceeded – to my annoyance – to try and tell me how to use a broom and shovel, then swear at me for not doing it the way he had always done it.

As autumn was not so far away, Jim went off ploughing while I spent the rest of that morning with this old chap who, like Bob, had a bark that was worse than his bite, or so I hoped. One of our jobs was to get some hay for the calves which were penned inside one of the barns, so George backed the trailer into the huge hay barn and told me to climb up to the top and throw some bales down. I looked up and saw how high this involved climbing, and fears came rushing back to me of the giant redwood tree back in Herstmonceux that I had always refused to attempt. As I couldn't see a ladder, I asked George where I could find one, to which he replied that I didn't need one as I could easily climb up the thirty-foot high metal stanchion. This did not in any way appeal to me, so I thought I'd try a bit of peaceful negotiation, believing that every man was willing to listen to reason and be open to a change of plan.

I explained very calmly that since I had a fear of heights, I wondered if he would mind doing it, or at least let me go and find a ladder. I'm just glad this old loud mouth had not been our Minister of Defence, because with his lack of reason we would now have been entering World War Ten. My calculated and reasoned comments didn't just fall on stoney ground, they actually got buried in concrete. To think that I had got the nerve to even want to discuss the issue seemed to incense him more than if I'd run over his wife with the combine harvester. He started to shout and swear at me so much that in the end I didn't know if I was more scared of him or the mountaineering feat I was about to begin.

I began my long climb very carefully and slowly, making sure my footholds were secure. Strangely the nearer I got to the top the more I could hear the verbal assaults from the little man on the trailer which was now a long way beneath me. Eventually I made it to the top, and wondered if there was a flag around anywhere that I could stick in to commemorate my success. However, this moment of elation was short-lived as I was about to discover the literal meaning of the expression 'Pride comes before a fall.' As I started to crawl near to the edge to begin throwing them down to my totally impatient co-labourer beneath me, my heart suddenly started beating faster than any role that I had been able to do on the drums. To my horror all the bales that I was gripping onto like grim death had come loose and dozens of them were rocking and rolling uncontrollably above a now panicking George. Within seconds the trailer had been filled with haybales, I was spread-eagled on top of them and a very ungrateful George was wedged underneath them. Talk about being hard to please – he was still not impressed at the speed with which I had managed to fulfil his commands.

To give George a break from me I spent most of the rest of the day weeding and tidying up the back garden, which of course was the job I loathed the most. I'd watch the tractor go racing up and down the farm lane and long to be in one, but obviously that would not come about for a little while yet. I was called upon to return to the house of horrors, otherwise known as the chicken house, to collect the eggs. I found out what it was like to be henpecked without even being married. The mangy perishers hacked into my hand, even though I tried to explain to them that although I may have been nicking their potential offspring, I was only doing my job.

I also found time to nip into the milking parlour and watch George the cowman at work. (George had an annoying habit of shouting out 'Hey' and when I turned and said to him 'What', he'd continue saying 'Heyty one, heyty two', and so on. This wasn't particularly funny the first time I heard it, but imagine how tedious it became by the heyty-first time.) The cowsheds were made up of three stalls and there were about sixty cows to be milked. George encouraged me to have a go, which was totally in keeping with his lousy sense of humour. He let me enjoy my first experience of milking on some bad-tempered old animal that nearly kicked me straight into the churn. After he'd had his little laugh, he showed me how to wash the four long dangling things called teats. Being the willing student that I was, I bent over to watch him and as I did so he somehow managed to bend the teat to face me, gave it a mighty squeeze, and with more precision than any water-pistol that I had encountered squirted me straight in the eye with hot milk.

After more laughter he showed me how to wash the teats and then would squirt each one into a little cup to see if there was any disease present. Then he told me it was my turn. I must admit that due to my sheltered upbringing I was a little embarrassed at the thought of touching what could correctly be termed a cow's private parts, and even wondered if it was a very Christian thing to do. But, I thought, if I don't hurry up and get on with it this old girl's going to take another swipe at me. So I rapidly lost all my inhibitions. After that I simply had to put four heaving, sucking, metal and rubber objects onto the teats which hopefully would squeeze out whatever remained of the milk, bearing in mind that most of it thanks to George's frolics had found its way into my eye. These would remain on until there was no milk left, or the cow kicked them off again, or George had finished his cup of tea. I soon left the excitement of the cowshed and returned to the less dangerous and quieter life back in the garden weeding. As the day ended, I returned to my bedroom, my Bible, my drum-sticks, my *Farmer's Weekly*, to look forward to another restless night's sleep.

The following day was my first visit to the sheep. I knew even less about sheep than I did about chickens, except when I tried counting them the night before as a last resort to try and get some shut-eye. On approaching the field I tried to do exactly what Jim did, as I didn't want to rush in and look more of an idiot than I had done the previous day with the chicken incident. I was told we had to catch some of them as they needed to be examined, and I was surprised to find out that the dog that followed the farmer about was only for show – he would have had more chance of catching foot and mouth disease than he would of catching a sheep. So it was up to us humans to do the job. We herded them into a corner by a fence, then I was told that we were all to grab hold of specific ones and pull them to the ground, rather like branding steers in the cowboy movies. This was not an easy task, as I discovered when an angry ewe dragged me halfway round the field.

Eventually we both ground to a halt, exhausted, and Jim came running over with an aerosol-spray can, a knife and a pair of clippers. Then, right in front of my very eyes, he announced, 'Look, footrot,' and proceeded to cut the hoof right back to reveal foul-smelling, festering matter which he sprayed with his aerosol. Then, turning the unfortunate animal over and looking at a bald patch on its back, he grunted, 'Look, maggots,' and set about digging them out with his knife. As my colour was changing to a whiter shade of pale, someone muttered, 'Always remember the sign of a good shepherd is a warm heart and a sharp knife.'

The autumn came and with it the potato harvest. The eleven acres allocated to us would have given even Samson back trouble, as we spent all day bending over, picking up these horrible little lumps of starch, and then putting them into a sack. At the end of the day we would collect up all the sacks and tip the contents out into a barn to dry. They would then be sorted, put into paper sacks, weighed and sold. And all this had to be done by hand – it seemed to take for ever.

The winter brought new jobs like hedging and fencing, which meant making nice big wood fires to keep the cold out. It also brought such wonderful tasks as cleaning out the chicken houses and calf-pens, which again all had to be done by hand as a tractor couldn't fit into the buildings. As the weather got colder and the ice and snow appeared, we saw less and less of Bill which meant we had to spend more and more time out braving it. It was winter feeding-time, and with no grass growing, substitutes like hay and root crops were fed to the animals. This is when I discovered what mangolds were, for each morning I had to dig these large bulbous roots out of the frozen ground and cut the leaves off with a sharp billhook (a sort of chopper) and throw them on the trailer. I wonder if my fingers ever really recovered from the severe frostbite they encountered over those weeks.

Amidst all the pain and rain though, I was really enjoying my work. It was during the winter season when life on the farm was reasonably quiet that I had my chance to learn how to drive a tractor. I practised on an old Fordson Major. Now, one of the assets about learning to drive on a tractor is that there is very little on them that can be damaged, especially the old one that I was learning on. Mind you, in the course of learning I did leave behind a trail of broken hedges, fences, gate-posts, brick walls and the odd building, which all happened because I loved speed and could never drive anywhere without going flat out.

Although I loved farming, I felt at times that it was very cruel, I hated the smell of burning flesh as a red-hot iron was pushed into the skull of a young calf, just to stop its horns growing. No one could convince me that a shot of local vaccine made this more humane and hence acceptable. I tried to imagine the pain a young lamb would feel as it had a tight rubber band put round its testicles and tail, which would stop the blood flow and eventually allow both these 'unnecessary' items to drop off. Up until then I had always thought that young lambs playfully bantering around in a field were doing so because they were full of the joys of spring, now I knew otherwise. I also had questions that I couldn't answer. Why were we artificially inseminating our cows with the semen from a different breed of bull, which was so large that there was no hope of the cow being able to give birth by herself? Surely it was not God's way that men should have to use ropes and even tractors to assist with calving. And was it right that small calves should live their whole lives on slatted floors in darkness, just so man could enjoy a plate of veal?

Christmas was the saddest time of the year though, because this was when we had to slaughter hundreds of cockerels and turkeys. I was never really upset when we sent things to market to be butchered, only when I was the one who had to break necks and end lives. Each year I would give one or two of the birds a reprieve though, rescuing them and giving them to Dad for his Christmas present. One year I gave him Psychedelic and Freakout, two ducks who managed to turn our small back garden into a quagmire. And another year he was presented with Henry the cockerel, who was not only an early bird himself, but by crowing at the top of his voice at five o'clock each morning he encouraged all of Littlehampton to be early risers as well.

My body was developing and growing stronger, as was

my self-confidence. Most nights the lads from the farm would visit the local pub which was called 'The Racehorse'. Whereas at one time I would not have been seen dead in a place like this, now I was starting to feel that frequenting such places was what living was all about. To begin with I would only drink soft drinks because I was a Christian, then I would only drink soft drinks because I was under age, and finally I would only drink soft drinks if the barman refused to sell me alcohol.

Living away from home and church life meant that my faith was suffering badly, and I soon discovered that I was not quite such a strong Christian as I thought I was. At first I bought a BSA Bantam motor-bike which enabled me to get home at weekends and also to attend church. Then I progressed into being a mod which meant I had to buy a Lambretta scooter and parka anorak. I was at a stage in my life when I was having to make choices, and as 99% of my time was spent with people who not only didn't share my faith but also strongly opposed it, my decisions were coloured by them.

I chose to spend more time with my mod mates and less time with Christians, I chose to spend more time on the farm and less time at home. And I chose to stop attending church because I was finding it totally boring and unrelated to real life. No one was to blame for my moving away from spiritual things except me. I chose to do this because I thought my parents were naïve and missing out on life, and I wanted to make sure that I lived my life to the full. But if anyone asked me if I was a Christian, I would always say yes.

The only reason that I would drift back to Littlehampton was to be with the boys in the band where, with my new-found confidence, I had taken on the role of lead vocalist. We had been through a few name changes and had come up with the bright idea of being called 'St James' Infirmary' which is probably where we should have been sent for treatment.

Dorothy, the farmer's daughter, had become like another sister to me, and although we would often argue and fight, we remained good friends. The only addiction I had at this stage was to chocolate swiss rolls. Every tea-time Dorothy would attempt to deprive me of my major pleasure in life by snatching the swiss roll out of my hand. This was followed by the daily punch-up, which brought laughter all round, and even old Bill seemed to smile on the odd occasion.

Peter Bradshaw and I were also very good friends, and whenever Pete came back from college we would spend a lot of time together. In the spring of sixty-six, Bill suffered a serious kidney problem and was rushed up to hospital in London. Pete felt he should visit him so I went along to keep him company. We took the train to Victoria, popped in and saw Bill, and then thought that we would make a day of it so we went to see some rude film in Soho. Well, we got a bit carried away and didn't realise the time, so when we eventually got back to the station we found that we had missed the last train home. Having no money, we spent the night trying to sleep on benches in Hyde Park. And very little sleep we had, as we kept getting told to move along – not by the police but by other vagrants who claimed we were sleeping in their beds.

Soon after that Bill returned and Dorothy had her sixteenth birthday. I was thrilled because she chose to have a party and wanted our band to play. We cleaned out the big barn, disposed of all the old spuds, grain and fertiliser sacks, swept it out and decorated it, and just left some straw bales around the edges. The big night came, and what a night it was. Bill was encouraged to go out for the evening, and once his car had disappeared down the driveway the festivities began. The band struck up and loud music echoed around the barn. Everyone danced, laughed, ate, drank and then drank some more. Even though we might have been rather merry, the only evidence that all was not one hundred per cent normal was Alfie's conviction that he was a bird. He spent a lot of the night perched on a gatepost trying to fly. We were also convinced he was a bird and kept trying to push bread down his throat to feed him. When the parents came to pick up their dearly beloveds, they first had to find them, which meant a thorough search of the haybarns, dairy and even the old pigsties, but I assume everyone was found eventually.

Early morning came, Bill returned and blew his top, but nobody seemed to take much notice. By four o'clock we were starting to fade and even our feathered friend Alfie thought it time to roost, so we all crashed out on the bales in the barn. We were so exhausted that we didn't even feel the gentle scurry of the paws of the rats and mice as they had a busy night running all over us and polishing off the leftovers of food and drink.

After a cold winter came a hot spring and summer. The grass started to grow again and we started working very long hours making the silage, cutting and collecting the haybales, and then bringing in the harvest. It was extremely hard work, but again I loved it. I was strong, fit and healthy, except for the odd migraine, and a wonderful golden-brown colour due to wearing shorts and no shirt. All in all I was very happy. On the last night of the harvest, when all the corn had been safely gathered in, which was by the way long after most harvest thanksgivings had been held, we rushed off to Littlehampton beach to celebrate. We ate, we drank, we swam, we lit a fire, and we were told by the police to put it out. But we didn't mind – we had worked hard and now we played hard.

A few months earlier I had applied to go to the West Sussex School of Agriculture, and soon after harvest I heard that I had been accepted. I'd built up such a good relationship with the Bradshaws that they kept a room for me, and although I still loved my family back in Littlehampton, home was now Petworth. I seemed to have more in common with this non-religious family.

It may seem strange that whereas I had been so keen to leave school I was now very keen to return to the world of education. The difference was, as in the Congregational Sunday school all those years ago, I enjoyed the subject. Farming, music and fun were now my life, and agricultural college would be the place where I could have the best of all worlds.

6

What's the Point?

Why try and be a goody-goody?
You'll never be perfect anyway.
What's the point of missing all the fun,
Why not just go your own way?

I did feel a bit strange arriving at Brinsbury Farm, otherwise known as the West Sussex School of Agriculture. I seemed a bit big and old to be going back to school, and although I had a government grant this would not be the same as receiving a wage packet at the end of each week. Being a residential institution, the first people I was introduced to were the Housemaster and his wife, Bill and Betty Sparks. To say that they were a couple of bright sparks would be inaccurate, but to say that it wasn't too long before I saw the sparks fly would be totally true. (Sorry, I just can't resist it.) They were both of a similar humpty-dumptyish build, and both had jolly, round faces giving a great welcome to new pupils like myself. And I felt very secure in the fact that they were quite a nosey couple and nobody could get past them in the corridor without being spotted. In fact, nobody could get past them in the corridor full stop.

After my introduction, I was shown to my dormitory. Although this was a large room containing six beds, I had my doubts as to whether it would be large enough to hold six up-and-coming young farmers whom I imagined were at least six feet tall, bulging with muscles and speaking with a worzel accent, having spent all their lives on their fathers' farms. But this couldn't have been further from the truth. What a motley looking bunch they were! Tall chaps, short chaps, fat and thin chaps. Some suffering from acne, asthma and – would you believe it – even hay fever. And to top it all there was one called Nigel, whom we nicknamed 'The Toff', who spoke as if he had come straight from public school.

The farm was much larger than Kilsham. As well as arable land there were sheep, a dairy, a piggery, a beef unit, poultry and a special site for those interested in weeding – sorry, horticulture. It also had all the latest farm machinery which I was really looking forward to playing with. Our days were divided so that half the time we would be working practically out on the farm and the other half we would be getting our heads down to learning theory in the lecture hut. We were split into working teams so we all got a chance to experience the fun and games of the different departments.

Although I have eaten pigs and even eaten with pigs, I was quite excited when the chance came to work with them. I never realised they were such interesting animals. My first task was to feed them. I had to start with the 'porkers' which were in about thirty indoor pens with a dozen pigs to a pen. For the uninitiated, I am not being rude about these little pink squealers when I call them porkers. All pigs have different names which are not supposed to be insulting but to let the unfortunate pig know his ultimate destiny – whether he will be served up with eggs or roast potatoes. So as well as porkers there are 'baconers' and 'heavy hogs'. What a din those porkers made as they waited for their food – they literally screamed. I hadn't heard such a terrible noise since back in my choir days. As I rushed round to each pen as fast as my wellies would allow me, I tipped buckets full of slushy meal into their troughs, whereupon the noise would immediately change to a very satisfied slurping sound with the odd intermittent grunt.

After feeding the porkers I had to feed the large older females known as sows. They were a vicious lot, as I discovered the minute I leapt over the corrugated fence into their pen. I could see that they were not going to be part of *my* fan club. These big girls not only weighed more than I did, but when they stood on their hind legs they were taller than me. As I approached them they started grunting and moving towards me with military precision. It was like Orwell's *Animal Farm* revisited. I quickly tipped their food into the bins, but even while I was doing this one of them had started chewing my boot. I hurriedly gave it a gentle kick with my remaining welly, then leap-frogged over two others, fell over a third, and threw myself over the fence to safety. As I returned to our bedroom no one needed to ask me what I had been doing that day, they could smell the truth for themselves. I had a hot, soapy bath, shampooed my hair twice, emptied a bottle of after-shave over myself, and put on clean clothes. On entering the dining-room I was greeted by old Sparks who took one sniff, screwed his nose up, asked me how I got on with the pigs, and told me that I needed to go and have a bath before I sat down for my meal.

From that day on I decided they could keep their stinking pigs. With a surname like mine the last thing I wanted to do was live up to it.

The farm had a special calf-unit consisting of four nurse cows, which basically fed and fostered young calves, numerous little calves, a mechanical teat (which we had to convince the calves was their mother, and if they didn't believe us they would starve), and a miserable old stockman called Ted. Now, Ted and I shared one thing in common – we both disliked each other immensely. I used to think old George back at Petworth was grumpy, but compared with Ted he was like a stand-up comedian. Admittedly Ted only had one proper leg (the other one was artificial), but that was still no reason why he should pursue and persecute me like Captain Ahab chasing after Moby Dick.

I could never do anything right with Ted. He would use sarcasm, temper and even ignore me if I accidently did anything that was not perfect in his eyes. Some of the lads would lick his boots to get on into his good books, but God never made me into a creep, and neither was I brave enough to stand up to him; I just lived in fear of the next time I was due on the calf-unit again.

I used to think that it was only school kids who were cruel and bullied, but this went on even at the agricultural college. I mentioned earlier Nigel the Toff. Sadly, no one liked him much as he was rather stuck-up, so any chance that anyone had to have a go at him they would take with great pleasure. Nigel was never cut out to be a farm worker, and it would be wrong to think that he ever could be. He was a classic gentleman farmer who would end up owning his own farm, driving around in a brand new Range Rover, and owning a bulldog called Bertram. Although he would always look as though he was busy, he would actually never be capable of doing a day's work in his life.

Poor old Toff. He was once told to top up the radiator on a Ford 5000, but when he reached the tractor he didn't have a clue where the radiator was. He asked one of the other students to show him where it could be located and they wickedly pointed to the oil-filler cap. Toff topped it up only to discover that oil and water don't mix. Another time he spent the day ploughing on a new tractor. One of the farm workers noticed that there was more smoke coming out of the tractor than out of the exhaust, and rushing over discovered that Toff probably was one of the few people on earth who have tried to plough a field with the hand brake on.

As you can imagine, our bedrooms were far from quiet at night, which was one reason why many of us overslept when we should have been on the early shift at the dairy. When the noise grew above a certain level each evening, a naked and hysterical Mr Sparks would rush into our rooms telling us to shut up. We were rotten to the Sparks, and it's quite understandable that Mrs Sparks observed that we were the worst students ever to darken their doorstep, especially after the morning she woke up to see a pair of her knickers flapping in the breeze at the top of the college flagpole.

Another one of the students, called Richard, was not only a very heavy sleeper, but snored more loudly than a tractor with a hole in its exhaust. One night it was so unbearable that once he'd dozed off, six of us opened the french windows onto the balcony and carefully and quietly moved him, his bed and his mega-loud hailer to spend the night under the stars. On reflection, it was not a nice thing to do in the middle of January.

We also had our own way of dealing with the overzealous (swots). One chap, called Clive, was always keen on impressing the cowman. On the five a.m. milking stints he would get up extra early, not bothering to wake us up, and have all the cows in the parlour before we'd even arrived at the dairy. Of course, the cowman was very impressed, but we were not – and Clive had to live with us. However, we found an appropriate cure for his overenthusiasm. One night at eleven o'clock, while he was fast asleep, we crept over to his alarm clock which he had set for four-thirty and changed it to twelve-thirty. We also altered his watch and the clock in the bedroom, then we lay down and waited. Sure enough, when twelve-thirty came and the alarm went off, we saw him dutifully jump out of bed, not quite as energetically as usual it must be noted, and by one a.m. sixty sleepy cows were in the parlour waiting to be milked. It would not be edifying to relay what the cowman called Clive, but suffice it to say Clive's newly defined relationship with his once-beloved cowman certainly made him more easy to live with.

I won't say too much about the theoretical side of my studies. Although I was quite keen on both animals and machines, I never realised that maths had so much to do with farming. We had to calibrate seed drills, ration foodstuffs, and even work out profits and losses. All I knew was that when it came to this dreaded subject, I was still a dead loss.

I mentioned in the last chapter that I liked to think that I was a mod, riding a motor scooter. Well, that was a slight exaggeration, as I must have been the only mod who couldn't manage to turn a corner without falling off. Now

Dad noticed this and, obviously wanting me to live for a reasonable length of time, decided that I might be safer on four wheels, so he started giving me driving lessons. He was a good teacher and although I failed my first test because I knocked a lady off her bike, I did manage to pass on my second attempt. As a reward Dad treated me to my first car, which happened to be a sit-up-and-beg Ford Popular.

My years at agricultural college were in the mid 60s. Any old hippies will remember that this was the height of the flower-power, love-joy-peace man era. Everyone was wearing ultra-wide flared trousers, multicoloured kaftans, and little bells and beads around their necks. I could not afford a real kaftan, so I made do with an old dressing-gown. With so much colour around, the old black Ford Popular looked right out of fashion, so the lads from the band back home in Littlehampton decided to help me customise it. Trevor, our lead guitarist, always fancied himself as an artist, so with the help of some red, blue, yellow and white paint, he proceeded to cover my machine with angels, medieval priests, dragons and anything else he thought he was good at painting. Once Picasso had done his worst, the rest of us welded on some aluminium mudguards, put in gas-cooker grills where some of the windows had been, blocked off the doors so everyone had to climb in through the boot, installed union-jack headlamps and hunting horns, and finished the masterpiece by hanging a painted toilet seat on the front grill.

Dad, now a deacon at the Baptist church, and Mum, being as spiritual as ever, no doubt found it a great blessing when I parked my creation outside their house on one of my occasional visits. Neither my car nor my kaftan were receiving a favourable reaction from my agricultural school. I thought that flower-power would fit in well with farming, especially with the horticulturalists, but the principal thought otherwise. He threatened to expel me if I ever wore my way-out clothes again. Fortunately my year was nearly up, so even though it was the age of the protest song, it seemed pointless to protest. Anyway I would have looked silly protesting all by myself as all the other students seemed happy to carry on wearing Barber jackets and Tuff working boots – and that was on their day off.

In the June of 1967 I took my City and Guilds exams, and just managed to scrape through. This allowed me entrance into further education at Plumpton Agricultural College which would begin in September.

So it was goodbye West Sussex School of Agriculture, goodbye miserable old Ted, and goodbye work because I now had eight weeks' holiday – and I was going to make sure that I made the most of it.

I got together with Alfie and another couple of friends and we decided to give my multicoloured car its first long-distance trip. So we set off towards the West Country for a camping holiday. As my car was not the fastest thing on four wheels, we only got as far as Somerset on the first night. Feeling in desperate need of liquid nourishment, we pulled in at a pub and noticed a drink we had never heard of before called scrumpy. I thought it was amazing value at just a few pence per half-pint, and we couldn't understand why the barman would not serve this mysterious liquor – until we started drinking it. After a few half-pints we began to feel the full effect of this fire-water. We couldn't and didn't drive far that night – just a few hundred yards in fact, to set up our tent.

It wasn't until dawn that someone's alarm went off. Of course, everyone shouted at poor old Alfie and told him to switch it off. Alfie, after searching around, remembered that he didn't have an alarm clock, and shouted out that it wasn't his. Gradually, with heads banging like bass drums, courtesy of the previous night's scrumpy, we all sat up and looked at each other trying to work out the culprit. We then discovered that the ringing seemed to be coming from outside our tent. Gingerly, we poked our heads out of the flap and to our horror realised that we had pitched our tent in someone's driveway, having tied two guy-ropes to the car headlights and the other two to the house gate-posts. We had camped outside someone's bedroom window and it was their alarm clock we had heard. I think that we should have secured a place in the *Guinness Book of Records* for the fastest demolition of a tent in history.

That day we thought we would go and visit the lions of Longleat as this would make a pleasant change from the semi-domestic wildlife that I was spending all my time with. On arrival, we saw a big notice that laid down some basic rules for the protection of humans, one being that car windows must remain closed. Now this posed a bit of a problem as we didn't have any windows, just the odd gas cooker grill. The white hunters came over to us, eyed the car up and down suspiciously, and then told us that my vehicle couldn't go into the park as the colours and paintings might upset the lions. After a bit of negotiating however, plus the fact that with so few people around that day they needed our money, they let us go through. They also gave us an armed escort – for our protection; or was it for the lions'?

That night we had our second and last go at the scrumpy. The following morning we were again woken by a noise, only this time it was the sound of busy traffic. It wasn't till we looked outside the tent that we realised we had camped on the grass in the middle of a dual carriageway, and the passing lorries and cars seemed to pay no attention to the fact that we, more than most, were in great need of our beauty sleep.

Once off the scrumpy, the rest of the holiday went without a hitch. The only thing that did tend to annoy me was that we were every policeman's dream. They would stop us and check the car over, basically because they could not help but notice us. To show my protest at such regular interruptions, I purchased a picture frame and carefully mounted all my driving documents on it. Every time I was stopped I would hand them this 'to put them in the picture'.

I was now eighteen. Although I had attended the occasional church service to keep my parents happy, now I had 'come of age' I had no intentions of going any more.

I wasn't taking life, including farming and my studies, seriously at all. I was going to go to Plumpton Agricultural College to have fun and enjoy myself, and woe betide anybody who was going to get in my way.

7

That's Life

We like to shock and cause offence.
A bit of aggro, a bit of aggro.
We will not obey our parents.
Ma, ma, ma, ma, ma and Pa –
That's the miserie life.

Plumpton Agricultural College was situated right near the famous race-course at the foot of the South Downs in East Sussex. The college was much larger than the school that I had just left and the work was a lot more academic, aimed at achieving a college qualification plus the National Certificate in Agriculture at the end of the year's studies.

The college was linked to two farms; one specialised in beef and calves and the other contained the dairy and piggery and was also the base for all the arable work. Again, the year was divided into theory and practical, although due to the higher qualification at stake, there would be less labouring and more studying.

There were over a hundred students living in two halls of residence. One was adjoined to the college and was more for those whose fathers were rumoured to be friends of the principal. The other, a couple of miles down the road, was a rambling, slightly dilapidated large building which went under the grand name of Middleton Manor. In our year it contained most of the odd-bods and riff-raff like me.

I was put into a large dormitory, and an oldish gentleman who only had one arm introduced himself to us, informing us that he was our housemaster as well as one of our tutors. His name was Charlie Catt. Charlie was a very nice man with only one really bad habit: he kept all the drain-pipes smothered in axle grease which meant that any student coming in late after the doors had been locked either spent the night in their car or arrived with one or two nasty stains on their clothes as an everlasting reminder to all that they were dirty stop-outs.

On the first morning we discovered all the disadvantages of living in medieval conditions miles from anywhere. The main drawback was that we had to get up earlier if we wanted breakfast because the canteen was part of the college, and with all our old bangers littering up the driveway we had to try and find one that would start each morning, or else we could kiss our breakfast goodbye.

On arrival at the college we were introduced to the staff and the other students. I was surprised to see that a couple of girls were also residential. As my years were progressing, so was my interest in women. Although these two were farmers' daughters, and at first glance it was hard to see any difference between them and the other lads, I had a feeling that by the end of our year of hard labour, having spent all our time with smelly animals and greasy machines, they would look like a couple of ravishing beauty queens to our deprived eyes.

Now I won't waste time and bore you by going through all the farming detail that I was expected to learn, although that was important. As I said, I was here to have fun. If I could do that and study, fine. If not, I would just drop the lesser of the two, which of course was the study. There were some important things to learn if I was to live the normal non-Christian life. Luckily I had many friends who were more than willing to give me instruction, both practically and theoretically.

Back at the Middleton mausoleum, on the quiet evenings when the swots were diligently studying, I was being taught the gentle art of giving all one's hard-earned money away to others, or gambling as it's more commonly known. Now, I had always chosen to steer clear of this pastime, not particularly on religious grounds, but more because I knew at some stage that it would involve me in the dreaded mathematics. Win or lose, there would come a time of reckoning when I would either have to count up my winnings or subtract my losses. As it happened it was only the latter of these two that really affected me, and even I could work out how much money I had left when I was broke.

I was also learning about the refined art of boozing. Up to now, apart from the odd scrumpy, I always went for half a pint of beer. As I couldn't stand the taste of it, this was purely for social reasons. It always seemed so bitter. I was sure that I might have enjoyed it more if it had been acceptable to add sugar and stir it. But I was mixing with hardened drinkers, and in our local I would stand and watch with great admiration as they would take it in turns to drink a yard of ale in seconds. It was quite an effort for me to knock back my half-pint by closing time. But I was always a willing learner, and one of my instructors informed me that my attitude of mind was wrong. He told me that you don't drink because you're thirsty, you drink to get drunk. It wouldn't matter if I didn't like what I was drinking, after a few pints I wouldn't be able to taste it anyway. I found this logic sobering and reassuring, and from then on I tried to keep up with my leaders.

It didn't take us long to discover that neighbouring Eastbourne's reputation for being a geriatric stronghold was absolutely true. However, it did have two large girls' colleges, and when I say large girls that is no understatement. They would often have dances and parties which we used to gatecrash. We actually had a lot in common with them as we were muscular young farmers and they were strapping physical education students. The dance floor looked more like a tag wrestling match than a disco, as both male and female boogied around, biceps bulging, with the finesse of a couple of JCBs with punctured tyres.

I was still quite shy of girls though, and by the time I had plucked up the courage to ask one of them for a dance, last orders had been called and the disco had been packed away. I was also never very confident in my dancing ability, and though I found the slow ones easy and most enjoyable, these fitness freaks always seemed to be going over to the DJ and asking him to put on very lively Tamla Motown records. So while all the girls were dancing in one corner as if they were limbering up for the 1,000 metres, we farmers would be in the other corner bouncing around like decapitated chickens.

I had several girlfriends throughout this year, but my relationships were always very moral, as all I really wanted was a good-looker to show off to my friends. I found the kissing and cuddling side of it a bit sissyish and a bit of a waste of time. I would much rather be having a laugh, or listening to music, or having a laugh while listening to music.

While I am on the subject of stupidity, I still had my old dressing-gown-cum-kaftan and I had invested in a great big lady's straw hat which I had bought from a jumble sale and dyed purple. Fortunately the college was sympathetic to eccentrics so I never got in trouble for the way I looked. Even the principal and lecturers would encourage my antics by calling me 'Flower-Power Fred'.

College also initiated me into the musical experience of singing rugby songs. Up till now I would use the odd swear word, but thanks to the literary genius of books like *Why Was I Born So Beautiful?* I could now learn a whole new language. I bought all the songbooks that were available and, thanks to my lead vocalist training, I easily memorised what few words there were. As a lot of the tunes were old hymn melodies, I at last began to see a purpose in my religious upbringing.

I had now found a place in the hearts of all the other students. I was accepted. I may have shown a total lack of interest in farming, but I would go down in the annals of Plumpton Agricultural College's history as Flower-Power Fred, the best man at leading community singing.

Now on the subject of singing, the band was the busiest it had ever been. We just seemed to be around at the right time, because audiences were more interested in the visual presentation than the actual music being played. If you had heard our music you would understand why we made it a priority to spend time concentrating on our visual presentation. We first tried employing one of our friends, who was into doing outrageous things, because we thought he would win over both organiser and audience.

At one gig in a nightclub he informed us that he had just the gimmick to light up our act, so halfway through he walked on stage wearing a stunning metal crown. To give it a finishing touch he got out his cigarette lighter and set it on fire. Now this looked really effective except for two things. One was that he had long hair and the singeing smell was foul. The other was that the club had a low ceiling which was made out of fishing-nets, so both audience and organiser couldn't believe their eyes when they saw the ceiling start to go up in flames. (Fire our nets song ....)

Realising that we were the first band to be thrown out for being a fire hazard, we not only dethroned our more than helpful arsonist, but also crowned him properly.

A great venue to play was Worthing Assembly Hall. A big-name band would play once a week, with local bands going on first and providing a din while people arrived and waited for their heroes to appear. We were given our audition on the night that a soul band called 'Jimmy James and the Vagabonds' was due to appear. Before we went on stage we thought it was important to look good, so one of the band member's girlfriends told us to remove our shirts. She then proceeded to paint various designs on our chests with her lipstick. All went well until she came to Alfie who had been blessed with so many pimples that she found it easier just to join up the dots. At this stage I was trying in vain to grow a moustache, so while I was being decorated she also obliged by putting some mascara on my top lip. Errol Flynn, eat your heart out.

Once the artwork had been completed, the MC introduced us and we rushed on stage and went bashing into our first number. Sad to say, the audience was not really tuned into our sound. It was made up of skinheads who had come to hear their favourite soul music, but at least the one or two farmers specially imported from the college clapped enthusiastically at the end of each song. Following that, people started throwing money, not exactly to us but more at us. I'm convinced that our sound wasn't enhanced by the fact that our bass player stooped down and started collecting it up rather than carrying on playing like the rest of us. By the end of the evening though, we were not too despondent. OK, we were not going to hit the charts yet, but it hadn't been a total disaster as the bass player had gathered up enough money so that we could at least go and have a pint.

News spread around college that an agricultural trip to Sweden was being arranged. As I had never been further abroad than the Isle of Wight, I soon put my name down to go. I wasn't that enamoured with the fact that we were going to be visiting farms, but Sweden had a very risqué reputation and I was quite keen to find out if it lived up to it. Once on board the ferry we all went wild. There was a disco, plenty of girls, and – most important of all – plenty of bars with plenty of cheap drink. On arrival we realised a more than tight schedule of visits had been arranged. Within two hours of treading on Swedish turf, we were in fact treading on Swedish other things as we walked around a dairy farm. When I say we, I mean just a percentage of our party, as the rest were taken straight to our hotel to sleep off the effects of our overindulgence on the ferry. As we went around the Swedish farms, what amazed me was that all the workers wore clogs. I couldn't help wondering what their wives thought when the time came to wash their socks.

After what seemed endless farm visits, we were told that we were going to take the hydrofoil over to Copenhagen. To a round of cheers we were told that we were going to visit the Carlsberg factory. It was very interesting being shown how our main pastime was made. Needless to say, there was a 100% turnout for this trip. At the end of the visit there was a long table set out before us littered with different types of lager. We were told to drink as much as we liked, compliments of the brewery. For once in our lives, we didn't need to be told twice.

Once our lecturers told us that they thought that we had honoured the brewery enough by the amount we had been able to consume, we walked outside and were suddenly hit by the cold air. The change of temperature brought about in me an instant need for the gents, and as all the party boarded the coach to take them back to the hydrofoil, I made for a park across the road with plenty of trees that would be ideal for a man with such a pressing problem as mine. Wandering back feeling much relieved if rather light headed, I boarded the coach, sat down, and fell straight to sleep. It must have been a good fifteen minutes later when I was roughly shaken by some foreign coach-driver asking to see my ticket. As I looked around to ask the lecturers who had them, I suddenly saw that not only were no lecturers present, but all the students had disappeared. Only then did I realise that after leaving the trees I had got on the wrong coach, and instead of heading back to the coast and Sweden, I was now somewhere in the middle of Denmark. Fortunately, the one sober person in our party had realised that I was missing and the coach was still waiting outside the Carlsberg factory for me as I arrived back from my personal sightseeing tour of Denmark.

Although I enjoyed the trip, I was glad to get home, especially as the one girl that I fancied, but had never had the courage to chat up, spent the return journey enjoying herself in the arms of one of my friends.

As soon as we returned I was faced with exams. During that week the band was busier than ever, and all the late nights made it very difficult to concentrate on two things at once, so I chose to concentrate on my music.

After the papers had been marked, I was called into a very stroppy vice-principal's office where I was informed that although I had just scraped through and got my National Certificate, I had failed the college exam. But in my opinion that was only the equivalent of being moaned at by Littlehampton Borough Council for not being good enough to play a gig at the local day-centre and then being invited to play at the Royal Albert Hall. I'd made it – I'd got the exam I came for.

As I left college, just like my old school reports had said, I knew I could have done better. But, I thought, at the end of the day what would it achieve if I had done? I was losing interest in work. Why shouldn't I just drop out of society like many hippies were doing? But, having found the freedom I'd longed for, why wasn't I totally happy? The answer seemed clear to me: I still had one or two Christian principles that were preventing me from getting the best out of my life, but if I ditched them I would be completely happy. If people thought that I was already extreme, they'd better watch out, because I was about to show them that I hadn't even started yet.

8

Father God I Wonder

Father God I wonder how I managed to exist
Without the knowledge of Your parenthood and
Your loving care.
But now I am Your son, I am adopted in your family
And I can never be alone,
'Cause Father God You're there beside me.
I will sing Your praises ... for evermore.

While I had been away studying, my family had moved to a village called Rustington, which was just a couple of miles away from Littlehampton. They had chosen to live in a wooden bungalow which again was situated right next to the railway line. I often wondered if Dad had some sponsorship deal with British Rail, or was it that he had a major flaw in his character and was a compulsive train spotter. Either way here they were again, down by the railway side.

Although there would have been a place for me to join them as I had now left Plumpton, I knew that I would be restricted in my activities, ambitions and personal pleasures if I returned to live at home.

I chose to move back to the Bradshaws at Petworth. Although Peter was back at home and they didn't need another full-time worker, they agreed to take me on over the harvest period which would give me time to look around for another job. Bill, the farmer, had rented some more land and this contained quite a large old house next door to an old-fashioned, noisy but working water-mill. Although half of the house was occupied by sitting tenants, Bill asked Pete and me if we would like to take over the remainder of the property – to which we said an immediate yes. We had grand visions of making it into a batchelor pad the likes of which no one had ever seen before.

The flat itself had two upstairs bedrooms, a large living-room with a huge open coal-fire, a kitchen and a dining-room, plus a toilet which was only accessible by walking through our co-resident's accommodation. The whole building was rather damp and run-down, and we knew that quite a bit of work was needed to transform it into our dream penthouse. Our neighbours were rather a strange family, so our first task was to board up all doorways through which they could gain any access into our property. But the trouble was that as fast as we would block them off, they would drill holes in them so they could peep through to keep an eye on what we were up to.

We then toured all the shops, cinemas and garages in the area to ask if we could have all their old publicity posters. These made stylish and functional wallpaper as we could sit in our armchairs and work out our shopping lists, see what was on at the pictures, and fix our cars just by staring at the walls.

Once we had moved in, the flat became the youth centre of Petworth. People were always dropping in and out, most of them girls. Not content with being a half-pint heathen, I was now out to show not only the Christians, but also the pagans what it was like to have no rules of conduct and to live purely for one's self. We had parties most Saturday nights and everyone did what was right in his or her own eyes. It was nothing on a Sunday morning to clear up well over a hundred empty wine bottles, and that didn't include the beer, cider and spirits that were liberally consumed. The next-door neighbours complained, mainly because we never invited them. On one occasion the wife decided to take the law into her own hands and entered our flat with a shotgun. One of the lads tried to push her out and ended up with the barrel shoved up his nose. It must have been painful, but he was too drunk to notice.

One other occasion of bad vibrations – and there weren't many – was when I caught Alfie chatting up one of my girlfriends. I dragged him outside and as we bundled and both rolled over in the driveway, I banged my head on a rock and knocked myself out. When I came round my first vision was of a very distraught Alfie broken hearted at the thought that he had killed me.

The morning after the night before was always hard to face. I usually got up early and, battling my way through bodies and bottles, would make some soup for breakfast, and go and eat it outside by the mill, – fresh air was vital. As I sat drinking it one Sunday morning, I noticed somebody else taking an early morning breather – a reasonably tall, good-looking, quiet bloke who was a loner if ever I saw one. I couldn't remember having seen him the night before. To be friendly I started talking to him, offering him some soup which he readily accepted. He then introduced himself as Andy Piercy. He looked quite intelligent and it came as no surprise to me that he had studied at Guildford Royal Grammar School and was now doing an apprenticeship with the GPO.

As we sat out in the sun he modestly told me that he could play the guitar a little, so I nipped into the flat and found him an old acoustic and watched with mouth wide open as he finger-picked through Bert Janch's instrumental 'Angie' as easily as spreading butter on toast. From that very first bowl of soup together, I knew that we were going to become best mates, even though over the next year or so I saw him very infrequently.

As the harvest was safely gathered in, so my work on Kilsham Farm expired. Fulfilling those prophetic words written on my school reports, I did something that I was qualified to do – I joined Petworth Dairies and became a milkman. Derek, the boss's son, was the most sincere and dedicated milkman that I had ever seen. He spent the first week teaching me my round. We sat in a Bedford van and drove out on the Guildford road to just past the village of Northchapel,stopping at every house along the way to deliver our wares. Derek was one of those horribly reliable sort of guys who was always smiling and saying good morning to everyone. I thought that no one in their right mind could be that cheerful at that time of the morning.

I hated the predictability of the job. Every morning I would stop at a couple of old dears' houses for a cup of tea and a biscuit, and once I had said thank you all would go quiet because I would run out of conversation. Next stop was the primary school's kitchen where I was given a bit of the pudding that was about to be inflicted on the pupils later that day. Then old Mrs Fishface would complain that I hadn't shut her gate, or mustn't take shortcuts to the next garden by treading on her flower-bed, or I'd given her silver top instead of gold top or I'd forgotten to put her precious cup over the cap and the birds had eaten the cream. With all sorts of wars and disasters going on around the world, the ultimate crisis in Northchapel was that I had put somebody's bottles on the wrong side of their step. It all seemed so trivial to me.

The worst time of all was Friday afternoon, when I had to work out what everyone owed me that week (calculators hadn't been invented yet). Whatever I had worked out that my customer owed me, they always disagreed. Because I was never confident that my mathematics was infallible, I always ended up agreeing with them. On my round there was a council estate where I had to refuse milk to a number of houses that hadn't paid up. I found it very embarrassing to have them shouting and swearing at me all the way down the road for my 'lack of social conscience'.

I never believed that my social life should be affected by mere work, so after completing my milk round it was time for the next round – of drinks at the pub. I would still continue to drink excessively each night because I knew that I wouldn't have had the nerve to do half the things that my body wanted me to do had I been sober. Once I got back to the flat I would make myself sick and swallow a dose of Eno's to prevent a hangover at 4.30 the next morning. From this time onwards my nickname changed from

Flower-Power Fred to Eno, as I was told that I was going down as fast as a dose of salts.

My staple diet was cornflakes and cream, courtesy of the dairy, and the big three Bs: baked beans, black pudding and brandy. With this sort of diet I was not only becoming unhealthy – I was not very acceptable company either.

By Christmas I'd had enough of delivering daily pintas, so after I'd collected all the tips from my round, I resigned. They seemed disappointed and when they asked me why, I lied about having trouble with my back from lifting the crates. In reality I was getting trouble from my kidneys from lifting the glasses.

I needed more and more money to maintain the standard of happiness that I was fighting so hard to keep, so I got a well-paid job with a veterinary firm. It involved travelling up and down the country to poultry farms, and vaccinating chickens against infectious bronchitis and fowl pest.

A crew of about half-a-dozen of us would climb into a big coach which was kitted out with bunks, cooker, shower etc, then travel away for about a week at a time. As well as getting our normal wages, we would also receive subsistence for being away at nights. We would arrive at a farm, don our smart green overalls and little caps, hang the vaccine around our necks, prepare our syringe guns, and head off into the darkest deep-litter sheds and battery cages. The mortality rate was very high as the foolish chickens would all rush into the corners and crush each other to death. The battery cages were even worse as we would always find dead birds enmeshed in the bottom of the cage, that had been lying there for at least a month. To relieve the boredom we would often have water-pistol fights with the vaccine, and I got soaked so many times that I was soon thoroughly immunised against fowl pest.

Although the job was pretty earthy, I worked with some great people. I got on particularly well with a lad called Ali. At this stage in my musical career I had finished with the drums and was learning the acoustic guitar and the three chords that would prove to be a major influence on the rest of my life. Ali was at about the same stage musically, and started to interest me in traditional folk music. The two of us would tour the various folk clubs and even attempt to perform the odd number alongside our nationwide chicken tour.

Our HQ was in a town on the coast. The boss was a bit of a playboy, seeming to spend more time with his racing car than his business. One night after a long week away we went into his local, appropriately named 'The Lively Lady', the boss insisted on buying drinks all round. I thought that night for a change I would try barley wine. I knew it was extremely strong and I felt like getting canned. By closing time we all staggered out, and while some of us were trying to remember which car was ours, others were in the middle of the road with blood pouring from their fingertips as they vainly tried to scratch up the white line. This, we thought, was really living.

My life was full and busy. Everything was going my way, as it always had. Yet when I returned to the flat and lay in bed and allowed myself to think, I was feeling increasingly empty. But I couldn't understand why. I'd had the best of everything. I'd had more experience in a year than the average Casanova would have had in a lifetime. I had more laughs than anyone I'd seen around me. I had more friends than I needed, I had no fears of death, hell or damnation. Yet even by not allowing the word 'self-control' to enter my vocabulary, I knew I was far from happy and satisfied. I had to keep on having more and more of everything, becoming increasingly overindulgent. I also knew that I was nearing a time when my body and mind would not be able to keep up with my excesses.

It was early one morning soon after this that a gang of us went off to a job in the firm's Land Rover. We were travelling at a reasonable speed and I was just dozing off in the back when we suddenly hit some oil in the road. The next thing I was aware of was the Land Rover rolling through three different front gardens. I was thrown out of the back door and landed on top of a hedge. The Land

Rover was written off, but fortunately we were not. We were taken to the local hospital, and although we were all suffering from shock, thankfully no one was seriously injured. As I left the hospital I noticed that the collar on my thick leather flying-jacket had been ripped straight off as it caught the metal side of the vehicle, and I realised that had it been another inch, it would have been my throat or neck. I must admit it got me thinking. Did someone up there want me to stay alive for some special purpose?

Once back on the farm I was again shaken as I got talking to one of the most foul-mouthed, debauched individuals I knew. Throughout all my pleasure-seeking times I would never blaspheme as I had never been in doubt about the existence of Jesus or God. I would never deny them, nor did I wish to hurt them in any way, so I would always claim to be a Christian. What sent me reeling was when this godless fellow turned round and asked me in an accusing tone what right I had to say that I was a Christian when I lived a more unChristian life than anybody else he knew.

I tried to ignore my conscience by not allowing myself time to think, filling every minute of the day with work, drink or girlfriends. But I knew I was on the run and just using any thing or person to keep me well away from reality.

At this time I was driving a souped-up Morris Minor 1000. One evening my latest girlfriend, a couple of others and I went to a folk club in Guildford. We were about to return home, having had a good night out and all being rather inebriated, when I spotted an ice-cream sign sitting on the pavement. As no one seemed to own it, I decided to take it back to the flat as I thought it would make a perfect coat-stand. With its large concrete base it was heavy, and it took a couple of us to get it onto the back seat. As we did so the suspension almost collapsed, but at the moment a coat-stand was more important to me than a car.

As we were returning home, a thick fog came down and visibility grew very poor. But as usual I was in quite a hurry so I pulled out into the middle of the road to overtake the old curb-crawler in front only to discover that there were another three cars in front of him. I started to panic a bit as the car that was behind me moved up which meant that I couldn't get back into the queue and was wedged on the wrong side of the road. Things got worse because I could see some headlights just coming into view and heading straight for me. Quickly I pushed my foot down on the accelerator as hard as I could, hoping to race it to the front of the queue and save a head-on collision. But I was not fast enough and the car coming towards me swerved to the left, avoiding me but flying off the road out of view into the fog.

Even though I was the sort of person never to allow my conscience to get the better of me, the fragments of Christianity still remaining within me prevented me from racing away from the accident. Someone might be seriously injured. I pulled the car into the side of the road and ran back to see if the poor victim was all right.

I couldn't get too close as I discovered that the car had ended up in a pond, but as the owner paddled out towards me shouting, I realised to my horror that he was dressed in a uniform, and through the fog I could just make out the outline of a floating police car.

The poor man was so shaken that he couldn't even write my name down, so he called in reinforcements and took us back to the station. Once there I was led to a cell and told to remove my shoelaces, to which I replied that I was hardly going to strangle myself over a motoring offence. They then set about searching the car, and discovered some of my chicken vaccination needles in the boot. These needles were so large that if a junkie had used them he would have leaked, but the police did not consider this as they searched every inch of the car looking for dope. Of course, all they discovered was fowl pest vaccine.

A little while later one observant officer noticed a rather large ice-cream sign sitting on my rear seat, which he guessed did not belong to me as I was not wearing a white coat with Walls written on it, so I was charged with dangerous driving and robbery.

Having spent most of the night in the cell I was eventually released. I explained to my father what had happened, and he took it very seriously. His first course of action was to resign from the Baptist church diaconate on the basis of the Bible's insistence that a deacon must be able to manage his family. Then he acquired a reputable Christian lawyer for me who instructed me to smarten up, get my hair cut, and wear a suit in court as this always impressed the magistrates.

Well, I was blowed if I was going to creep to some senile old magistrate, so when the day of judgement came I wore my usual old clothes and kept my hair long. First came my robbery charge. Two policemen lifted Exhibit A, the rusty old ice-cream sign, onto the table. It was then discovered that no one had owned up to owning it, so this charge was dropped. Then came the dangerous driving. As they hammered me, so I became more and more angry until I completely lost my temper and started shouting back. At this point my good Christian defence just put his head in his hands, gave up, and sat down. Although it was my first offence, I had obviously upset them as they gave me the maximum penalty which was a heavy fine, endorsements, and a ban from driving. As I left the dock I shouted out to them for my ice-cream sign back, but no one answered me.

It was nearing Christmas, and I had failed to realise just how much of my life had hinged around a car. I lost my job because I could not drive, I lost a lot of my friends because I couldn't chauffeur them around any more. Even the girls wanted to be driven round and did not want to spend all their time in my flat, and I had very little money so my sources of entertainment were drying up. The parties came to an end, the damp crept through the walls so that all the posters decorating the lounge fell off and lay all over the floor. Even Pete had become ill and had moved back to the farmhouse. Everything seemed to be collapsing all around me. I allowed myself to start thinking and I became very depressed. I even contemplated suicide, but knew I would not have the nerve to carry it through.

It was Christmas Eve, and after a few drinks to give me courage I decided to go home to Mum and Dad. It was only about nine o'clock when I arrived, but after my parents smelt my breath they decided to go off to bed. I sat in my bedroom and for the first time in years I started talking to God. I knew that I was faced with a major problem. I had tried everything that could possibly bring contentment and happiness, but I hadn't found it. Yet I hated the thought of being like all the Christians I knew because they seemed so boring and lifeless. I wanted something very special, even though I knew I deserved nothing. I'd almost forgotten what prayer was, but with every bit of meaning and sincerity that I had in my body I pleaded with God that if he could give me a really exciting Christian life, one that was not necessarily easy but one I would really enjoy and that would provide peace and satisfaction, then I would do whatever he wanted me to and try to stop doing all the things that made him unhappy.

I felt no lightning bolts come out of the sky and strike me, no flashing, blinding sensations, but for the first time in years that night I slept well, knowing in my heart that I would never be the same again. I was about to start a different life, where old things were going to pass away and all things were going to be made new.

9

Spirit of God

Spirit of God,
Please fill me now to overflowing,
Spirit of God,
Give me the words You want me to say.
Spirit of God, release my tongue
To praise the Holy Son,
Spirit of God, fill this spirit of mine.

When I eventually awoke the following morning I can't say that I felt any different, yet somehow I knew that I was. I told my mother that I had given my life back to God, to which she quite calmly replied that she would wait and see if it was real. I was a little shocked at her lack of hysterical joy. I thought I would at least have received some new clothes and jewelry, and that the fattened turkey would have been brought out of the freezer. After all, the prodigal had returned. Now I was left in the position of having to prove the reality of my newly-discovered faith before the celebrations could take place. I often wondered what made me receive such a revelation of God that previous evening, but now I know it was a culmination of many years of persistent prayer by my parents that brought it all about, for which I was very grateful. As the Bible says, 'The prayer of a righteous man is powerful and effective' (James 5:16).

I returned to preach at Petworth, telling all my sinful friends my good news. Remembering the results after Pentecost when Peter preached and thousands became Christians, I would have been happy with a similar response even if it had been on a much smaller scale. As I started expounding, however, I realised that I was not quite the Billy Graham I thought I was, as within a few moments my preaching had not only lost them, but within an even shorter period of time I could see that they were wishing I would get lost. The next few weeks were very difficult as I tried to readjust my whole lifestyle. I wasn't without my failings, and these were all eagerly noticed by the watchful eyes of my friends and relayed back to me. But even though the verbal persecution was very painful, nothing was going to make me go back on what I had promised to God.

I started to attend two churches, both for different reasons. On Sunday morning I would go with my parents to Littlehampton Baptist Church where I had been given the job of a Sunday school teacher which was very handy as I still found the services and sermons a little tedious and longwinded, so having to up and leave during the singing of the second hymn suited me fine. Also I had all the little uncontrollables in my class and I loved being with them as they were kids after my own heart. In the evenings and mid-week I would attend Fittleworth Evangelical Free Church which was near Petworth. Because only a dozen or so people attended and they had a great young minister, the service was much more informal and the preaching seemed more simple and relevant to where I was at.

Although I had proved to be very much a non-evangelist in Petworth, I was enjoying more success in Littlehampton. After many hours of debate, argument and discussion, but fortunately no violence, Alfie had become a Christian. Together we set about some more of our friends and they followed suit until there was quite a little nucleus of us wild, untamed young Christians who were out to attack the devil and clobber some stuffy church traditions at the same time.

One Sunday I invited an old school-friend Paul along to the Baptist Church. Although I hadn't seen this guy for years, I remembered that while we were at school we used to talk about Christian things together, and I also knew that he had attended the local brethren assembly. I sat in the front row waiting for him, and about ten minutes after the service had started he arrived dressed in a very smelly yakskin coat and laughing his head off as he sauntered down the aisle to join me. As non-religious as I was, I felt he was going a bit over the top when he put his feet up on the pew and lay along it, only to wake up when the collection came round at which point he threw some money up in the air shouting, 'Pennies from heaven!' frightening the life out of all the older members of the church, especially the treasurer.

Paul made it very clear to me afterwards that the only reason he had agreed to meet me was because he was heavily into drugs and he thought I was missing out and wanted to convert me back to the good old life. But neither Paul nor his girlfriend had the power or influence to make me turn away from God. Even while Paul was talking I knew he was not only trying to convince himself by the lies he was telling, but he was also being spoken to by God. It wasn't long before Paul had committed himself to the Lord Jesus Christ.

A priority for me at this point was a job. The only farming job that I could find was near a village called Bolney, about twenty miles from my parents' home. My parents were a little scared that I might lose my new-found faith once I left Christian circles, but I had no fear of that. As I packed up all my worldly wealth to move, I felt that God was telling me to destroy my massive record collection. I argued with him at first, but he made it clear to me that the reason that it had to go wasn't because all the records were evil, though I knew that some of them were, but because the songs would have brought to mind some of the ungodly things that I had been participating in whilst listening to this music. I couldn't destroy them myself, so I gave them to my dad who burnted the lot. I must admit, once they had gone I did feel a lot cleaner inside.

It was in the spring of 1970 that I arrived at Bolney. The farm was a small, very intensive and very well-run dairy farm. John, who was the owner, was to be my only co-worker. John was in his late thirties and an extremely hard worker. He was certainly out to get his pound of flesh from me. Having to work very long hours together gave me a great chance to talk to him about Christianity, but I got the similiar non-response that I had received at Petworth, so I began to believe that it was impossible to be a farmer and a Christian.

For the first time I had a house to myself, a tied cottage about a quarter of a mile away from the farm which was close enough to get there by five o'clock in the morning to milk the cows, yet far enough away to get the peace and quiet that I needed to spend time getting to know God better. I had hardly any furniture so I just lived on the ground floor and kept upstairs free for what I called 'grovelling times'. In these times I would just lie on the wooden floorboards and pray for hours about anything and everything. I had just finished reading Norman Grubb's book *Rees Howells, Intercessor* and I not only wanted to be a man of prayer but also a man of faith. Not knowing quite how to go about this I started in very practical ways, but with little success. Once my car had a flat tyre and seeing this as an ideal opportunity to get my faith going, I not only spent hours praying for it to get mended and refilled, but I also went out and laid hands on it as I had read about in the early church. I was very disappointed when nothing happened and I had to get out the jack and put on the spare tyre as anyone else would have had to do.

I would always try and be home for Sunday and Wednesday nights. On Sundays were the church meetings and on Wednesdays I went to my sister Heather's house. Heather and her husband David, a Baptist church deacon, would hold a very informal meeting every Wednesday evening in their flat where all us eager young Christians would meet and listen to various speakers.

It was at Easter when the new minister Alan Pringle, whom we all grew to love, gave a talk on being baptised. I had been christened and confirmed many years ago, but when I read the words in the Bible 'Believe and be baptised', I knew that this was what God wanted me to do, and preferably in that order. So I went along to a series of talks which were called baptismal classes, which on reflection could have been said more concisely in sixty minutes rather than the six weeks allocated. First, I was told about the spiritual significance of baptism where going under the water portrayed death to the old life and coming up out of the water showed the brand-new life I now had with Jesus. Then came the practical instructions. I was told that I was to stand in a tank in the floor at the front of the church which would be filled with warm water: I was to stand rigid and keep my mouth shut except for saying yes a couple of times to questions about whether I was sure I was a Christian, and I must remember that when I went to get changed I was not to go into the first Sunday school room because that was where the girls would be changing.

Sunday night came. I was very nervous. I stood in the water shivering. It was nothing to do with the temperature of the water – it was just plain fear. Then splash, under I went. When I came spluttering up out of the water I could not put into words how fantastic I felt. Somehow it was so much more than just a declaration to those around me, something inexpressible had happened inside me.

Although I was getting stronger spiritually, I seemed to be lacking in power. Apart from my dad, who still had no problems from the ball-bearing in his brain, I had not seen any real healings or miracles such as I had read about in the Bible. I also could not understand that when people were praying for those who were sick, quoting James 5:14–15 – 'Is any one of you sick? He should call the elders of the church to pray over him and anoint him with oil in the name of the Lord. And the prayer offered in faith will make the sick person well,' they then had to tag on the words, 'But your will be done, Lord.' I gradually realised that this little clause was added in case the person got worse or died, then we could all assume that it was God's will that the person should either remain in their sickness and suffering or snuff it. It was, of course, a cop out, and it all boiled down to the fact that none of us had a clue as to what the word 'faith' really meant.

A short while after I was baptised, a young Baptist minister called Terry Virgo came to talk to our ever-expanding tribe of hot gospellers at our Wednesday night meeting. At first sight Terry appeared to be nice, quiet, typical ex-Bible college material, but once he started talking he seemed to get very excited which I thought was quite out of character for a Baptist minister. He was telling us about something called the baptism in the Holy Spirit, which he himself had only experienced just a short while earlier. He pointed to Bible verses showing that this power from on high was not just for the early church but also for us today. And he talked with great excitement about some of the supernatural presents that God gave to those who had been filled with the Holy Spirit. Not only did his voice get so loud that I thought that we would have complaints from the neighbours, but his face went rather red and I was frightened that he was going to burst a blood vessel. He obviously had discovered something that stirred him up like nothing else he had ever found.

As he concluded his talk, Terry asked any of us who would like to be baptised in the Holy Spirit to go into the next room where he would pray for us. Terry was nearly trampled to death in the rush and within seconds he found that he was the only one left in the meeting room. We didn't understand a lot of what had been said, but being a bunch of naïve young Christians, if we heard that God was giving anything away then we wanted it whatever it was. We all sat in a long line while Terry and Alan started at one end, putting their hands on people's heads and praying over them to receive the power from God. I was about halfway down the line, so I was watching intently to see what was happening. Some stood there and made funny sounds through their mouths which we had been told was speaking in new tongues, which simply meant using a brand new language to praise God in. Others fell on their knees thanking God in English, and some just stood there as if nothing had happened. The closer they came to me the more excited I got. With all the strange noises going on around me I can't say that I felt fearful, but rather more apprehensive as to what I would do when I was prayed for.

Then it happened, the moment I had been waiting for. Two pairs of hands were firmly clamped onto my head and the prayer was prayed. I stood with my eyes firmly shut and felt what can only be described as a surge of electricity passing through my body. I stood there rigid as they moved on to pray for others. I was receiving a very special experience, so I stood totally still, frightened to move in case I lost the amazing sensation that I was feeling.

I didn't have a clue how long I stayed static, but eventually I knew I had to come back down to earth so I tried to open my eyes but found that I couldn't. I screamed out at the top of my voice, 'Help, I've gone blind!' I couldn't see a thing and no one had warned me that this might happen. I could sense that those who had already been prayed for were quite relieved that this hadn't happened to them, and those who were yet to be prayed for were starting to get nervous. Terry and Alan rushed back to me and kept saying the obvious, telling me to open my eyes, to which I replied that I couldn't. All I could see was this incredibly bright light dazzling me.

Within a short while I regained my vision, much to the relief of everybody, especially Terry, Alan and our patient heroes at the end of the queue. But I had tasted just a tiny part of God's power, and it had nearly blown me apart. From now on nobody, whatever their argument, could convince me that I was not in tune with an almighty God who was capable of doing anything and nobody on the face of the earth would be able to stop him. I would never forget that evening.

I wasn't too disappointed that I hadn't spoken in tongues; I knew that I had now been baptised in the Holy Spirit and was filled with a new power. For the next three days back at Bolney, the poor farmer could not get any conversation out of me as all I could do was shout out praises to God. My grovelling times back at the cottage took on new dimensions. I spent many hours in Bible reading and prayer which meant that I was constantly being refilled with the Holy Spirit. This stopped me from getting that horrible drained feeling which comes after spending many hours working with atheists and trying to preach to them without any visible success. I was also getting quite inspired in my songwriting. As well as writing many little parable songs, like 'Eli the Fly', I was surprised that immediately after I had written a praise song called 'I'm So Happy', within ten minutes I'd written the words and music to a four-verse song called 'The King of Glory', which was used to help many people become Christians.

It came as a surprise to everyone that Sussex was about to be put on the map. A three-day rock festival called Phun City was to be staged in a field very near to Clapham village. From past personal experience I knew that it would be a breeding ground for immorality and drugs, and that some of the bands were, by their own confession, well into pushing the occult.

We had a special time of prayer about this, and I felt God speaking to me. Rather embarrassed, I announced to all present that I had been given a picture of Moses while the battle was going on against the Amalekites. Moses was sitting on a hill with his hands in the air, and all the time that his hands were held high the Israelites were winning, but when they dropped the enemy gained control. I felt that three of us should go up on the hills overlooking the field, and as my hands were held in the air Satan would not gain any ground, but if they dropped he would. Many other churches in the area were organising evangelistic campaigns into the enemy camp, but when I posted letters to them telling them what I thought we needed to do, they obviously thought that I was some sort of loony as they didn't even bother to write back.

Not to be deterred, on the first night of the festival three of us stood on the hill, me with my hands held high and the other two making sure that they stayed that way. It wasn't the aching arms that proved to be the main problem, but all the people out on a summer evening walk who kept passing by and looking at us as though we were some kind of nuts. After a few hours it started to pour with rain. We believed that this was an answer to our prayers, so rather than drown we went home.

The festival was a complete wash-out. Half the bands didn't bother to turn up, and the few punters who had attended spent all their time under plastic sheets trying to keep dry. The only time the rain stopped was when a Christian called Nigel Goodwin was given permission to take a Sunday morning service from the main stage as it was far too wet to put any bands on. Nigel loudly declared to everyone that God was going to stop the rain for one hour so people could come along to the service. We were all amazed that as Nigel preached the good news of Jesus the weather remained clear and dry, but as he finished his closing prayer it poured down. I drove a couple of the rock fans to the station afterwards, and all they could talk about was how pleased they were to have seen a real miracle, and I must admit that I was quite chuffed that I had been there to see it too.

My contract to work on Bolney Farm only lasted until the end of the summer as I wanted to learn more about the Bible and thought that the best way to do this was to go to Bible college. I applied to one in South Wales. After a journey of two hundred miles I arrived for my interview, but the length of my hair and failure to sport the obligatory gospel grey suit must have put them off as they didn't even offer me a cup of tea. They literally pushed me out of the door, making it very clear that I was not the sort of student they desired. Having sampled their teaching on hospitality, there was no way that I would trust their teaching on theology. The farmer wanted me to stay on and work for him, and though I did not have a place at a Bible college I knew that God had other things in store for me, so I thanked him but declined his offer.

Between March and July of that year I had organised a series of evangelistic folk-music evenings in conjunction with the Baptist church's youth group, which had now gained the grand title of Littlehampton Youth Outreach. These were called 'Saving Offer', 'Teach In' and 'Reach Out'. We even did one in Bolney called 'Let Bolney Live', but somehow I don't think Bolney wanted to. Apart from the latter, these evenings were very successful. Many people outside of the Christian faith would come, and by the end of the evening many of them had decided that they too wanted to become Christians.

In August 1970 I left Bolney. I was unemployed but that didn't worry me because I felt that God was pleased not only with me but also the events that I had been organising. I knew that he wanted me to develop these and take them to neighbouring villages. How would I live, who would support me, would I be welcomed by the local churches, let alone the unsaved? Would my minister and Littlehampton Baptist Church agree with my guidance? Would I be the first evangelist in Britain to die by faith? These were minor details. All I had to be assured of was that this was God's plan for the next stage of my life ... and I was.

10

I've Made Up My Mind

I've made up my mind that I'm going to follow –
Wherever Jesus leads me I will go.

Being totally convinced of my 'hit-a-village' calling, I had a temporary setback when I thought that God was telling me to do something else. Being a young Christian, I was never quite sure if what I was hearing was God's voice or just one of my ideas. Consequently, I never spent too long in thought and prayer because I found that these more usual methods of guidance tended to confuse me further. It wasn't that God kept changing his mind, but that my erratic leadings took me up so many blind alleys. I could not even go to any Christians for advice because they would simply recommend that I got a job and became a 'normal' Christian like them.

Christian Publicity Organisation and *Challenge* were now flourishing in Worthing and becoming a great resource to the church. Meanwhile Uncle Allan, always the great visionary and never willing to give up, had acquired a large house in Cornwall, and armed with words from Haggai 2:9 – '"The glory of this present house will be greater than the glory of the former house," says the Lord Almighty' – he was prepared to resurrect the now almost extinct Turn to Christ organisation.

Dad refused to join Uncle Allan, but I thought that maybe this was the start of a new 'Old Rectory', and maybe the baton would be handed on to me and a new generation for this vision and work to prosper again.

With this in mind I set off for Cornwall. When I got off the coach at this way-out-west village called Linkinhorne and saw just Uncle Allan, Aunt Margaret and another lady who happened to own the house, my heart sank. Even with Uncle Allan's masterly way of sharing his heart, I just could not catch the vision. For the next few days I did some gardening and built a wall which fell over, but my heart was not in it. To me the house seemed more like a place of retirement than a strategic place to attack from. A short while later I left. I did not want to upset my uncle, as he was one of my greatest heroes, but I knew that my calling was to be at the heart of where people are, not in the heart of the English countryside.

On returning to Littlehampton I met up with Paul again. Unfortunately he still wore his smelly yakskin coat, but at least he had given up drugs and become a very committed Christian. He too had left his job, and as he not only played the bongos but also had a very old Bedford Dormobile which was handy for sleeping in, we thought this sufficient guidance for us to form a partnership and hit the villages together.

Paul, while famous for a kind heart and a willingness to help anybody, was probably better known for his manual skills in bodging. Whatever the task or job that needed to be done, Paul would not only attempt it, breaking every craftsman's rule, but guarantee it for at least ten minutes. Hence he rightfully earned the nickname 'Bodger'. Due to excessive drug-taking Paul's memory was not brilliant, but the incredible thing was that God had fixed it so that he could just remember Scripture, therefore, even if he forgot who he was he could at least look it up in Acts and find someone with the same name. Just one other thing about Paul's character, which was both a strength and a weakness. He was always cheerful and joking, and even during the most serious crisis he would find something that would tickle him and set him off chuckling.

One of our first ports of call on our countywide village crusades was a place called Uckfield. Although we did not actually have an invitation to do anything there, we did have the name and address of one of the leading Christian businessmen in the area. We hit Uckfield with a bang, as the first confrontation we had was with another car which Paul had managed to drive into. With the irate driver of the other car jumping up and down swearing and Paul going into one of his giggling fits and all this in the middle of a busy high street, it would have been easy to question whether we were in God's will at all. Things did not improve much after our meeting with the Christian businessman. After wanting more information out of us than the Spanish Inquisition, he made it very clear that he did not want us doing anything on his patch. We argued with him that we felt it was what the Lord wanted because we had run out of petrol and couldn't go any further anyway, at which point he altered our guidance by filling our vehicle up with petrol and wishing us *bon voyage* to go in any direction as long as it was out of Uckfield.

We now had just enough petrol to get to London, so we thought that we would break into Soho. Shaking the dust of Sussex off our feet, we went for the capital, sin-city itself.

As we wandered around outside all the strip clubs and girlie revues, we glanced at the life-sized photographs and were disgusted by them. The only trouble was that due to our not-so-distant and dubious past, we found it very hard to talk to people about the Lord. Our eyes seemed to keep wandering over to look at those pictures.

As we walked down Wardour Street, I saw some very large premises for sale. Without actually asking the Lord whether he wanted it or not, we immediately claimed it for him. We then went straight to the estate agents and offered to buy it with the Lord's money, even though we were not quite sure where he kept it. I will spare you what they said to us when they found out that we had no jobs, no capital, and not even enough faith to fill our tank and get us back to Littlehampton. Far from downhearted, we just jumped into the Bedford and drove as far as we could, ending up back in my other sin-city, Petworth.

We took up residence in the car park under a street lamp, as this made it possible to lie in bed and read our Bibles. Many a night we would be annoyed when the lights went off at midnight, for we were invariably just halfway through some exciting passage. It was now late autumn and very cold, but we couldn't complain. After all, we were blessed with an en-suite bathroom courtesy of the local public conveniences. Then there was the joy of being run into the local nick for vagrancy, always a nice place to warm up.

Our days were spent knocking on every door in the town. As well as confronting the occupant with a questionnaire on Christianity just to get conversation rolling, we would also invite them to a concert on the Saturday in whatever venue we could get hold of.

There was, however, a very kind Christian family in Petworth called the Snellers. Not only did they seem to own half the shops in the town, and were financially loaded, but they were also from quite an exclusive open Brethren denomination. These things tended to cut them off from Mr Average whom we were trying to reach, but it didn't exclude them from us, even though we were in many ways opposites. They were very generous to us. As well as helping to fund our little work, every tea-time they would give us the most enormous meal that I had ever seen, so a friendship over food was quickly built up.

We were also building up a lot of other good relationships with those we were contacting in Petworth. It was great to see how God was starting to use us. We were never totally needy or hungry, even though God always seemed to wait till the eleventh hour before actually providing our essentials. We could see that having to rough it was all part of God's training programme for us, teaching us to look to him and not to people.

If you cast your mind back to our Petworth parties, you will remember that I told you about my friend from the GPO called Andy Piercy. Although most of our little group of friends had become Christians, many after much argument and debate, there was no one to compare with Andy when it came to sheer stubbornness. I would argue with Andy and he would completely disagree with all I said. Then he would come to a concert, break down in tears, say a prayer of commitment to Christ, then the following day deny that anything had happened. This became quite a regular occurrence till we had almost given up with him.

On a Baptist youth weekend at the Elim Bible College, Andy was in the library with Alfie and me, looking through a book on revival. We were easily excited and a book like this was all we needed to start us praising God. In no time we ended up in our usual position face down on the carpet. We felt the presence of God come into that room in such a tangible way that we could almost reach out and touch it. In our excitement we clamped hands on Andy as we were never ones to miss an opportunity. After being stuck to the carpet stunned for a while, he suddenly leaped up and went rushing out of the room. We didn't see him till the following morning. When he staggered in at daybreak, he was a broken man. He had obviously spent the whole night fighting with God, but eventually he conceded and was now a new person.

Andy was totally committed, a radical disciple if ever there was one. How many people do you know who, after reading in the Bible about only possessing one set of clothes, would immediately take all their other clothes to the jumble sale? Andy and I started working on some projects together. Our first major production was a nativity play called 'Emmanuel'. This was to be held in a theatre on Littlehampton sea-front on the two nights previous to Christmas. Andy wrote the script and between us we wrote all the songs. Both young and old folk from the Baptist Church were our actors. We billed it 'A Portrayal Surrounding the Birth of Mankind's Saviour', and tried to keep it completely accurate to the biblical account. Our local paper printed a notice about the event on December 4th 1970.

It all went off very well, even if Andy did get stroppy with the girl portraying Mary, and with less than two minutes to curtain up we had a very upset, weeping Virgin on our hands. In some ways the production was way ahead of its time. There was no scenery – we relied for effect on the actors, use of lighting, and probably most important of all, acoustic music. The local press applauded our endeavours with such statements as, 'A huge success,' and, 'The play was beautifully produced with original songs.' Many people became Christians during these two evenings, and many non-Christians were brought along, not least a tiny, dark-haired, teenage lassie from Perth in Scotland whose name was Irene Cochrane.

On Christmas Day we went carol-singing around some of the local old people's homes, and that is where I was first introduced to our latest, as yet unconverted member of the ever-increasing bunch of young people that seemed to be joining us. Irene made it very clear that she thought both Andy and I were a couple of bigheads. What made it worse was that the previous night she had thought I was oriental as I'd been squinting in front of the bright lights. I didn't really mind what she thought of me as she was unavailable anyway, and was preoccupied with trying to sort her life out.

A few weeks before Christmas she had taken an overdose but was miraculously caught in time and whisked into hospital for a stomach pump. The Christian family who had taken her in had brought her along, after much persuasion, to 'Emmanuel' and then to church on Christmas Day. Unbeknown to her my Mum had actually been sitting in the Baptist Church that morning behind Irene praying for her. Irene was desperately searching for something to live for. Her life so far had not been a happy one as her parents had separated and her father had become an alcoholic. Although still very young she had certainly seen life and didn't like it and had found no reason to go on. That was until one night after much battling and arguing with God and shouting at poor old Alfie – she was a typical fiery Scot – she eventually gave in and totally and utterly gave her heart to God on January 6th 1971.

Paul, Alfie and I had now become members of the Baptist Church. At our first members' meeting we wanted everyone to see that we intended to be fully active members, so when any other business came up we leaped up with about half a dozen things that we felt were unbiblical about the way the leaders were running the church, which was probably not a great blessing to them. We were allowed to hold a youth service one Sunday night. Here I had my first opportunity to preach formally. Everything was going very well until I read out a couple of modern poems to put over one of my points. OK, so they were written by people presumably outside our faith who tended to use colourful, descriptive language, but it was a youth service and I thought the old dears would understand that. But they didn't, and from that time on I was banned from speaking in the church unless I scripted what I was going to say and let one of the leaders vet it.

In addition to all this, after much pleading Paul and I had at last got the leaders to send us out officially. In our interpretation of Scripture that made us the church's apostles which, again in our interpretation of Scripture, put us higher than the pastors, teachers and evangelists. So we were convinced that we should have been invited along to all the deacons' meetings to put our fourpennyworth in. Not surprisingly, our local leadership had a different interpretation of those scriptures. I think in the end they would have been wiser to have kicked us out rather than sent us out.

Paul and I did quite a lot of travelling over the next few months and we often called in at the haven I had spent so many hours reading about, the Rees Howell's Bible College. The folk there were very kind and obliging to us vagrant apostles/evangelists, though I could never have coped with their strict discipline. We were not even allowed to eat in the same room as the women, so with such little contact with the opposite sex we never stayed there for too long.

An organisation called Musical Gospel Outreach had by now been formed, and they had set up a national concert tour involving such then-famous names as Roger and Jan, and Judy McKenzie. As they were playing at Portsmouth Guildhall they wanted some local talent, not only to help fill up the evening but also to make the main attractions sound better. I was asked to play as I was gaining limited popularity around our area. For me this was a big break, but I don't know whether the others saw it in quite this way. After I had done a song for a soundcheck in the afternoon, one of the young organisers called Pete Meadows asked if I was going to bother to tune my guitar up, to which I replied that I thought I had.

The big night came and I couldn't understand why everyone was so serious, because I certainly wasn't. We all queued up to put on some stage make-up, but as there was only one pot left by the time I got there I just covered myself in that and ended up looking like a very embarrassed Red Indian. We all waited at the side of the stage for our cue to appear. I had to follow Pete singing, 'A froggy went a courting'. I had great trouble working out why a man of God should be singing such a strange song, unless it had some deeply religious connotations that I knew nothing about. I later discovered that it was nothing so spiritual, it just happened to be the only song Pete could play.

Then I was introduced and on I went to rapturous applause from my one row of friends and silence from the rest of the auditorium. I only had to do two songs and in the first one I snapped a string and immediately stopped playing. All went quiet and I wondered what I would do next. I turned to the side of the stage and shouted, 'Oi, Pete! Lend us your guitar,' at which point a very embarrassed Pete came on stage handing me his instrument. Now, Pete was nearly twice my height, so when I put his guitar on it ended up around my knees and the audience roared with laughter. It was at that moment that I realised I was never going to be a brilliant singer or guitarist, but through sheer cheek and humour I could communicate better than any of them. Throughout the rest of the evening whenever people saw me they laughed. And even during the big finale when we all stood around the grand piano singing 'Amazing Grace', I could see people looking at me and smiling.

'Uncle' Philip Vogel had now become the Director of British Youth for Christ and lived just along the road in Brighton. One day I decided to go along and see him. I felt a bit silly asking him to hear a tape with some of my songs on it, but I felt even sillier asking him if he would mind if I stopped calling him 'Uncle'. I was thrilled that he both liked my songs and preferred being called Phil, and that after spending some time with me he asked if I would like to become an associate evangelist for British Youth for Christ. Although I wasn't quite sure what this meant, it sounded good. And so along with four others, two being well-known old-timers, Mervyn Morgan and Tony Stone, and two being little known but up-and-coming, Ken McGreavy and Clive Calver, I signed on the dotted line. I was now an evangelist and, moreover, an official one.

My old mate Andy Piercy was still getting into trouble because he too felt that God had told him to leave his job, even though he only had a few months left until he would have finished his apprenticeship and been a qualified GPO technician. His parents were very distraught. They called in various ministers who all gave Andy the same advice which was to finish his training then he would always have something to fall back on. Andy, as usual, would not listen. He insisted that if God had called him now then that meant now, and he argued that he would never need anything to fall back on as it was God who had called him. He was logical if totally irrational. Andy left his job and the two of us went to a Youth for

Christ conference together. Paul, meanwhile, had now been so attracted to the celibate lifestyle of the Rees Howell Bible College that he had decided to join them. This left everyone thinking that Andy would now join up with me, which was the last thing that Andy wanted to do as his pride would be hurt if he had just done the obvious.

One Saturday night a crowd of us piled into a minibus to do an evening at Crewe Youth for Christ. Phil asked if I would do a couple of songs and, always willing to please the boss, I agreed. On the way over one of the girls who was sitting directly opposite me in the minibus was sick all over me, it even went right inside the red patent boots that I was wearing. When we arrived at the tiny little church that was packed with over-sixties – more like Grannies for God than Youth for Christ – I got someone to walk in and make an announcement that we were going to have a perfume offering. Within minutes I squelched into the gents and was pouring every sort of cheap scent possible down my front. To my frustration, by the time I'd emptied the lot I came to the conclusion that the previous smell was better than the present one.

Eventually I entered the church and enquired as to where all the young people were. I was promptly told they had been banned and were not wanted because they spoiled the meetings. Frankly, I felt more sick than the poor girl on the minibus. In my opinion the meeting wasn't making God happy, it was just a mockery. I only sang about half a song, then I had to sit down as I felt I was wasting everyone's time. Nobody needed to be saved here, and I didn't even feel like giving anyone a good kick up the proverbials as my boots were still filled with more than just my feet.

As I arrived back at the conference centre, I realised that God had been speaking to me. He wanted radical people: people who didn't mind getting into trouble, but people who were willing to shake up the apathy present in churches like the one we had visited that night. I couldn't do it alone, however. I needed a friend to travel with me – after all, it was biblical to go out in pairs. At that very moment Andy appeared, having spent a good night back at the centre listening to the Lord. He said that he no longer cared if he was being predictable, he now knew that God wanted us to work together. We both gave each other a celebration hug, and from that moment on 'Ishmael and Andy' was born.

11

Like Electricity

Like Electricity I've been wired up for power,
Wired up for power, ready for action.

Ishmael and Andy hit the Christian community with all the subtlety of the proverbial bull in a milk bottle factory. Our main source of stability at this time was British Youth for Christ, with whom we felt it right to be associated. Thus we were not looked upon as just a couple of weirdos travelling around the country doing our own thing.

Andy and I never had any relationship problems, but because we were so close we certainly gave some of our organisers and friends a hard time. If we argued we would fight it out either physically or verbally, but if someone dared argue with us we would stand together whether we were right or wrong and never let them have the slightest chance of proving that they were right, which of course they invariably were.

We officially began our work together on May Day 1971, and in no time we had masses of bookings coming in. My mum kindly agreed to look after the secretarial side of things which never appealed to either of us. We felt very strongly that we should not charge a fee for our work, but just share out between us whatever the Lord provided or the organisers provided which at most times was one and the same thing. We travelled about in Andy's rather aging Ford Anglia van. This always leaked and had a pool of water on the floor in the front, but we didn't mind as it was a reliable little vehicle and we that foot washing was very biblical anyway.

Our songs were always very down-to-earth, but they were like loaded guns. Once on stage we would pick them up and fire them in any direction, hoping to hit everyone from the self-righteous Christian to the poor unfortunate non-Christian. We were certainly no respecters of persons and we would knock any unbiblical traditions, even though we knew that many people in our audience might get upset by our frankness and sense of humour. We had many little parable songs, some riotously funny, others very sad. We sang lots of simple praise songs, as well as songs that simply told the message of who Jesus was and why people needed to become Christians. Our whole repertoire was made up of audience participation interspersed with humorous patter, and we could guarantee that any sensitive person was sure to be offended by something that we said throughout the evening. At one event in Chelmsford Prison, all the long-termers walked out and asked to be allowed to return to their cells because we had upset them. But many people still became Christians.

In the beginning we took any and every engagement that came in, believing that they were all sent by the Lord. It wasn't until after we'd experienced a few that we realised they were not. Barbecues and outdoor events were the first to get the chop. Sausage Sizzles were then the 'in' evangelistic function, and often our job was merely to provide the cabaret while the hungry heathens lined up to get first pickings at the burnt bangers. Of course, no one could hear us shouting away or was even interested in listening to us. And with the beautiful aroma penetrating our nostrils, in no time our thoughts had drifted from wondering if people were going to get saved to wondering if the people were going to save any sausages for us after we had finished going through this ordeal.

We also did numerous outdoor concerts and festivals which we were convinced never had God's approval as he would always send down the rain just as they were about to begin. One such wash-out was in Guildford where a Christian promoter had done the church a favour by inviting a group of Jesus People over from America called the 'Children of God', but due to the torrential rain only they and we performed. Being rather hippyish they wore no shoes and seemed totally oblivious of the weather, while we, being great men of faith, had come armed with wellies, raincoats and umbrellas.

In July we had to start rethinking our attitudes towards music. Although we were fairly way-out in many ways, the good old Evangelical brain-bashers had 'shared' a few of their major doctrines with us and we had allowed certain traditional yet unbiblical ones to become part of our theology. For instance, we had great trouble believing that God could use or would ever consider using heavy rock music. In fact, we were under the impression that it was all satanic. However, a three-piece band of headbangers called 'Out of Darkness' wrote to us asking if we would play support for them at a concert in Lewisham. Still being under the impression that all bookings were heaven-sent, we agreed.

As we prayed beforehand with them the drummer reminded the Lord that in the past he had mightily used the jawbone of an ass and he prayed that tonight the Lord might use his. That really tickled me. As the hall started filling up and Andy was tuning up both our guitars (I still hadn't mastered this skill), we were both a little apprehensive as to how our funny little ditties would go down among a pack of loud music fanatics. But we needn't have worried. Once we had started we took the place by storm, they loved us. Even our infamous 'Grunting song', which was specially written to insult people's intelligence by encouraging them to join in with farmyard noises, caused an uproar and won an encore. We'd made it, we'd become rock stars. Even more important than our achievements was the fact that we saw God using the music of the over-amplified band and in the light of this we were forced to change our opinions about this sort of music. Dozens of people who were definitely not Christians were keen to know more about who this band was singing about.

It didn't take long to reach the top as there were no other full-time Christian musicians around at this time. Britain was no longer big enough. Although I had hardly ventured further than Sussex, I felt that the world was my oyster, and there was no way that I was going to be shellfish with the pearls of wisdom that I had to impart. International fame came hammering on our door and we were invited over to a small town in Holland called Zwolle to join the Dutch Youth for Christ for a mission in a monastery. I don't think the Dutch knew what to make of us. They didn't understand our humour, they didn't understand our language, and they couldn't understand why we showed so little interest in music. From our point of view we could not understand why nearly all of them smoked while we had packed up such evil habits a short while earlier. The only time we could convince them that it was not acceptable to worship and puff at the same time was when we taught them to raise their hands to the Lord and the ash rolled down their sleeves with painful results.

Once back on home territory, it hit me quite hard that our minister, Alan Pringle, who had given me much patient encouragement, was moving back to his hometown of Newcastle. A rather square but very likable keyboard fanatic, Derek Moon, took his place. Ministers may come and go, but the work of the kingdom must continue. I organised a beach mission for our local church in Littlehampton called 'Saving Offer', and invited a young student called Graham Kendrick down to give him a bit of experience in evangelism. Now, Graham amazed me on two accounts. One was that he had written some very good rocky little numbers, and the other was that I had never quite seen anyone tune up a guitar so quickly. He wasn't quite as talented at street work because he was rather long-winded, so we left him to get on with the music which was proving to be very popular.

We still had a heart for the hippies, so after the successful 'Saving Offer' we hurried down to St Ives in Cornwall to find the rest of the 60s left-overs. Apart from Sausage Sizzles, the other dangling carrot to coax in the poor unsuspecting unconverted was the coffee bar. These spread faster than an epidemic. Every lively church, Youth for Christ centre, or youth group had one, and the two things that made them different from a normal coffee bar was first, the lousy coffee, and secondly, the name which always had some embarrassing religious connotation. Basement coffee bars were usually known as 'The Salt Cellar', while anywhere above ground floor was invariably called 'The Upper Room'.

St Ives was a little different in that their coffee bar was very well decked out and was known as 'The Minelamp'. Each evening we did our Salvation Army bit and gave the ever-hungry hippies their free soup. Then, after entertaining them along with other guest Christian musicians, we would spend the rest of the evening philosophically analysing their beliefs which were usually anything that happened to be passing through their minds at that time. On the positive side, we did learn to canoe and surfboard; on the negative side, Andy and I had to share a double bed for a fortnight, which was not a great blessing to either of us.

This was also the era when you were either a musician or a preacher, you could not be both. So when they held their crusades most churches would need to book both. The musician would be the bait while the preacher would be congratulated for his fishing skills. Although our reputation was that of not being very easy to work with, we were quite popular, always available, and most important of all, cheap. One preacher that worked with us a lot was Tony Stone. He was one of the clearest, most precise and effective speakers I had heard. I learned a lot from him, particularly from the way he said things and how he used his humour to communicate.

In September 1971, we were working with him at an Assemblies of God church. We were having rather a tough time because as fast as we were bringing gangs of little thugs into the church to hear Tony, the pastor would run down the aisle shouting, 'Drive them out!' afraid that they were going to steal his hymn books or get his carpet dirty. He certainly didn't approve of us wearing jeans, so he gave us some money to smarten us up and buy some awful cavalry twill trousers like his own. We accepted the money and bought multicoloured jeans that were twice as outrageous as the pairs that had offended him. Of course, we wore them to the meeting the following day, going to great pains to make sure that everyone knew they couldn't object to our clothing, for these were the trousers that their pastor had so generously bought us.

While at this venue, vintage ex-rock-and-roller Terry Dene came and joined us. We had to walk around the streets with sandwich-boards proclaiming 'And I Thought Terry Dene Was Dead' to advertise his arrival. Sadly, his 1957 smash hit 'A White Sports Coat' was not enough to bring them out of their homes to see Terry live. In fact, as they saw our sandwich boards they just agreed with its statement by telling us that they thought that Terry Dene was dead too.

Finally at this venue our trusty old public address system, after a last defiant screech of feed-back, croaked out on a blaze of distortion. We trekked down to the local music shop and saw one system which, although second-hand, would have been ideal for our needs. The only trouble was the price which at a hundred pounds sounds cheap, but when you live on a budget of zero is out of the question. The salesman asked us what we did and who we worked for. When we like good dutiful Christians replied evangelists and God, he challenged us that surely our Boss could come up with the cash to which we in great faith replied that he certainly could and we would be back in one week to pick it up. What we had done suddenly hit us as we left the shop. These two great men of faith felt this horrible sick feeling inside. God surprised us both though, and throughout the next few days we received gift after gift until we had the hundred pounds plus enough money to buy our godless salesman a copy of the New Testament.

When we arrived at the shop one week later as promised, both the salesman and we had a shock. He was shocked to see us standing there with the cash, and we were shocked to hear that he had so doubted that God would provide the money that he had sold the system to somebody else. The poor chap didn't know what to say. But suddenly he looked at us and pointing at a much better and more expensive system he asked us if we would mind having that at the same price. We were over the moon, thanked God, thanked him, gave him the money and his New Testament, and carried the system out of the shop knowing that he would think twice before putting God to the test again.

We had now started working with Clive Calver, just fresh out of Bible college. Clive was one of the nicest chaps we had ever met, but unfortunately he did not share our sense of humour. I must admit that we gave him a really hard time. We did a lot of schools work together with him. Now Clive had the knack of using phrases which are acceptable to Christians but, unbeknown to Clive, had a completely different meaning to dubious-minded fourth-years. Clive would look so serious wondering why everyone, including us, was rolling around the floor laughing when all he had made was an intelligent statement, but without realising its double meaning.

Prison work was no better for Clive. We had noticed that when it came to packing up the gear and carrying it down numerous little stairways, he always made it his priority either to counsel the chaplain or go to the loo. At one top-security prison we got so fed-up with this that we quickly loaded the truck, drove across the courtyard, and got through one of the gates only to turn round and see someone dressed in a dog-collar running across the courtyard yelling, 'Wait for me!' at the top of his voice. The prison officer asked us if he was anything to do with us, to which we of course replied that we'd never seen him before in our lives. But Clive was soon released for good behaviour!

We even played a few times at Guy's Hospital in London. Two occasions in particular stand out in my mind. One was the afternoon we were given a tour around the museum and saw bits of body in various shaped bottles. We then went straight to the refectory but could not eat any food because the odour was not dissimilar to that of the museum. The other was when we did a gig in the crypt. Behind some curtains were a few stone tombs. Andy and I both decided that we could have some fun here, so Andy rolled his sleeve up, covered his arm in white chalk, and hid on the floor by the side of the tomb so that all you could see was his white arm and fingers tapping on the top. At this point I invited Clive and his girlfriend, Ruth, to come and see this phenomenon. But the joke backfired when Ruth screamed almost hysterically and Clive's face turned as white as his dog-collar and the poor chap needed reviving with a cup of tea.

In our lodgings things weren't much better. We would spend hours arguing with Clive about theology which was a subject that we knew so little about. We couldn't even spell the word. But it did help to pass the time, and although we would never give Clive the slightest hint that he could be talking sense, we were in fact learning from our numerous debates.

In Newcastle two organisers had loused up the bookings and through not communicating with each other had double-booked us into two venues at the opposite side of the city. We tried our best to do both and keep everyone happy, but we were continually got at for turning up late. At one venue the PA was set up, and we were just preparing to go on, when one of the organisers came up and tried to tell us that it was not his fault, it was the other organiser to blame. I was furious, I couldn't care less who was to blame, I was just trying to prepare myself to go out and give to the hundreds of teenagers that were now waiting in the hall. I told Andy to pack his guitar away as there was no way that I could go on in this frame of mind. Then we got hold of both the organisers and prayed with them both to get rid of any bad attitudes and from that moment onwards the tour really picked up. Poor Clive was left to do something with all these hundreds of young people in the hall who were waiting for Ishmael and Andy. Musically Clive would have had trouble getting a tune out of a comb and toilet paper, far less sing our songs. But Clive preached and he preached well, getting a better response than if we had played. It must have been a great encouragement to him to know that God had called him to his own ministry, not to a lifelong torture of being the third member of Ishmael and Andy.

It was in autumn 1971 that my recording career began. Musical Gospel Outreach and Word UK were getting into full swing, picking up anyone with any talent to join them on various solo and compilation albums. The labels they used for contemporary music were Key Records from MGO and Myrrh from Word. But neither of these short-sighted companies considered Andy and me suitable for putting down on vinyl. Rejection never set in, though, because if we felt that we were being left out we would attempt to do our own thing, which we convinced ourselves would be much better anyway.

We heard that the Elim Bible College in Capel had a small studio, so after praying in the two hundred and fifty pounds which was required for such a venture, we went up there, perched ourselves in front of the microphones, and made a single of two of our more musical songs. These were 'Benedictus', which was taken from our musical 'Emmanuel' and 'Song of Praise Number Two', which was not to be confused with our other praise song 'I'm So Happy'. The quality was not brilliant, and I couldn't quite reach all the notes in Song of Praise Number Two, but what do you expect for fifty pence plus ten pence p and p. It didn't quite make the charts, but it did make us quite a lot of money as the few hundred copies that we had pressed sold like hot cakes to a loyal if not musically discerning Christian public.

If you extracted the Christians from our audiences, apart from the odd sleeping hippy, they would be divided into two factions. The greasers with their long hair, motor-bikes, mopeds and push-bikes (depending on their age) parked outside. And the skinheads with their scooters and very short haircuts. With our medium-length hair and old van we usually got on fairly well with both sides. Outside of their gangs and underneath their fancy dress they were the same as anyone else.

One night we were playing in an Anglican church in a very posh part of Surrey – Ashtead, to be precise. It was the last place we expected to find any trouble. We were in the parish church and, having set up our gear, we were convinced that we were in for a nice quiet evening with a few old saints. As the doors opened at eight o' clock, a large gang of skinheads walked in and immediately got into the spirit of extreme praise by throwing some of the hassocks at the lovely stained-glass windows. As we peeped out from behind the curtain on the stage, we realised that these were not the nice little chaps that we were used to. You couldn't tap these on their bald heads if they got a bit over excited. No, they were larger and older than us. After convincing ourselves that we were filled with the Spirit of God and had nothing to be afraid of, we got up on the stage and with the accompaniment of our knocking knees started our first song. I don't think they were too impressed as they started throwing coke cans at us and one made rather a large dent in my guitar. I began to wish that they hadn't run out of hassocks.

The lights were bright so I couldn't see the audience at all, but suddenly I felt a real power from God, every bit of fear left me, we stopped singing and I started shouting at them and sharing the good news of Jesus. All went deathly quiet, but being unable to see from the stage that the police had come in and marched them all out, I carried on giving all I'd got, convinced that the silence was due to the fact that the Lord had closed the mouths of the lions. Although it was a slight anti-climax when I discovered what had happened, I had learned something very real. Even though I was a chicken and would not have any hope if faced with the slightest torture and persecution, I now realised that there comes a point when the supernatural power of God provides strength and courage that we never knew we had. No longer would I be afraid of anything that Satan might (literally) want to throw at me.

Along with the persecution and poverty came the perks, and they came in the form of nice young Christian girls. A sailor has a girl in every port, and we could see no harm in having a girlfriend at every venue as long as she was a Christian. We found that a pretty face more than compensated for a miserable organiser or duff booking, and life was a lot of fun. It wasn't long before the big chief of YFC, Phil Vogel, heard about our romantic involvements. He wrote us a very serious letter warning us that we were being labelled as Christian prima donnas and that we shouldn't use people in this way – after all, we were working for the Lord.

We had been to YFC training weeks but very few other conferences, so we decided a good one to start with would be the Musical Gospel Outreach Teach-In Weekend. Although we quite enjoyed this, we did find it frustrating that all some people wanted to talk about was which were the best plectrums to use, while others had only come to prove that they were God's gift to music. Very few seemed to be interested in looking at the most effective ways of using music to get people to turn back to Jesus, which was all we were interested in.

Christmas came and went. I never really enjoyed Christmas as I couldn't see the point in it. I didn't like religious festivals, primarily because so many hypocrites were pretending to celebrate someone whom they did not believe in, but also because all evangelism seemed to stop and we all overindulged in things we had been preaching against for the previous eleven and a half months. Another major factor was the presents. I could never get to grips with the scriptural fact that it was better to give than to receive; I always got more joy out of opening a present than giving something to someone then watching them open it. Then there always came that point where I had to lie and say 'Oh, thank you, just what I wanted,' when I knew full well that it was either too big or too small, that I wouldn't want to be seen walking around dead in it, or I already had three hundred pairs of socks, pants and handkerchiefs anyway.

Over Christmas I had plenty to do as we were preparing to stage a special New Year's Day extravaganza on Worthing pier called 'The Resolution Show'. This was to include Phil Vogel, Judy Mackenzie, Roger and Jan, and the band that we had spent a lot of time with in St Ives called 'The Southern Travellers' Handbook'.

As with the previous year's 'Emmanuel', we had a packed pier. As usual, Andy and I were looking forward to going overboard. The show started with us coming on dressed as schoolboys with short trousers and singing our version of 'Auld Lang Syne'. Then our guests came on and did their bit, with Phil doing a spot of preaching when he got the chance to get in front of the microphone. We all gathered on stage for a rousing version of 'I'm So Happy' to finish the show. This was the first time that I had seen so many people dancing seriously as an expression of praise, I thought that people only either danced for a laugh or to be romantic.

Although we were still rather unconventional as far as evangelists went, we didn't want to be thought of simply as musicians and end up going only to musicians' get-togethers. So we went to a conference where a lot of big-name evangelists would be present to try and chat to a few of them and learn from them. The sessions were very good, but the highlight for me was the Saturday night which was supposed to be a let-your-hair-down time. The organising committee sat on the stage and the various participants stood in front of them to do their party piece. This was all going very smoothly until a very funny fella with a North-country accent came on. He was called Gordon Bailey.

Being a poet, Gordon, had very cleverly put his own words to Stanley Holloway's poem about Albert and the Lion, and the committee behind him were in hysterics. Then came the verse with that naughty word 'ruddy' in it. Gordon, never being one to back down from a bit of controversy, had left the word in. Suddenly the committee stopped laughing and turned very straight faced, not sure if they should stop Gordon in case he got worse, or if by stopping him they would bring even more attention to his expletive. By now Andy and I were in fits of laughter, not at the poem so much as watching the expressions of the men on the platform as they tried to cope with something that was riotously funny but had in their minds gone way over the top. It goes without saying that from that moment on we struck up a real friendship with Gordon, learning ever such a lot from his masterly art of communication but tending to ignore his usage of the odd word prohibited to Christians.

I had now reached the ripe old age of twenty-two, and although I still had a lot of girlfriends, as a sign of my maturity and spiritual growth I decided that I would only have one at a time. It was on St Valentine's eve, that I plucked up the courage to ask out the lass from Scotland, Irene Cochrane. I didn't know her very well, but there was something about her that fascinated me and I knew that I would never discover what that something was unless we spent some time together. I'm glad to say that after a roundabout way of asking her to join me at a Valentine's party, not being too precise unless I would be humiliated by being turned down, she agreed to go out with me.

There was something special in this relationship. Although I was learning how to love God, I had never really loved a woman before. What I mean by that was that although I did have strong feelings towards past girlfriends, there was never that mutual awareness that we were both made for each other. But with Irene it was different. After we had finished a booking Andy would drop me off to see her, even if it was at one in the morning. After spending some time together I would not only walk the two miles back to my house but often dance it. This was not me at all.

As something serious was obviously taking place I thought I had better start praying about it. There was no way that I was going to break the promise I had made to God all those years earlier and get involved with something that would displease him and ruin the ministry that he'd given me. After talking it over with the Lord and discovering a wonderful sense of his peace over the whole matter, I then talked about it with Andy. We had a mutual agreement that after the Lord, our ministry always came first. So Andy was naturally quite shocked when I told him that I was about to propose to Irene after only six weeks of dating her. He knew I was slightly impetuous and therefore spent quite a while quizzing me on how it would affect our relationship. He only shut up when I told him that we would carry on as usual and I promised him that he could be my best man.

I didn't know that Irene had also been praying about our relationship. Being a younger Christian she received her guidance through the more fallible 'pot-luck' method of praying: flipping open the Bible and reading the first thing that your eyes set upon. This just happened to be the birth of Ishmael which seemed all the confirmation that she needed.

It was now Easter, and I decided it was time to tell my mum and dad. Although they had gone beyond being shocked by my original lifestyle and madcap ideas, they too interrogated me to check out my guidance. But when I had finally convinced them of my sanity, Mum gave me a family engagement ring as I could never have afforded to buy one to give to Irene. Now was the time to put my faith into action. I rang up our minister, Derek, and told him that I was about to propose to Irene and that we would both be round in an hour to fix up a wedding date.

As I sat in the car with Irene I was losing my nerve rapidly, I kept wondering how I would feel if she said no. In the end I thought I'd make it an open ended question: I'd ask her what she would say if I asked her to marry me, then if she said yes I would say well it just so happens that I have a ring in my pocket and an appointment with the minister in half an hour, and if she said no then I would make a joke and say that I wasn't going to ask her anyway.

This I did, and – praise the Lord – she said yes. Being quite spiritual she added that God had showed her I was going to ask her, at which point I whipped out the ring and rushed her off to see Rev Moon as time was running out.

Ishmael and Andy were always very busy, so as we sat in Derek's study, I realised that I had a few free days in six weeks' time or else I would have to wait for a year, so both Irene and I agreed on the 24th June 1972. Being only a matter of weeks away we had to move quickly. We found a cosy little flat in Littlehampton that we could rent and that was also available from the wedding day, Mum and Dad got the reception details organised, while Andy just flapped and bought a book on the responsibilities of a best man.

We spent many an hour arguing with Derek over such things as which Bible translation to use as I insisted that he use the *The Living Bible* and not his favourite King James version. Then I didn't want any of the usual boring old hymns so I chose 'Let the Fire Fall' and 'Years I Spent in Vanity and Pride'. They may not have been appropriate for a wedding, but they both had good lyrics and tunes and were the rockiest hymns that we could find.

Needless to say, tongues were wagging with my past reputation. The rushed wedding may not have looked good, but if only people could trust me and see that since I had become a Christian there was no way that I was going to get involved with immorality. Still, I always considered that while people were talking about me it saved them talking about somebody else.

My stag night was spent with Andy travelling back to Sussex from Norfolk. We pulled in at a hot-dog stand by the side of the A11, and in the dark early hours as we stood in the rain he treated me to a king size with masses of onions. As we stood there I knew that later on that day I was going to make some more promises to God which I knew I could never break till death us do part.

12

I'm Looking up to Jesus

I'm looking up to Jesus, His face is shining beauty.
I'm feeling so unworthy, yet His spirit leads me on.
I'm looking up to Jesus, His radiance surrounds me.
I feel so pure and clean, a taste of heaven on earth.

Our July newsletter read as follows:

> On account of Ishmael being on his honeymoon, this is Andy writing. Yes, it really happened. Ishmael got married to Irene on June 24th, although I still don't think he realises what he's done. So Ishmael and Irene are now happily married, but then who wouldn't be after less than a week? The wedding took place at Littlehampton Baptist Church and also involved me as best man (Ishmael said that he couldn't find anyone else at such short notice), Clive Calver who led the prayers, and Graham Kendrick who sang while the register was being signed. The bride wore a very pretty white satin wedding dress and Ishmael was forced into his suit (in both meanings of the word). The two bridesmaids, all two foot six inches of them, wore full-length white cotton dresses printed with blue flowers and flower head-bands, and they were gallantly supervised by a five year old page boy. Ishmael and Irene praise God for his wonderful provision of a flat for them in Littlehampton, which must be jam-packed with presents judging by the number I saw.

The wedding went off without a hitch, except for the fact that my mother-in-law, whom I had not yet met because Irene's family all lived in Scotland, approached Andy in the church and told him how wonderful it was to meet him and how pleased she was that he was marrying her daughter and how proud she was to have such a good looking son in law. Strange to say, but she didn't repeat the second part of her speech when she eventually met me.

My brother-in-law, David, kindly lent me his five hundredweight van. Apart from getting lost in Bournemouth, we were soon beginning our honeymoon in a luxury caravan right near the sea in a picturesque little village in Dorset. After a few days Andy joined us and the three of us set off for a booking in Norfolk. As they say in the business, the show must go on. Irene had left her very highly-paid job, as we didn't feel she should be the breadwinner and that we should all live by faith. It was the first time I heard of having a chaperone after a person is married. Exactly one week after the wedding we played in Upminster along with what was then called a classical rock band, 'After the Fire'.

Once we got back to our lovely little two-roomed flat (bathroom to be shared with eight other flat-owners) married life was like a bed of roses (have you ever tried sleeping in a bed of roses?). Irene and I were both very strong and independent characters, and we realised that for two lives harmoniously to become one was going to take a lot of working at for both of us. I'll never forget how in our second week of marriage we had an argument over a game of pitch and putt. I got so angry that I was all for calling the whole thing off, and then I remembered that I couldn't do that because we were married for life.

Although there was friction as we were learning how to live and cope with each other, we knew that our love for each other was stronger than any disagreements. We also knew that we would have to learn that we could not just live as individuals any longer, yet we needed to keep our own identities so that we didn't just become unreal 'yes' people. Learning to share our lives with each other fully was going to take a time, but we knew that we were aiming for a vital goal.

Although we had told everyone in our newsletters that just because I was married nothing would change with the

Ishmael and Andy ministry, inevitably things did change. There were times when I knew that Andy felt he had lost his partner in a way because he saw a lot less of me as I naturally wanted to be with my wife. There were times when Irene, although never wanting to hinder our work in any way as she was a strong, spiritual woman, would want to be more a part of what I was doing in order to be an encouragement to me. There were also times when I didn't want to upset Irene or Andy and found that I was upsetting both of them.

As the pressure grew I told Andy that it was time we finished. Andy didn't seem too upset by this and told me that he would carry on by himself and pursue a solo career. Later I felt this was a wrong decision and told Andy that I thought we should continue at which he got rather angry as he was already mentally prepared for his solo career. It was soon after this that on the way to London we both reached peak frustration level and started shouting at each other. It got so bad that I pulled the van over as I thought it was going to come to fists. After this we both went quiet and didn't speak to each other for at least an hour. This was followed by a time of tears and apologies as we both knew that neither of us had any future as long as these feelings were between us, and from that time Ishmael, Andy and Irene grew closer together. We had a very special bond between us.

As relationships were restored we seemed to become more aware of outright demonic activity. One day we were booked to play at a youth club attached to a church. To reach the room we were to play in you had to go up three flights of stairs and along a landing. The room that we were given to tune up in was on the ground floor, and while we were tuning up we noticed a large spider in the corner – one of the sort you normally see in the bath, about three inches across. Neither of us particularly liked spiders, but we ignored it as it was on the other side of the room. We then went up to do our bit and thought no more about it. When we started to play we found that the audience was not very responsive, but just as they were warming up we couldn't believe our eyes as there walking down the centre aisle came the ginormous spider. It climbed up onto the stage and joined us. By now it had grabbed everyone's attention and although our immediate response was to finish it off, we felt it would look cruel to do that with so many people watching. We never regained that audience. I don't believe that any spider could climb three flights of stairs, get through doors, walk through an audience onto a stage, and ruin an evening without some evil assistance. Needless to say, as soon as we were finished and no one was looking the spider gained an extra foot ... on his head.

Apart from demonic insects, we were also getting more and more people at our concerts who were influenced by the evil one, and I still felt very inadequate in dealing with them. I knew that I had been filled with the Holy Spirit, but I longed to speak in tongues. I read over and over again in 1 Corinthians where Paul says how much he would like everyone to speak in tongues, and at the end of Mark's gospel where Jesus says, 'These signs will accompany those who believe: in my name they will drive out demons; they will speak in new tongues.' I approached a few pentecostal pastors who left me totally unsatisfied by telling me that if God wanted me to have this gift then he would give it to me. I knew that God wanted me to praise him in a new language, but no one would tell me how to do it.

I became even more dissatisfied as Irene was already released in this gift, and when I went along to meetings with her it seemed to me that every Christian in the building was having a great time lifting their voices to God and singing and shouting words that they had never learned, while all I could say was 'Hallelujah', 'Praise the Lord', and the odd 'Glory'. Why was I getting left out?

One night as Irene and I walked back to our flat in the pouring rain, having just been to one such meeting, I could stand it no longer. I told Irene that I was going to go for a walk and stay out all night if need be as I wanted to know why I was not being given this gift. Being quite wise, she knew I meant it and said, 'Right, well, I'm going to pray for you at home. Off you go.' As Irene went into pray for her confused husband, I walked down to the beach and just wandered up and down in the pouring rain shouting to God and asking why he was holding back on me. I was far too engrossed to notice a few dog-walkers staring at me as though I was some deranged lunatic. After a long time of shouting I suddenly started listening to what I was shouting and believe it or not I couldn't understand what I was saying. It took me about another ten minutes before I realised that God had given me the gift of tongues and I had probably been shouting in tongues for half an hour without realising it. I don't know how long I stayed out there jumping around in the rain bellowing out my new language at the top of my voice.

When I eventually got back to Irene I discovered a new problem: I couldn't get my mouth to speak in English. By now she realised that God had answered prayer and we were both caught up in the Lord, praising him in tongues. From that time on I knew my praise language was going to be my native tongue and I'd have to work at my English. We both thanked God that night for all the wonderful things he had given us and the gifts we could use for his glory. That special night in the pouring rain remains vividly in both our minds.

This experience brought new life to me and I felt on cloud nine, but only for a little while. After playing in such venues as St Paul's Cathedral, and having been billed alongside such artists as Larry Norman and Cliff Richard, it was only a matter of time before pride crept in to such young Christians as us. We had come a long way in a short time and were becoming more performance-orientated and less ministry-based. We would travel to a town, entertain a packed hall, sign a few autographs, and move to the next town. We really had reached the top of the Christian circuit. We had no more aims, nothing more to achieve, and if we had wanted to we could have gone on for ever. From this moment on, Ishmael and Andy was finished.

Being in the big time we travelled down to Cornwall

where we found a guitar-maker. Without praying about it we ordered three custom-made guitars. God was not in this decision as when the three guitars eventually arrived, they looked awful, were unplayable and hence totally useless. We realised that we had done this for reasons of pride, and not out of necessity or God's leading so we sent all of them back except one which we kept as a painful reminder. We lost hundreds of pounds learning that lesson.

We were not slow in realising that something had to change. In our newsletter I wrote; 'Our ministry in the South of England is finished. Instead of outreach we are being crippled by Christians seeking entertainment. At least twice this month due to the hall having a large percentage of Christians, the unsaved have refused to come in, some even after buying tickets. Everywhere we seem to play we are overlapping with Christians who have travelled miles to see us.'

We thought that maybe the answer was to move to the North of England, but God didn't in any way confirm that. We really didn't know what to do. Fortunately, a short while later we were on a Youth for Christ conference and talked it over with Phil Vogel, Clive Calver and another evangelist for whom we had a great respect, Ken McGreavy. With reluctance they could see that our work together was coming to an end.

During that week Andy went through an incredible experience with God. I, on the other hand, spent the week either peaking in extreme worship and then being broken by God as he told me that my Christian growth rate was very poor. If I wanted to move on to greater things I must discipline myself and get down to learning more about God and more about the Bible.

Ironically, the minute news got out about our joint ministry finishing, Word (UK) said that they were interested in recording an album. So in one evening we took the young people from Littlehampton along with us to a studio, and within a couple of hours we recorded 'Ready Salted'. All we put on it were vocals and our acoustic guitars. It was just like doing a live performance because we only went through a song once, twice at the most. But we were very satisfied with the end-product.

Not only were we producing records, but a young Ishmael was also in the production line. After being married a few months, both Irene and I were putting on weight, me because of my insatiable appetite for chocolate cake which Irene got into the habit of baking nearly every day (she was extremely blessed in her catering skills), and Irene because, as we now discovered, she was pregnant. We were thrilled to bits as we had both wanted to have a family while we were young so that we would still be active enough to play games with them in their early years and also not be so ancient that we could not understand the pressures they would encounter when reaching adolescence.

This brought its problems though, as our housing contract stated that no children were allowed. As the nine months rolled on, we prayed very hard as the thought of being homeless was not very appealing, even for myself who lived in the van for a lot of the time. Then came the good news: the flat where my sister used to live had become vacant and the lady who owned it offered it to us. After the strain that we had been through this was wonderful news and everyone was praising the Lord along with us. Then a week before we were due to move in the lady died. She went to live in her mansion, but it left us in a state of confusion and without a home.

In this state I fulfilled the last of the Ishmael and Andy bookings. I had so many pressures I couldn't think of which one to worry about first. Even the accommodation seemed minor compared to things like how would I cope being a dad, was the child going to be healthy, how would Irene cope with a new baby and no home, where would our money come from, and, of course, what was my future?

As the last booking, apart from a tour which we were obliged to do later, came to an end we were all sad. We had a great love for each other and we had pioneered a different type of ministry through rough and smooth times. We had tasted supreme elation and great success, but we had also known what it is like to be financially broke and spiritually broken. We had lived a life of extremes. Even though we did not know what our futures held, we knew that we had learned a lot of lessons that would remain indelibly in our minds. Ishmael and Andy was over, but – praise God – the memories and the effects it had had on people would last for ever.

As we said goodbye to Andy we also said goodbye to the flat. My parents kindly stored all the possessions that we had collected in their garage, but we still had no home to go to. I had been asked by Phil Vogel to help with an evangelistic mission in Falmouth, Cornwall. So Irene, who was nearly eight months pregnant, and I set off down there in the transit van. The mission went well and I got the chance to have a go at preaching and not just singing which I really enjoyed.

On our return to Littlehampton we were involved in the youth outreach week. Quite a few church members were going on holiday and they were happy to let us use their houses. The only problem was that we had to move house every week for three weeks. Irene was getting exhausted as she was fully involved in helping with the counselling and running the coffee bar. I remember questioning God, but I seemed to get no answer except wait and be patient. I knew that God often answered prayer in the eleventh hour, but it seemed to me that we were in at least the thirteenth.

By the end of August we were running out of holiday homes and the only alternative that was left was my parents' house as they were going away on holiday. This was something that we had never wanted to do, believing in the scriptural principle that when a man marries he leaves his mother, father and home. But at this stage it was the only option. We had only been there a couple of days when Irene started having contractions. She telephoned the local maternity hospital but was promptly told that as the baby was not due for another three weeks she could not possibly be going into labour but that they would take her in for observation anyway. As we had no car at this point, Irene said that she would walk there as it was only a short distance away. I was to ride my moped there with her suitcase, but in our hurry to get there we forgot the suitcase. It was rather embarrassing when we arrived at the hospital without her change of clothes, so I had to about turn and rush back for them on my trusty moped.

Once Irene had settled in, and knowing that there was another three weeks before the baby was due, we decided that there would be time for me to hitch-hike back down to Cornwall as a very kind Christian there had contacted us saying that the Lord had shown him he was to give us his car. I eventually got there, and enjoyed driving a very nice car home again – without a hitch.

When I arrived back at the maternity hospital one of the nurses called me over and told me that Irene had been complaining of pain but the baby was nowhere near due so could I tell her to quieten down and give her an aspirin as they were very busy. Not wanting to argue with this rather large sister I did as she said, but to no avail. Irene just kept insisting that she was in dire pain every few minutes, huffing and puffing and telling me she was convinced she must be either about to give birth or she'd got food poisoning. As my only previous experience had been with four-legged animals, I didn't know what to think. However, common sense told me that Irene, who was not prone to making a fuss, must know more about what was happening inside her than those big ladies who looked like spinsters anyway. I called them over and told them to check it out, and although they were obviously annoyed I made sure that they did. The curtains were pulled round and within two minutes Irene was whisked down to the labour room with profound apologies from a very embarrassed matron. A couple of hours later I was the proud owner of our own little son. Irene was fine and together we thanked God for our new arrival. Joseph Gideon Smale had joined the tribe of Ishmael.

Gradually we became aware of God's timing. On the

day that Irene came out of hospital with our new little bundle of joy, a Christian came round and told us that the organisation he worked for had just bought a large house in Bognor which had been divided into four flats for young married couples that needed temporary accommodation while waiting to be housed. They also had various problems, and he wondered if we would like to go in as wardens of a sort. At the same time I heard that I had been accepted as a day student at Elim Bible College, even though I only had agricultural qualifications. The only question about my qualifications at my interview was, did I play a guitar? Fortunately there was no question on whether I could tune a guitar.

So at last the Lord was revealing the future to us. Within two days we had settled in our new home at Bognor and within a week I was back at school, chained to a desk. My Maker knew me too well; he knew that this extreme method was the only way he could get me anything like disciplined. Elim Bible College here I come. The trouble was that I didn't even know what 'Elim' meant.

13

All Scripture Is God-Breathed

All Scripture is God-breathed
And is useful for teaching, rebuking,
Correcting and training in righteousness,
So that the man of God may be thoroughly equipped
For every good work.

It's funny how even the very name 'Bognor Regis' brings a smile to people's lips. When we arrived in what was once a very nice detached residence but had now been transformed into a doss-house, although we were very thankful we had a roof above our heads, we didn't really have too much to smile about. The garden was cluttered up with dead cars. The front door, which all the residents had to use, was wedged wide open. Our little flat upstairs, apart from being filthy dirty, had obviously been carefully decorated by its former tenant who either must have been high on drugs or only been able to get his hands on dark purple paint.

Bringing our brand-new, clean little baby into this environment was a bit of a culture shock, but after many hard-working hours scrubbing, cleaning, polishing and painting, we soon settled in and made it home. The worst times were at night when little Joseph would enjoy exercising his lungs in one room and through our paper-thin bedroom walls we could hear the couple next-door screaming that they were going to kill each other. Happy families? Sorry, not at home.

My first year at Bible college proved to be an interesting one. Alfie, my friend of old, had just finished working for

Operation Mobilisation and felt that he should join me. So each day we would both travel the forty miles there and back and argue over everything in the Bible. (We were allowed to do this now, as we were becoming theologians.) There were over a hundred students at the college varying from the children of Elim pastors, who thought they already knew everything and had really only come to pick up a certificate at the end of the course, to a former all-in wrestler, who found it hard to both read and write but obviously had great potential in street work and dealing with difficult congregations.

Understandably, I got on best with the not-so-clevers and the ones who did not take the course too seriously. But Alfie, with his new-found grasp of the French language courtesy of OM, got on best with the foreign students. He could certainly speak better French than he could English.

My first surprise came after the opening morning devotions. Someone from across the other side of the room gave a message in tongues, but I could hardly hear it as many around me were showing no interest at all and just chatting amongst themselves. They had been brought up in a pentecostal denomination whereas I, having heard comparatively few messages of this sort, had my ears pinned back thinking that God might be speaking to me. They had heard this gift so many times that they had become *au fait* with it and didn't take any notice. I remember asking God to help me never to become that overfamiliar with his supernatural outpourings.

My second surprise was that some of the students were far more entrenched in empty traditions and religion than the lecturers. A small contingent approached me stating that because I had long hair and liked rock music there was no way that I could be a Christian. Of course, I was big enough and ugly enough to stand up for myself and give back as good as I got. I praised God that I was a day student and could clear off rather than endure their incessant trivial pursuits.

My first year's lectures ranged from the brilliant, where

qualified teachers came in to teach us, to the boring and abysmal, where pastor Joe Bloggs would come and share his devotional experiences which was about as exciting as watching paint dry. But I was kept so busy and alert with the former that the latter was necessary as it allowed me to get in a bit of shut-eye before the long journey home.

Back in Bognor I decided to try out the local Elim Pentecostal Church. This was rather a strange-looking building, semi-detached, three storeys high, and resembling a Western saloon more than a 'house of God', especially with the public house on the adjoining wall. As we entered we noticed that there were only about half a dozen people, plus an old lady who was sitting up the front playing an old harmonium. She was obviously amusing the rest of the congregation with her unique style of bouncing up and down on her seat as her hands laid into the keyboard and her feet pushed away at the pedals as if she was in training for the London Marathon.

We sat down quietly behind another couple of old ladies with young Joseph who was fast asleep. But he nearly got a rude awakening as one said to the other, 'Oh no, not a baby! I hope its not going to be noisy.' This did not bless Irene or me, but due to my Bible college training, I did manage to stop myself from refraining, 'Oh no, not another silly old woman!'

Eventually the service started. Apart from us there was only one other young couple, Malcolm and Margaret. Malcolm was obviously looking after the church, while Margaret was obviously looking after Malcolm. The rest of the meeting was taken by the remaining two old ladies that I have not yet mentioned. The service was nothing much to write home about, but then again there would have been no point in writing home as Joseph, Irene and I were all at the meeting. However, at least five out of the six people were friendly so I thought I would go back in the evening to see if that was any different.

It was good news to me to walk in and see that the number had at least doubled, but even though everyone was doing their best to look happy and screech along with the bouncy music being painfully extracted from the old upright squeeze-box, a heaviness was definitely in the air. After the meeting yet another old lady, whom I hadn't seen before, got up in the pulpit and looking very severe told us that she had something very serious to say. Her first comment was that it was time for the church to close down. This is brilliant, I thought, we've only just started coming. Then she continued by saying that they had been praying for a number of weeks for God and Elim to send them a new pastor and today was the deadline, God had not sent anyone, so it was time to close. The strange thing was that she seemed almost happy about this as she obviously had some argument with Elim and thought that by closing down the church she would in some way be having a go at them. Everyone around me nodded their heads in agreement.

At this point I leaped up, rushed to the front of the church, and with all the courage I could muster shouted out, 'You've been praying for a pastor, well here I am!' There was such a sudden silence that I wondered if I'd given all the poor old dears a heart attack. Nobody spoke, they just stared at me. On reflection, it must have seemed strange for them to see this young, scruffy, long-haired person whom they knew absolutely nothing about rush to the front and make such claims.

After the long silence the lady who was standing next to me at the front turned around and ignored me as though I was just yet another weirdo that the tide had dragged in and carried on with her closing down-speech. Again I butted in, this time using all the authority that I had not yet been given, and explained that I was training to be a pastor at Elim Bible College and even if everyone boycotted the meetings, God had sent me here and as from next Sunday I would be taking charge. The meeting instantly finished. I'd spoken as if it was my finest hour and hadn't even got a 'hallelujah' – well, apart from Irene who was quietly praying in the corner. However, at least three people were pleased: Malcolm, Margaret and the little old harmonium lady (she was pleased because she could carry on playing her beloved instrument, not knowing that at the first possible chance I had plans of dumping it in the sea).

After filling Elim in with the situation, they felt that I was not the man for the job, so they sent down a second year student from college to whom we grew very close. Over that period it was great to see that, far from the little old saloon church closing down, it actually started to flourish.

Life was never lonely in our little flat. As well as seeing Paul Carter, whose banjo playing was to be heard on my later albums, become a Christian, we also had an influx of Irene's relatives. We brought her younger sister, Valerie, down from the north of England to live in the little airing-cupboard. Then my usually very drunk brother-in-law, Stewart, dropped in after turning over his three-wheeler three times in fifteen miles. As he and his car were both in quite a state, we made the most of this opportunity of telling him about Jesus. Later, Stewart not only gave up drink and three-wheelers, but also became a Christian and is now an elder of a church.

Towards the end of my first year came 'Open Day'. This was a big annual event attended by all the Elim top brass, the local clergy, the odd pastor, plus anyone else who happened to be passing by the gates. A large marquee was erected and all the second-year students were awarded their diplomas or certificates. It seemed that however thick you were, everyone was rewarded with some piece of paper or other which gave me great hope.

I was then given my musical début and I chose a cheerful little number from my own pen entitled 'The Laodicean Church' which has in it a line which goes 'CofEPentyBaptandCo, MethyCongreFreequake, put them together and what have we got, we got an umptiunichurch break'. It was a song against the growing wave of ecumenism which was considering unity at any price, even by ignoring biblical truth. As I sang I noticed the students really enjoying it, but a few gentlemen with their haloes around their necks and the top brass sitting behind me started to shuffle, sweat, whisper and look terribly embarrassed. Needless to say, I didn't get a standing ovation. All I got was the principal whispering in my ear the spiritual equivalent of 'Don't call us, we'll call you.'

During the last week of term, I decided to stay on for a second year, and fortunately for me the principal decided to let me. He then read out a letter from a church in London that had a new pastor coming to it. The pastor wanted a student from the college to join him as his assistant. I immediately put my hand up, thinking that a year was long enough for anyone to live in Bognor, and that this would be my first real chance to be a pastor. After praying about it, Irene also agreed that it seemed the right thing to do, but again it meant that after less than a year in our flat we were off house-hunting again.

While I had been at college, Andy had not been sure what he should be doing. Despite being somewhat poverty stricken, he had managed to acquire rent free a flat with three rooms plus a kitchen and bathroom just outside London from a very generous Christian businessman, and when he heard that we were looking for somewhere to live in London, he invited us to come and live with him. We were very grateful, and although it sounded like fun at the time, to say that it was a tight squeeze would be a massive understatement.

Irene, Joseph and I shared the small front room along with nearly all our worldly possessions, Andy had the back room with nearly all his worldly possessions, and the lounge/dining-room was more like a narrow corridor which led to the kitchen. When we sat in the lounge there was only room to put all the chairs in a long line, so most evenings were spent sitting next to each other looking at the opposite wall a few feet away. As time went on though, we got a long narrow fish tank and would sit and watch that.

The upstairs flat was quite the opposite to ours. It was the tidiest place I had ever seen and was occupied by two members of a team that Clive Calver had formed called 'In the name of Jesus'. What I can't understand is why

Clive didn't invite Andy and me to join his team ... well, perhaps I can.

As already mentioned, Andy was unsure of his future. As I now had to drive about a hundred miles each day through the centre of London to college, and as Andy had nothing better to do for the immediate future, he decided to join me for a year there.

The second year was not as exciting for me as the first year. The academic standard was being raised which was bad news for someone like yours truly who didn't like reading and writing much. Also, we had to study Greek, apologetics, eschatology, homiletics and worst of all, the dreaded philosophy. I'd argue and argue with lecturers that I saw no point in learning about some heretic who had weird beliefs hundreds of years ago. All I had to do was walk around the streets and talk to people today if I wanted to pick up loony ideas. In the end I got so frustrated by the subject that I went out in the gardens and learned to be an excellent frisbee-thrower, which seemed much more useful.

Andy was not a good student. He would never agree with anything unless he argued about it first, and many a lecture hardly got started let alone finished thanks to Andy's vital interruptions. The students from his class would line up to warn me that if Andy wasn't careful he would get thrown out, but as this was coming from weaker brothers who would swallow anything rather than cause a stir, I didn't take any notice of them.

In between all the travelling, studies and frisbee-throwing, I also had to learn what a pastor was, and eventually I met the new head pastor whose job it was to teach me. He was a large serious-looking Brummy called Adrian Hawkes. He had been an Elim minister for a number of years and had just been transferred from a church in the North of England. His wife, Pauline, also shared his strange accent and had a great sense of humour.

I had never met anyone who was as ambitious as Adrian. He wasn't satisfied with one church, he had in fact taken over three: Finsbury Park, Palmers Green and Rye Park.

The main church was in Finsbury Park in a rough area just tucked round the corner from the famous Rainbow Theatre. My first meeting with Adrian was at a deacons' meeting. I'll never forget looking up at the outside of this miserable building and seeing the words 'The warm church with the friendly welcome' surrounded by a ten-foot high wire-mesh fence with barbed wire along the top, plus a wall with broken glass cemented in its top. It looked about as warm, friendly and inviting as a maximum-security prison.

Adrian introduced me to the four deacons who seemed as warm and friendly as the church exterior, and then he suggested to them that they should pay me two pounds and fifty pence per week. I never thought it possible that people could discuss so little for so long, and I noticed that Adrian was getting quite distraught by their mean attitude. 'Listen,' he said, 'You are getting two men for the price of one,' to which one replied, staring straight into my face, 'One and a half'. Now I knew that I was maturing as a Christian because I didn't even attempt to hit him, I just sat smiling thinking, what on earth am I doing here Lord?

The more time I spent with Adrian, the more I learned from him. Although he was so easy going, he was the best possible teacher. One thing that impressed me about him was that he never pulled rank on me although he had every right to do so. There were times when I would lay into him about the way he would do things or the need for taking days off, and although he always put up a fight he would often end up agreeing with what I said.

I don't know how he managed to cope with my humour. I remember one time when he was about to lead a church members' meeting and because of his revolutionary ideas and plans he knew that some of the people had come armed for war. He turned to me and asked if I could lead the worship to quieten them down a bit, and I remember getting everybody to stand up and announcing that we would start our worship with that well-known hymn 'Sound the battle cry'.

Adrian shared his house with the funniest person I had ever met. His name was Alistair Pirie, and he was a disc jockey for BBC Radio. Even though he was rather embarrassing to walk around with, as he wore windscreen wipers on his spectacles, he got me to do some recording for the radio with some professional session musicians which was transmitted on Radio Four.

There were all sorts of people with all sorts of jobs in these churches, including the percussionist from the English National Opera who gave Irene and me some free tickets to go and see *Carmen*. I think he felt that I needed some exposure to culture as all I had known was agriculture. I'm afraid that as much as Irene enjoyed it, it was wasted on me. All the shrieking and wailing reminded me of an amplifier feeding back, and with all that singing I couldn't make head nor tail of the story line. It was quite a relief that I felt sick halfway through and had to go home, but Irene kept insisting that my sudden bout of illness was just an excuse to go home. How could she say such a thing?

My first church baptismal service was also a memorable occasion. Adrian always liked to make out that he could not be shocked, and when I asked him what I should wear to go in the water he told me to wear what I liked. As we changed in the church office and the congregation waited patiently for us to return, while Adrian wasn't looking I slipped into a pair of bermuda shorts and a T-shirt with the words 'Beer is Best' printed all over the front. I knew this would go down well because to be an Elim pastor you had to sign a pledge that you would remain teetotal. I just wish I'd had a camera to take a picture of Adrian's face when he eventually turned round and saw what his assistant pastor was wearing.

I, of course, defrocked myself of such worldly attire before re-entering the church, but I was still rather nervous of baptising people. Thoughts were going through my mind like, suppose I drop them, suppose they don't go right under, will I have to do them again? The church was packed with our own people plus the friends and relatives of our baptismal candidates, which was another reason why I couldn't afford to make any mistakes. Adrian kindly informed me that I would do the first one, so I nervously got into the portable pool forgetting that we were going to sing a hymn first. As it was a long hymn and the water was rather cool I couldn't work out if I was shivering out of fear or because I was cold. When the music died down eventually I was handed a microphone and read out the name of the first poor person who was to experience my aquatic skills.

A little old lady of about eighty hobbled forwards smiling, and I thought, oh no. She then sat on a chair by the side of the tank and pulled her robe up. I wondered what on earth she was doing. She saw my eyes nearly popping out of my head and shouted over to me, 'Don't worry lovey, my doctor says that I mustn't get my false leg wet or it'll go rusty so I'm just going to take it off.' From that moment on my mind went bananas. It would be hard enough to get a two-legged person back upright, how could I possibly manage to get an eighty-year-old up out of the water to balance on one leg? Then came the classic statement: not thinking about what I was saying, with my microphone in hand I turned to her and said, 'Right, hop in.' The congregation's response ranged from hysterical laughter to utter disgust. Fortunately the little lady concerned thought it was hilarious and her baptism went very smoothly, which was a great joy and relief to all.

Pastoral visits in London, however, were not such a joy to me. Either I got lost or, even if I found the right house, people left me standing on the doorstep ringing the bell as they never seemed to understand that I was the assistant pastor, and would not open their door to strangers.

As I mentioned earlier, if Adrian had a plan which he was sure was from God he would go ahead and do it no matter what anyone said. Now, I never minded this until I was called upon to be a mediator and was told to go and visit the disgruntleds and try to pacify them. On one such occasion a couple came to the door and told me in no uncertain terms that they would never come back to church unless Adrian changed his mind on a certain issue. I saw no point in debating the subject so I just held out my hand and said, 'Well, that's fine. I guess therefore we won't be seeing you again so I may as well say goodbye now.' Needless to say I was not sent on any more of these missions of reconciliation.

During this time the second little Ishmaelite was born. Again, he was a little overkeen to enter the world, announcing his arrival fifteen days early and in the middle of a married couples' evening we were hosting in our home. Fortunately, one of the women at our meeting was a midwife, so when Irene had a sudden bout of pain she gave her a quick examination and told her to get to hospital straightaway as the birth was imminent. Much to my relief she agreed to follow us in her car, while I drove Irene the five miles to the hospital to make sure nothing happened en route. Much to Irene's discomfort I drove like a maniac and got her there just in time. Within half an hour our second little bundle of joy, Daniel Jonathan, arrived on the scene. I really enjoyed choosing my offspring's names as I would tend to use all my favourite Bible characters.

As my year at Bible college was ending, I had decided that as much as we had loved working with Adrian and Pauline they had given us excellent training and it was time to have a church of my own. So I applied to join the Elim ministry. I had a slight bit of trouble as being so busy with travelling and church work I had managed to get out of doing all the exams. The principal said that I would have to take them with me and do them over the next year while I was pastoring, but I knew I would never have time for that.

Graduation day arrived again, but it was a bit quiet for me as I had been banned from singing and due to missing the exams I must have been the first student to go through Bible college without so much as a receipt. My future destination was kept quiet until my last week when I was given a large envelope which had my destiny sealed inside it. I tore it open and stared in unbelief as I read the big letters 'ACCRINGTON'. Although I had heard about some fellow called Accrington Stanley, I had to get out the world atlas to find where it was and discovered it was right up in Lancashire. It seemed to me that I was being sent as far away from Elim civilisation, and the college, as possible. Other details on the letter were: average congregation fifty, average offering thirty pounds and debt two thousand pounds. Now here was a challenge.

Even though I may have fought all the way, I know that my time at Bible college did me a lot of good. It gave me disciplines that I had not encountered before and that I knew would be of great use in the future. It was sad to leave Andy (who had managed to get through the year without getting thrown out). He had in fact got fully involved with the rock band which we had played with on my honeymoon, called 'After the Fire'. It was also sad to leave our good friends, Adrian and Pauline, who at least attempted to teach me how to be a good pastor. Still, I returned the favour by leaving them good old Alfie who was to be my successor. The tribe of Ishmael was off, the North was our oyster. My now dried-out brother-in-law, Stewart, packed all our belongings in the back of a truck, we packed both the children in the back of the car, and we were off.

Pastor Ishmael – well, it sounded good. Now to find out if I could actually live up to my title.

14

God Is Here, God Is Present

God is here, God is present, God is moving by His Spirit.
Lord, I open up my life to You,
Please do just what You want,
Lord, I won't stop loving You.

As our little convoy passed through the beautiful rolling Lancashire countryside, weaving its way through numerous small towns where the derelict cotton mills once thrived but now stood sad and empty, our excitement was building up by the minute. Questions ran through our minds: what would our first church look like, how would the people understand what I was saying, what would our first house to ourselves be like?

As we entered Accrington we were first greeted with a large pie and pudding factory, then more tall chimneys than I had ever seen before, some disused ones having been sawn off as the town planners obviously didn't see the same artistic beauty in these monsters as Lowry did. When we reached Blackburn Road all eyes were gazing out of the windows, who was going to be the first one to spot the church? 'There it is!' shouted Irene, and what a fantastic building it looked – large, detached and stately. Not bad, I thought, for my first church. On closer examination we discovered that this was the Catholic church. We turned the car round as we had obviously driven right past the building without even noticing it. Moving even more slowly along the road we suddenly noticed it. Set mid-terrace, it was sandwiched between a small sub-post office and a house. If it was in an 'I Spy' book I would imagine you would have collected at least a thousand points for finding it.

As we made our way up the steps and entered the building, my heart sank somewhat. It was not quite what I had imagined. A lot of the windows had been blocked up since the War, it was dark, smelt musty, and had no carpets. It would be the last place that would inspire me to burst into a round of 'All Things Bright and Beautiful'. The decor comprised a surround of dark brown panelling and the colour scheme was a sort of two-tone yellow and damp. We didn't need to say a word to each other, we both knew what we were thinking. As I opened a door which was in fact a cupboard, I noticed that it was packed with hundreds of old newspapers that had obviously been collected to sell and hence swell the church funds. These were an ideal breeding ground for the rats and mice which felt they had a right to be there seeing there were more of them than there were members in the church.

I had previously met the outgoing pastor who was a nice chap and had undoubtedly done a grand job. With all my observations of its deterioration now, I couldn't even imagine what it was like when he had arrived a few years earlier, but with no money and a large debt only so much could be accomplished. As I tried to be more spiritual, I reminded myself that the church was not the building but the people, and I was convinced that the whole place would brighten up once it was packed with fifty smiling faces.

The church house was about a mile away at the top of a steep hill, but it was sheer luxury to have three bedrooms having been cramped in one room for the previous year. I noticed that it even had a back-garden which was unusual as all the other houses only had small backyards. At the bottom of the garden was a large pond, and although this looked nice it did have the disadvantage of being a first-class breeding ground for toads. Consequently, the garden was often like one of pharaoh's plagues and you couldn't walk anywhere without squashing the poor little perishers.

Well, the first Sunday came and I was so excited at the prospect of my first meeting that I made sure that the whole family was down at the church an hour early. I felt good strutting up and down. I sat in the church office, which was like a large cupboard off the main hall, and noticed the hardboard ceiling bouncing about above my head as furry vermin were using it as a playground. Being rather nervous that they were about to come through and join me, I decided to seek sanctuary in the sanctuary.

It was Elim's tradition to have breaking of bread in the morning and what was known as a gospel service in the evening. In other words, the morning was supposed to be for the saints and the evening for the sinners. Now, if by chance a sinner crept in in the morning you would treat him like a saint, and if there happened to be no sinners in the evening you would carry on and preach salvation to the saints, pretending that they were sinners. It sounds confusing, but once you get into the swing of it, it runs like clockwork.

By five to eleven I was getting a little worried as still the only people present were the four of us, but then the door flew open and in walked one large lady and one thin lady who made their way to what must have been their usual seat in the back row without saying a word to us. Although nobody else arrived and I was disappointed at the turn-out, I felt that eleven o'clock had come and the service must begin. As the pianist wasn't there and I'd left my guitar at home, we struggled through the first couple of hymns with our only accompaniment being the patter of tiny rodents' feet.

As the meeting ended, and I must confess that I had been to better ones, the cliché of preaching to oneself took on a new meaning as I think that I was the only one interested in what I had to say. After my final amen, I walked up to our Laurel and Hardy look-alikes in the back row and said good morning, holding my hand out to them in a friendly gesture. The large lady just stared at me and said, 'I don't like men with beards and I don't like you!' and with that they both walked out. Here endeth my first lesson: beware of big ladies in back rows who have bad attitudes towards bearded pastors.

During that first week I was encouraged to discover that the entire church had not had some premature insight about me and left, but it was Wakes Week when the whole town seemed to close down and everyone went to Blackpool or Morecambe for their holidays.

I was still disgusted at the state of the church, so I told Irene that we would suprise them all when they returned as we would set about painting up the building. She agreed that this was a good idea and a kind thought and would be a lovely surprise for them when they all returned. I must state that this step was one of necessity as DIY and I are about as compatible as curry and chocolate. Due to an extremely low budget all I could afford was some pots of purple emulsion and white gloss paint. Irene, Joseph and I worked hard, while little Daniel, now six weeks old, lay fast asleep in his pram – well, most of the time. By the time we had finished slapping the white gloss directly onto the dark brown woodwork without any rubbing down or undercoat, and had attempted to cover up the damp stains on the walls with the purple paint, there was no doubt about it – it certainly looked a lot worse than it did before we started, but it certainly smelled a whole lot cleaner. It was very interesting to watch people's faces as they arrived on the following Sunday. I noticed that one lady actually came in and went back out to read the sign outside the building to make sure she had come to the right place.

At this point I met what leaders there were, who were really nice guys, and explained that the church building which, even before my attempts to brighten things up, was depressing and miserable, was not honouring to God, and would not attract anyone to join us. They all agreed about this and from that moment they started to redecorate, leaving me out. Seeing my previous attempts they felt that my gifting must lie in some other direction.

A few weeks passed till my District Superintendent, whose job it was to keep an eye on me, arrived to induct me. Now, that is not as painful as it sounds. An induction service was just a welcoming service where other Elim ministers and congregations came to see what I looked like. Pastor Alex Tee, who I had never met before, was late arriving. As I stood outside the church waiting for him, I suddenly saw him arrive. I went up to him to say hello, but he said in his Scottish accent, 'Sorry laddie, can't stop to talk to you now, I must go and meet the new minister,' and with that he left me on the pavement and disappeared inside the church. I won't tell you how embarrassed we both felt as we were finally introduced. Alex was a good man though, and as he was immaculately dressed and I had long hair and a trench-coat, his slight error was quite understandable. Although we were opposites in nearly every way, in all the time that I was under him, he never once questioned my rather outlandish ideas. As long as God was blessing the church, he would not interfere.

Financially, life was extremely hard. There was not a lot of money around and the church's debt loomed over us like a very heavy sack of spuds. The church could only afford to pay us, at most, fourteen pounds per week. I was so sure that God would not bless us as a church until we had cleared our outstanding account that I told the deacons I would pay back half of my wages until we were in the black. However, four into seven pounds doesn't go very far, so both Irene and I felt we should fast once a week on Thursdays in order that the Lord would bless the work and we didn't have to worry about finding money for food that day. This was fine for a few weeks till Irene became ill due to the fact that she was still continuing to feed baby Daniel at the time who was growing at a terrific rate and this was cheaper than buying milk. The hardest times were when we had invited guest speakers to the church and they came to tea with us. But Irene did brilliantly with the little she had in the cupboard, even if on one occasion some had to suffer chocolate cake iced with chocolate blancmange.

I tried doing a part-time job as a sales rep for Kingsway

Publications, but I must have been the worst they had ever employed. I either spent my time arguing with the shopkeepers for refusing to stock my records or, due to the pressure of the work that I was involved in, was unable to get to them at all. Kingsway were too kind to sack me, they just politely told me that my talents lay in making records and not distributing them. But God was doing some great things with us, and even though we were close on poverty level at times, we were thankful because God saw that we never actually starved and our babies certainly never went without.

One of my mottoes has always been 'Play to your strengths', and though my pastoral expertise was questionable, when it came to music and Christian bands, I felt myself somewhat of an expert on the subject. So one of the first things that I arranged was a series of Saturday night concerts. A baptist minister friend of mine called Mike Huck, who was the most way-out man of the cloth that I had ever met, opened up the series for us. I made it, as far as I could, a three-line whip that all my deacons and congregation should attend as I wasn't sure how many people would turn up.

Mike and his group were known as 'Movement Banned'. I wouldn't say that they were loud, but as they thrashed their first chord a window-pane at the far end of the building went hurling out of its frame and smashed onto the pavement below. The church was packed with many people who had never entered such a building before, thus giving them the chance to hear the over amplified gospel for the first time. As real kids off the street were wanting to become Christians, we payed little attention to the moans and groans of some who decided to fellowship elsewhere as I had turned the sanctuary into a youth club. Due to the success of that night, I invited Andy and 'After the Fire' to come and play. Although their equipment filled half the building, we still managed to squeeze people in.

I don't mean to sound hard and uncaring, but I really only had one aim: to see the church filled, not with transfers from other denominations but with the sort of unchurched people that I mentioned earlier. I hasten to add that I was not only interested in teenagers, I wanted to see all ages packed in. To do this we put on other events such as meals, sacred concerts, film-shows, choirs etc., and within a year the church was full, with only about 10% being Christians for more that two years. I praised God for this, but it did bring its own problems as none of these had any idea about Christian ethics and morality, and with some of my 10% being just passive pew-fillers, it did leave a fair amount of work for my leaders and myself.

As these folk began new lives as Christians, we didn't just want to give them a list of thou shalt nots, yet we couldn't let them carry on as they were. They were learning, but we did get the odd problem such as having to check the whole building out after each meeting to make sure that no courting couples were hoping to get locked in, or encouraging them not to stand up and make rude signs at the church secretary when he sometimes said things they didn't want to hear – all teething problems.

I was keen to get ordained, and though I managed to get out of the college exams I knew that I would have to do three very long theses before the Elim Executive would give me the works. I was supposed to have three years to do them, but I had been told that due to my previous full-time work that if I completed them by Christmas then I could be ordained the following year. This left me the two Christmas weeks to do three years' work, and through the sheer challenge I not only managed to complete it and deliver it to the college by hand in time, but I also came out with a credit for each paper. Later that year I was ordained at Westminster Central Hall at a very moving service which meant a great deal to me. But can you imagine a long-haired, scruffy young chap now being called the Reverend Ian Smale? If your mind is boggling, don't worry – so was mine.

Prior to this, a whole family had come to know the Lord: Tom, his wife Delia, and their son Paul. I had been praying Tom in for a long time. He was an odd-job man who seemed able to do anything from building walls to painting high ceilings. He was so dedicated that after he had worked on night-shift he would come straight into the church and spend his days completely renovating it. In no time, as long as I kept out of his way so as not to distract him, he had turned the miserable building into a place that people actually enjoyed coming to. Again, the street kids had never been taught to respect property, and many a time I had to step in to stop a head-on collision between them and the newly converted Tom while trying not to lose any of them.

Baptisms still brought me problems, and as we baptised more than a hundred during that year it's not surprising. Before my first baptismal service many hours were spent scraping green slime off the sides of the tank. When it was reasonable we filled it with water, put the heater in, covered it with a plastic sheet, and left it for a few days to warm up. When the service began and the plastic sheet was taken off, steam belched out and to our horror we noticed that due to an unforeseen leak we had hardly any water left. As those waiting to be baptised were getting ready, it didn't bless me to notice that one of the lads was wearing a T-shirt with 'Jaws' written in big letters on the front and a picture of a half naked woman underneath being chased by a shark. I quickly glanced down to check the small amount of murky water beneath me to see that there was no such monster lying in wait for us. When I eventually got into the water I realised that it was boiling, but determined that nothing was going to ruin the evening I proceeded. The only way to get them totally immersed was to roll them over in some fashion, and due to the heat they all came out as red as lobsters – but they were praising God.

As the church was quickly filling up I was thrilled that it was the young Christians that were doing all the work. They were so pleased about what God had done for them that they would literally drag their friends along because they wanted them to receive the same. I like to think that all our meetings were totally unpredictable and that anyone from any background would feel the presence of God there. I also found it interesting to note that the mid-week prayer meeting was the most popular meeting. All we would do was have a time of praise and worship, then allow God to come and speak to us. With no tradition to follow, these young Christians would stand, kneel or lie flat on the floor as they worshipped God. Looking down from the front it resembled a battlefield rather than a church meeting.

I never taught anyone to call me pastor. In fact, when some of the older members called me by this title as a sign of respect, I told them not to bother because if they really respected me I would see it in their attitudes, not in a title.

I spent very little time visiting because most people had their televisions on all day. When I sat down to talk to them I could never concentrate on what they were saying as I could see the box out of the corner of my eye and whatever programme was on always seemed more interesting than the conversation that I was trying to have. I spent a lot of my days doing door-to-door work, but I was always faced with the language barrier. Basically, they found it hard to understand me and I found it hard to understand them. On one doorstep I thought I heard the lady ask me if I wanted a coffee to which I replied, 'Yes thank you, two sugars please.' She looked at me as though I was mad and proceeded to open a paper bag and handed me a toffee.

It didn't concern me that all my folk were very working class, but I believed that to be a balanced church we needed some professional people as well, so it was a great joy to me when a heating consultant called Ken Taylor and his family came to join us. Ken was also great on the keyboards and he and I formed a good little musical duo, doing the odd gig in-between meetings in the neighbouring towns. We may not have been brilliant, but because so few other people were doing what we were doing it was well received – that seems to be the story of my life.

During this time Kingsway Music approached me to do another album, so leaving Irene to hold the fort and preach at the mid-week Bible study, much to her delight, I set off. I wanted to do something that few Christian artists had done before: to put over some very serious points by using humour. So with the very able John Pantry as producer, I set about recording the controversial *Charge of the Light Brigade*. We had great fun in the recording studio, and I was convinced that everyone would rush out and buy this very original album. Sadly it bombed. One person said, what's the point of spending all that money just to get offended. Another time at the Elim Conference I saw my record on the counter, but the people, not realising that I was standing there, told prospective buyers that it wasn't worth buying. To top the bill some large record shops even refused to sell it.

To compensate for that, though, I did feel that my preaching ministry was improving. I will never forget one talk I did at Easter. I had copied an idea from Phil Vogel. This was to do something outrageous and then tell the folk in church that when they left the meeting and told others what they had seen they would never believe them, just as people had not believed the Apostles' reports of the resurrection.

As a packed church sat and watched me, I told them that I hadn't had time for tea and out of my brief case I took a table-cloth, plate, knife, and a slice of bread that I started to butter. Then, asking them what I could put on it, I turned round and saw a vase of daffodils. Smiling all the time, I pulled one out stems and all, put it into my sandwich, and started to eat it. As I munched away I could see that their eyes were nearly popping out of their heads. When I finished I said to them, 'Now, the reason that I have done this is ...' and I clean forgot what the point of the illustration was. Then my stomach started churning and they watched as I slowly turned as green as the now digested stem. As soon as the meeting was over, I leaped out of the pulpit, raced towards the loos but didn't quite make it and was sick all over the floor. Well, it's true that the congregation never forgot my preaching, but they still wouldn't have had a clue as to why I had done it.

My three main methods of relaxation were golfing, potholing and watching Burnley football team. The first was expensive as I would lose numerous balls every round I played, the second was exhausting as it involved walking miles in the pitch dark with the odd waterfall pouring on top of your head, and the last was exasperating as every time I went they never seemed to win. Still, we all need our hobbies.

It was during this time that I first heard of charismatic house fellowships. Friends of mine had told me that these were just over-the-top weirdos who thought they knew better than us denominational churches. They were classed in with other cults and heresies. On one Sunday night just as I was about to start the meeting, I noticed two of them walk in. Now, you don't have to be a genius to recognise charismatics as they always have loud clothes, loud tambourines, and most of all loud voices. I suddenly became scared and went and hid in the church office. What would I do if they jumped up in the middle of the meeting and said that they had a word from the Lord that I should not be there, or even worse that God wanted to close the church down? I waited for as long as I could, then I rushed out and raced through the meeting making sure there were no gaps so if they wanted to say something they wouldn't have time to say it anyway. As soon as I had finished I ran straight back into the church office.

Within a few moments there was a loud bang on my door,and being loud I was left in no doubt as to who it was. As I opened it they came straight to the point and said, 'Brother, we'd like you to come and preach at our fellowship.' Everything within me told me to say no, but I didn't have the courage so as I nodded out came the diary and whilst I was still shellshocked the date was fixed.

On the night of their meeting I dusted off my best sermon. Fortunately, Irene had agreed to come with me for moral support, and we drove out to a place that I had never heard of called Barnoldswick. As we crept into the building, one of the leaders came rushing up and not only hugged us but actually kissed us. I nearly died. I struggled to get out of his embrace but he was much bigger than me so I just had to wait until he had finished his peculiar welcoming procedure. Once out of his clutches we made our way to some seats. I closed one eye to make it look as if I was praying, but kept the other one open so that I would be ready to ward off any further advances. As we looked around we saw something that we had never seen before: the room was full of young people, but although the meeting had not started they were spontaneously praying for each other. Some were laughing, others crying, but I'd never seen such a group of people who seemed to care for each other so much.

As the meeting began, everyone suddenly jumped to their feet and leaped around like a bunch of lunatics. That is, everyone except me. I had my tongue released for praising, my hands released for raising, but for my feet to be released it would have been amazing as I felt that God had not made me the shape and size for all this fancy footwork.

After a while I had my chance to preach. As I said before, I'd carefully chosen my best message so if it had not sounded coherent I should have been most worried. As I wound up, I realised that time must have gone and the end must be nigh, and as I sat down the leader told me how much he had appreciated my word, to which I duly patted myself on the back and grinned at Irene.

Then he told everyone to stand in a big circle and put their arms around each other. We wandered about trying to find two people to stand next to so that we didn't look too silly. Then he asked me to come and stand in the middle, at which point I nearly had a fit. Oh no, I thought, not piggy in the middle. I stood there motionless facing him while he announced that anyone who needed prayer should join me in the centre and I would pray for them. A very large young girl was the first one to join me in the ring. The leader whispered to me, 'Over there.' I said, 'Where?' but due to her size I couldn't have missed her if I had tried. I went over and tried to start praying for her, but it was very difficult for two reasons. The first being that if somebody needed prayer back at church, I would whisk them off into the church office then at least no one would know if my prayers hadn't been answered. The second was that this rotten lot were so free that instead of closing their eyes to pray they all kept them open to see what I was doing.

I'm sure, unless the grace of God intervened, that neither myself nor the poor girl I was elected to pray with were any better after this experience. But as I left the meeting I felt that some of these young ones who were more than half my age knew their heavenly Father more than I did, even with all my Bible college training.

I returned to see them again when they were having a meeting in a barn, and as the first chorus invaded our eardrums it was nothing short of Brands Hatch around the bales of hay. This time I had taken another Elim minister with me, and the more I talked and laughed about them, the more ill I felt. I left that meeting feeling physically sick knowing that while they were praising God in the heavenlies, I hadn't even touched on praise. And that while they were receiving an anointing, I was criticising the Lord's anointed ones, and I knew that God was not going to let this go unpunished.

As the church was now full and the debts had all been paid, we had moved to a larger three-bedroomed terraced house in the town which, apart from the cockroaches and the mice, was fine. I knew that my time was running out. These people needed a Bible teacher and a real pastor. It was great to have people becoming Christians each week, but someone had to take them on further into God and that person was not me.

Although our time in Accrington did more for us than I can ever explain, I knew I had to move back into travelling evangelism. I was becoming frustrated and had itchy feet having stayed in this town for nearly two and a half years. God was clearly calling us on.

While on holiday down in Sussex with our family, I realised that God was calling us back to Rustington. Mum, Dad, Heather and David had been sent out some years ago from Littlehampton Baptist Church to start a daughter church in Rustington. However, they were moving further away from the traditional Baptist position and becoming an independent fellowship. This was where my heart was because I knew that if I was to get back on the road again I would need a secure base that would not only look after me but also care for Irene, Joseph and Daniel. God spoke to me and showed me a nice little two bedroomed house for sale that would be ideal. Then he said, 'Put on your suit, go to the building society, and ask for a mortgage.' Everyone thought I was mad, but I didn't care as I knew what God had said. I arranged an appointment with the manager of the building society and he questioned me as to what kind of job I would get in Sussex and what the income would be. I told him that I didn't know, he looked at me in a strange sort of way. But when I told him that there was no need to worry about the repayments because God would give me the money, he turned round to me and told me the loan was mine. A true miracle!

It was sad goodbyes in Accrington, for we had made a lot of real friends. Elim had allowed me a year's leave, but after that they wanted me to go back into a church and work in local evangelism. As we drove down to Sussex, I knew that this would never be. Like Bible college, my few years in pastoral work had been a vital part of my training, but now it was goodbye local priorities and hello again national work. But what would I do?

15

The Fields Are Ripe

The fields are ripe – Lord, here am I,
And I want to be a worker bringing the harvest in.

What a fantastic sensation it was to walk through the doors of the first little house we were to own. The family had been in before us and cleaned it through, and our little two-up, two- down, was sheer luxury to us.

At first I felt that maybe I should resort to overseeing Bognor Elim Church as it was only a few miles down the road and at this time had no pastor. But it wasn't long before I realised that I would soon be back in the local trap which would not allow me to expand in the national work that I believed the Lord had stored up for me. But I also knew that it was important to be committed to a local work where my family would be cared for as I would be away from home a lot. I could think of nobody more qualified to do that than my dad and brother-in- law, who just happened to be the two elders at the local Rustington Christian Fellowship.

Those first few Sunday mornings were quite hard to come to terms with though, as I was now an ordained minister and for the past few years had not only been used to having a lot of say in the running of the church but also the last say. It had never been my strong point just to keep my mouth shut and say nothing, and as I saw things being decided and implemented which I didn't really agree with I would often throw a spanner in the works, which I sensed at times made Dad feel rather intimidated.

Although I knew that there was no way I was going to

stop poking my nose into things even if they were not my responsibility, I also knew that my priority was to develop my music and ministry. At first I wrote around to other minister friends whom I knew from previous years and told them of my availability. I also put an advert in the now popular Christian music magazine *Buzz*, which simply said something like 'Ishmael is back on the road again and is available for anything'. Over the next few months I got anything and everything.

My first visit was for a few days in Eire and then Northern Ireland. Of course, I had heard about all the trouble over there and was rather scared of going by myself. I was also anxious as to what sort of reception I would receive. Actually, I had a very good time except for two minor hiccups. People had warned me that the border counties were like a wild frontier, and as I sat in the train passing through them I was half-expecting some sniper to be hiding on a bridge with his gun carefully aimed towards a sitting target – me. At one point the train slowed down, and as my heart started beating faster I suddenly heard a crack against the glass window. After a brief examination of my person to check if I had any blood coming through my clothing, I was relieved to see that it was only some perishing little kid who at that very moment had chosen to throw a stone at the train.

The other embarrassing incident happened at a concert arranged for me by my friend, Rodney Cordner, in the hospital on the infamous Falls Road. Little did I realise that I performed the whole set with my guitar amplifier switched off. Still, that may have been a blessing in disguise.

I was not really content just to be a lone, wandering, acoustic guitar strummer. I still had great ambitions of being in a band and playing the rock music that I love so much, and on a couple of occasions Andy Piercy and Pete Banks of 'After the Fire' actually backed me. One booking I will never forget was the first 'praise party' I ever did. It was at the large outdoor festival of Greenbelt. We were the finale on the Bank Holiday Monday night, and we did a rock/worship set that was really anointed by God. One person from the enormous audience came up afterwards and told me that when our set began a white bird like a dove flew down and perched above the huge stage shining brightly in the spotlights, and it wasn't until we finished the last song on a crescendo with 'Kiss the Hand of Jesus' that the bird disappeared into the night.

The reviewers for *Buzz* magazine failed to mention my set, but they did print a letter the following month which went as follows:

> Dear Sir,
>
> To do a summary of Greenbelt and not even mention Ishmael's praise party is almost unforgivable. It was advertised as a festival to the glory of God and nothing came closer to this than Ishmael's finale backed up superbly by 'After the Fire'. I have very few complaints about any of the other artists, but I felt the finale was so excellent and so full of the presence of the Spirit that it at least deserved a few words.

I found this very encouraging as it wasn't even written by one of my relatives.

I never wanted to abuse my friendship with 'After the Fire'. At this stage they were pursuing their own career into rock venues where no Christian would usually want to be seen dead, but they did do the backing tracks to a worship cassette I did called 'Its Amazin' What Praisin' Can Do'. John Pantry came down to a small hall and we put the tracks down in a portable studio. My aim was to produce a rock album of praise songs, but John had great trouble with this concept as he thought that you could either do one or the other but to put the two together would be irreverent to put it mildly. While John held his head in his hands, ATF and I did not take what we were doing too seriously, spending most of the days laughing and joking. In fact, just for fun on one track we told one of the lads who was not the lead guitarist to go straight on and do a lead break, telling him he had only one take. Yes, it was quite awful, but we left it on. After all the laughing and shouting, when the time came to do the vocals I had completely lost my voice. So we either made the last few tracks instrumental or I literally croaked and whispered as best as I could.

When the cassette was released it was terrible. The lads in the band were too kind to say what they really thought and told me that it wasn't so bad, but I was totally embarrassed by it. Within a year I managed to get Kingsway to delete it, but the worst thing was that it not only sold very well but numerous Christians approached me and told me that it was the best thing I had ever done. They were serious, but to my mind they should have gone and got their hearing tested. From that time onwards I did a Bible correspondence course for 'After the Fire' and their wives, as the last thing that I wanted to do was to slow them down musically in any way.

By April 1978 everything was about to change. On the Fellowship front I had been approached to join the eldership team. On the one hand I knew that we would be criticised for being a family affair, but on the other hand I believed that it was what God wanted me to do as I knew I had things to contribute on that level. I was also keen on forming my own band which was to be called 'Ishmael United'. The first recruit was a bass player and ex-social worker called Laurie Mellor. As he and his wife, Bren, sat in our lounge talking and praying about whether we had a future together, although we were very different personalities we felt that God was saying yes.

As Laurie and I considered the rest of the band, his brother-in-law Dave Evans, who was just completing teachers' training college and was a good guitarist/keyboard player, said that he too would join us full time once his course had finished in the summer. Finding a drummer was more difficult, but I remembered a drummer I knew in Bognor called Pete Wills (we used to call him Pedro) and I suggested to Laurie that we should go to his house and see what he was up to. When we finally found him he was very low spiritually, and being a lover of nature was even growing his own cannabis plants in his wardrobe. However, as we talked with Pete we knew that he was our man. He immediately opened up to God and within a very short time he was not only right back on top spiritually, but he also weeded out his wardrobe.

In the early 'Ishmael United' days we really never had a clue where we were going musically. Dave was the only authority on current music trends, and at this stage he was only with us part time. I suppose we could best be described as an evangelistic variety show. Our concerts consisted of singalonga Ish songs, loony sketches, card tricks, guess the tune as Laurie plonked away on his bass guitar, and any other ridiculous thing we could think of. The performance got longer and longer as our silly ideas grew, but what amazed us was that it was so effective. Loads of people actually gave their lives to God either because of or in spite of the concert.

We could not afford to be discerning about our bookings, so we ended up in the strangest of places with Pedro constantly repeating his catch-phrase of 'What on earth are we doing here lads?', to which none of us could answer. Many a time we would just be tuning up and the organisers would tell us that we were too loud. This seemed strange to us as we had very little equipment. We were actually quite embarrassed by this, so at times we would pile up drum cases, suit cases, in fact anything black and bulky to make it look like we had more gear.

We were invited to tour with the Don Summers Crusade. Now, anyone with very little imagination could see that we didn't fit in with them and that we were complete opposites. Don would be dressed in his immaculately cut, American, tailor-made suit, and we would be in our scruffy jeans and T-shirts. Extremes went even further when we worked with people like Nicky Cruz. We had the knack of making the most serious sentence sound funny, and Nicky couldn't help but make the most funny sentence sound serious. These contrasts were valuable and made for a balanced if somewhat extreme evening.

Kingsway decided that they wanted us to record later on in the year, so they asked if we would go into a studio and put down one track which was to go on a promotion sampler called 'Music for the King'. Musically, we were now gradually finding more direction. The secular music scene was reaching post punk and pre new wave, and we felt that we could slot into this category with no problem as the style was sheer energy without relying on flashy lead breaks, which we would never have done even if we could.

We chose to record a very simple but powerful song called 'Bartimaeus'. We went into a Christian studio that we had not been into before. The engineer was a smashing bloke, but he tended to spend more time giving us his testimony than actually discussing our recording. I felt that we were being treated like a bunch of little boys as he wouldn't even allow us to stay in the studio while he did the mix-down, but had to go and sit in the garden – it was just as well it wasn't raining. Still, he was a good engineer and at the end of the day the main thing was that we finished up with a recording that we were pleased with, and as he played it back to us it sounded very raw and contemporary.

A little while later I was standing by our van talking to one of the Kingsway staff while the band was listening to my conversation from inside. He told me that on hearing the track he felt that it was lacking something, so they had decided to go ahead and add a lead guitar onto the track. Well, to say that we were furious would be an understatement. In our opinion, it not only took the whole feel of the track away, but also took our music back into the 60s. Sadly, that was where most Christian bands were happy to remain.

Our official first gig as a full-time band was a big one. It was held back at the good old Greenbelt festival where I am pleased to say that we went down very well. Many organisers got our address with the prospect of booking us up. During this time we went back to Holland to play at a Festival called 'Kamperland'. The audience went wild, but sadly the organisers disliked us as they wanted quality musicians not a Christian punk band as we were fast becoming labelled.

In September my little Joseph, who was growing up rapidly, started school. It's a funny feeling when your first child gets to that stage. I felt quite emotional as he was already becoming independent, and eventually one day he wouldn't need his dad as he continued to mature and trust more in his heavenly Father.

In October we were back in our favourite studios in Eastbourne recording *If You Can't Shout Saved, You'll Have to Face the Penalty*. Andy Piercy had agreed to come in and produce it, and the album ranged from manic numbers such as 'Song of the Last Generation' to a fun number about some happy little charismatic characters I'd invented called the Glories. For this track my sister and my children came along to provide the backing vocals. Although the styles were too extreme, we had a lot of fun making it, and it was the first of its kind on the Christian music scene. It gained mixed reviews from the Christian press. One paper said:

> 'Ishmael United's' sound is loud, muscular and rather heavy handed. One refreshing aspect of the band's music is its recent espousal of a new wave style with its fast, aggressive approach to a number of songs. However, the quality of their attack disguises a fundamentally propagandist approach to music. In fact, most of the album is characterised by bruisingly banal lyrics redolent of the coffee-bar beat-group era.

Another said:

> I had vague memories of 'Ishmael United' being slightly amusing, so when I was asked to review this album I looked forward to a bit of a giggle. Nothing was more removed from the truth however. Along with other bands 'Ishmael United' have adopted a punk pose. However, as they all must be getting on a bit, it hangs on them like a loose coat. They lack the total assault of a genuine new wave band. A curious mixture of styles, a few weak ones outbalanced by the good one however, and done with considerable integrity. Ignore the lousy cover and lack of bass in the recording. I think you should buy this record.

It seemed as if even the Christian critics couldn't make their minds up as to whether it was hype to like it or hate it. I read all the reviews and was hurt by some of the cruel, unthinking comments that some of the reviewers made. I would ask myself what made them an authority to praise or slam records; why not let the listeners decide for themselves? I knew that if I allowed those feelings of hurt to remain, then in a very short time they would turn to anger, so I found the best way to get my attitude right was to spend time worshipping the Lord in tongues.

One lousy review that I praise the Lord for was written in *New Musical Express*. We'd only sent them the record for a bit of fun, but ended up with a large review and an equally large photo of us all. This is what it said.

In large headlines: *Christians 0. Lions 15*.

> When reviewing 'After The Fire' recently, I made no mention of their Christianity – it's hard enough for new bands as it is. With 'Ishmael United', such discretion is impossible.
>
> On the evidence of 'Saved', produced by After the Fire's Andy Piercy, these boys should have stayed in the closet. At their best they're a second-rate 'After the Fire', but mostly we're in the sub-Rice / Lloyd-Webber country – tepid 'rock' music subordinated to stilted lyrics. Whatever their source, vitality and conviction are a likely basis for good music. You could enjoy 'All Things Must Pass' without heading guruwards and 'Volunteers' without storming the barricades for instance. But 'Ishmael United' aren't exactly the Edwin Hawkins Singers. Leader / singer/ lyricist Ian Smale (nickname Ishmael – get it?) is generally leaden and literal, though the title track labours the metaphor of life as a football match: 'And when the final whistle blows/ You're gonna lose your soul,' etc. Easily the most offensive is 'Caroline Robbins', a breathy, unctuous sermon to a lost girl: 'You can't turn to sex/ You can't turn to drugs.../ Your life is such a mess/ And Jesus keeps calling your name.' Come back Terry Dene.
>
> Musically, there's some irritating cod reggae and even some punk mannerisms ('Song of the Last Generation'), all rendered equally unpalatable by Smale's preach-a-go-go.

Strangely enough, this did not hurt me half as much as the milder comments made in some of the Christian press. I still could not understand why my own brothers wanted to stab me in the back and even twist the handle.

By autumn 1978, just as with Ishmael and Andy, Ishmael United was becoming very popular. In a Christian magazine popularity poll, we not only came third after Dire Straits and After the Fire as the best new group of the year, but we also came joint second along with Blondie for the best album of the year with only Electric Light Orchestra beating us. Of course, we knew that these were nonsense polls, but even such fantasies as these can be very encouraging!

We were now moving further and further into the new-wave musical direction. Off went my lovely shoulder-length curly hair, leaving me with a vogue prison cut. Even the treasured flared jeans found the dustbin as we donned our straight-legged trousers. It was the first time I had seen my feet for years, and without the flares to hide them they looked enormous.

With our change of image also came a much more serious approach to ourselves and what we were doing. When we played at the first Spring Harvest in 1980, our concert frightened some of the organisers not only by the aggression of the music but also by the response of the Christian audience who were pogoing around the floor in a similar way to the unsaved at a secular concert. This sort of movement and atmosphere was not expected at a Christian function, and many understandably found it hard to take.

As a band we never really became friends. We had no idea of what commitment meant, and when it came to honouring each other, that was the furthest thing from our minds. There were three main reasons for the pressure. The first was that I was still an elder of the Fellowship and all the band were members. It was always hard being on the eldership because we were all related, and it didn't help that Laurie and Dave were part of a large family which was also very vocal. So we always seemed to be living under a bit of a family feud, even as we travelled around the country.

The second reason was that I was supposed to be the

leader, but the other members of the band increasingly believed that it should be run democratically. They made it very clear that they didn't want to be known as Ishmael's support band, they wanted to be known in their own right. I found this hard to take because I knew that it was largely due to all my previous years' hard spadework that they were where they were today. Feeling that they were using me, I fought them all the way. The icing on the cake however, was financial. We were broke and couldn't make ends meet. Our overheads were enormous and it was no blessing to do a six-hundred-mile round trip to Liverpool and get handed two pounds sixty three and a half pence expenses at the end to cover costs.

The strain showed in different ways in all of us. Pete would arrive at a gig and kick his drum cases around the stage, Laurie would get very hurt and angry, Dave would become ultra-critical of the way the band performed. I would spend most of my time shouting at the organisers and the band. Our humour changed from inoffensive fun to cutting remarks aimed at each other's weak points, and although we would all team up together when attacked by outside critics or organisers, we showed little love to each other once we were by ourselves. After much debate we decided that we needed to define where we were going and maybe also move out into a new direction. We failed to see that we were the problem not the organisers, music or even the name of the band.

Amidst all the dark clouds however, came a little ray of sunshine. On the twenty-first of June, little Suzannah Joy was born. She was a tiny bundle of blessing, born to us in a time when we had little to laugh about, and it was her constant chuckling and beautiful smiling face that lit up our home.

In August 1979 Ishmael United decided that as we were no longer united we would implement some major changes. From Greenbelt onwards we would now be known as 'Rev Counta and the Speedoze' as this would take the other members of the band away from the Ishmael stigma. Our main aim was to play in secular venues and try to get a record deal with a major company. Pete, who had recently got married to a young lady from Wales, was to move up there. So as well as employing a new drummer called Dave Bickley, whom we soon nicknamed Jimmy, we also took on another Dave who had been with me at Bible college but was now sadly separated from his wife, and he was to be our sound engineer and roady. The latter Dave, who became known affectionately as Pugwash, had a couple of slight minor defects. One was that he was deaf in one ear which was not a great advantage to him when he attempted to balance up our stage sound, and the other was that he was not the world's best driver, so he was one of the first roadies to be banned from driving the group van by the band itself. But our two new recruits were soon to get used to our funny little ways, and as our arguments continued, Jimmy would just go quiet and wander off to phone up his girlfriend, and Pugwash would just add any silly comments to try and be part of it which then encouraged us to turn on him rather than each other.

Granted, this was not the best basis to form a band. Even though we thought that we could survive without being close to one another, we knew we could not survive without being close to the Lord. So in every spare minute that we were not with each other, we tried desperately hard to retain some sort of spirituality. The areas we were about to move into were Satan's territory. Only time would tell if we were strong enough and had enough spiritual resources not only to keep our heads, but more important to keep our sanity.

16

Be Merciful to Me, O God

Be merciful to me, O God, be merciful,
Because I come to You for safety.
In the shadow of Your wings I find protection
Until the raging storms are over.

At this time, we met the members of an up-and-coming Christian band called U2. The lead singer, Bono, told us how the Lord was leading them to become famous in the rock-music world, and seeing that they actually had Scripture to back up their claims, this gave us heart. If this band could achieve the impossible, why couldn't we?

'Rev Counta and the Speedoze' were off. Described in a magazine as Britain's most eccentric rock band, and noted for our less than tidy appearance, who was I to let the public down? On stage I was now attired in scruffy blue overalls, stripy socks, sandals, plus a long white coat with 'Rev Counta' sprayed on the back so that I could remember who I was.

We had our philosophies and were quoted as saying, 'At present Christians don't go out to where the people are, we expect them to come into our churches. We are far too quick to quote John 3:16 and to press for decisions; we are far too slow to make friends and get alongside people.' We continued by saying that we saw ourselves as primarily getting a message across and not after money or fame (but a little would have helped), that we weren't budding popstars, we weren't that sort of people, and anyway we were probably too old. Our most-quoted comment was, 'Having a fellowship behind us is very important. People in this area of work can go spiritually off the rails very easily'. We relied on our home fellowship for two things: first, prayer backing, and secondly, regular check-ups by the elders on how we were doing spiritually.

Now, all this sounds great on paper, but in reality I felt so vulnerable that I spent most of my time being on the defensive. I had little relationship with the other members of the fellowship because I was away so much and wasn't convinced that many people spent a lot of time praying for us. And as much as I was willing to listen to what my fellow elders had to say, I found it hard to take their advice because I was under the impression that due to their lack of experience in the type of work that I was involved in, most of their comments would be irrelevant. However, with all our shortcomings we genuinely believed that we were in the will of God and that our motives were pure. We wanted to see people become Christians.

Although we wrote to dozens of rock venues, sending what we thought was quite a reasonable demo. tape, they didn't seem quite as keen to have us as we thought. Having cut off a lot of contact with the Christian world and its gospel circuit, it wasn't long before we found that we had less work and money than when we were in 'Ishmael United'. Irene and I struggled like mad to pay our mortgage, feed and clothe ourselves and the children on the sixty pounds per week that had been allocated to us. At one stage we all decided to go and get part-time jobs to supplement our income until the Lord opened up the big time for us. I took to taxi driving and I must admit I quite enjoyed it. It was the first time that I had worked with non-Christians since I was back on the farm, and it was so refreshing to hear their problems rather than the griping of Christians that I had been used to for the previous ten years.

Our first secular gig finally came. We were to support a cockney fun duo, called Chas and Dave, at Brighton Polytechnic. We were all a bit nervous when we arrived, and seeing all their gear set up we asked their sound-man when we could set ours up. He made it very clear that until they had had their sound check we were to go nowhere near the stage, so we just sat waiting patiently like obedient schoolboys as the hours ticked by. As time passed and it was obvious that Chas and Dave were happier in the bar than sound-checking, we were eventually allowed to set up. Our equipment looked so poor against theirs.

The evening came, but due to a union dispute only about a hundred people came in. However, we didn't mind because then came the big moment: ladies and gentlemen, let's give a big hand for 'Rev Counta and the Speedoze'. About two people clapped as we trundled out on stage and rushed through our set at a nervously manic pace. I gave little introductions to each song, praying like mad that not only would the lyrics get through to the audience, but also that Pugwash had got the sound right and they could actually hear them. As we hacked into the ever-popular 'Bartimaeus', I could sense that every time I mentioned the name 'Jesus' it was having a similar effect to someone swearing in church. As soon as we had finished our last number we rushed off stage, not having a clue as to how well we had gone down. I could hear some shouting for more, but I guessed that they were being sarcastic as nobody outside the faith would demand that a bunch of Christians get back on stage and preach an encore. At that moment the promoter came rushing up to me and told us to hurry up and get back on stage – couldn't we hear that they wanted more? Shellshocked I headed back to the stage, bumping into Chas and Dave who told me that they had really enjoyed our set and that we were one of the best support bands they had ever played with. They then instructed me to get back on and play that ******* Bartimaeus song as it was brilliant.

What an evening and what a surprise! Christians are not all hated after all. Maybe it's just the way we Christians communicate the good news that gets people's backs up, and not the good news itself.

However, not all secular venues welcomed us with open arms as we were soon to discover when we were in a bar at London University. It just so happened that the Christian Union had booked us into the same place that the rugby team were hoping to celebrate one of their team's twenty-first birthdays. As we walked in we couldn't help but notice a life-sized, nude, inflatable doll being thrown around the room with the word 'Christian Union' inscribed in large letters over a part of her anatomy where most Christian ladies wouldn't dream of writing it. As we started playing we were a little disappointed as most of the CU walked out as the music was too loud for them. This left us with our rugby friends who were getting rowdier by the minute. To begin with they started to throw empty plastic beer glasses, but when they saw that these were having little effect, they started to throw full ones.

Now, I was reasonably all right at this point because I just kept dodging them and they would fly past me and hit the drummer. Then two of the biggest guys that I had ever seen, who must have been descendants of Goliath, came down to the front and put their mouths right next to the microphone that I was singing into. I turned round to see how Dave was coping on the keyboards, but he had sunk down behind it and all I could see was his two hands – his head was way out of sight as he did not want to get in the flight path of the plastic, beer-filled missiles.

Turning back to my microphone I noticed that my two giant, drunk, backing vocalists had started to sing a song which I knew quite well but had refrained from singing since I had become a Christian. So there the three of us stood, each trying to be louder than the other. After what seemed like forty-five years, but was in fact only forty-five minutes, we had finished our set and started to pack up. Picking up the twenty-four empty glasses scattered around us a couple of the lads came up to me looking very perplexed, so I asked them what was wrong. They started to explain that a week earlier they had been listening to a punk band called 'The Damned' in this same bar, but the band only played for ten minutes with less aggro than they had given us. They couldn't understand why I kept smiling all the way through and we never walked out.

This, of course, was just the opening we needed to talk about the strength that the Lord gives, but I didn't dare tell them that the truth was that I had a beer glass stuck sideways in my mouth, and anyway we didn't dare walk out of the door because they were standing in front of it.

As encouraging as this was, work was still slow. We were realising that we may have cut our own throats by instantly chopping all the Christian work, and in our efforts to move from the light to the darkness we had ended up in the dusk. Therefore we quickly made it known that we were also available for some Christian concerts, though the secular was our priority. Although this seemed a good compromise, it brought back all the old problems back with it.

One of these concerned the sort of music we should play at these gigs. To me, the 'Rev Counta' set seemed inappropriate for church settings and I was all for going back and doing some of the old 'Ishmael United' songs. But the band thought that we should preserve our musical credibility and that it was not necessary to give the punters what they wanted. As we were now a democracy, I was outvoted as everyone else preferred the serious set and kept reminding me that God had moved us on to this type of music. But 'Ishmael United' fans would still flock along to our concerts and infuriate the rest of the band by screaming for the Glorie song despite our impressive new numbers.

During this time I was still on the Elim books as one of their ministers, and even playing in all the bars not one strong drink had passed my lips (passed by my head, yes, but not my lips) due to the pledge I had signed on total abstinence.

Elim wrote to me and summoned me to their Headquarters in Cheltenham. I was under the impression that they were going to help me financially. As I walked in I was greeted by one of the heads for whom I had great respect, called Tom Walker. Firstly, he asked me when I was thinking of going back to be a pastor of a church, to which I made it clear that I didn't really believe that was the way the Lord was leading me at all. He then told me that some of the Elim young people had been at one of our Concerts in Birmingham and our style had upset them. This came as no surprise to me, as our style upset most Christians. Being ordained I could not be sacked without it passing through the Conference, as I had done nothing morally wrong, but I realised that the work I was now involved in would hardly be of benefit to Elim and remaining an Elim pastor would hardly be of benefit to me. The most sensible thing all round was for me to resign from the movement, so with a touch of sadness that is what I did. Elim had been very patient and good to me. Right from my early Bible college days they had stood by my outlandish ways and irregular methods of doing things. Even as I got up to leave Tom told me that if ever I wanted to go back into the pastoral ministry there would always be a welcome on the mat.

Elimless I still had to get on with the job, and our next port of call was back to good old Holland. Frank Van der Gaag was a Christian promoter whom we had worked with many times before, and although he did his job well and looked after us over there, he was as mad as a march hare. His practical jokes ranged from dressing up as a customs inspector at the ferry port and pretending to interrogate us, to throwing food at us in his front room. Come to think of it, Frank had an obsession with food. On one occasion he asked us to perform a couple of songs at a friend's wedding in a Dutch Reformed Church. I could hardly believe my eyes: in the middle of the service they took up an offering which Frank snatched away from them. Pretending to run off with it, he clambered over all the pews with the infuriated ushers in hot pursuit. Things didn't improve when the guests had to walk down some steps to the hall underneath where Frank was waiting, armed with chocolate eclairs which he with great pleasure pushed into their surprised faces as they turned the corner to meet the bride and groom.

But as I mentioned earlier, we were a serious band now, and when Frank's jokes came our way we did not always see the funny side of them. The Dutch tour looked good, though, as we were to play at more secular venues than we had played in England total. But what places!

The first was a gay club where everyone walked out in our first song except for one poor little guy stuck in a wheelchair whom everybody forgot to take with them. Then we played joint billing with a heavy-rock British band called Girls School. The organiser got worried about us when all the on-the-house perks such as drugs, drink, girls, even boys, we turned down because we were Christians. The audience were amazing: I'd never seen so many hippies since the sixties, and they all arrived at our high-energy concert armed with sleeping bags and enough dope to ensure that they could pass into oblivion however loud the volume was going to be.

I had never been on such a tour. This was to open my eyes to how the so-called other half lives. One night we were playing at Amsterdam University, and I felt quite ill as I noticed a guy injecting heroin into his arm on the side of the stage. Although Britain was in a post-punk era, Holland had not quite come out of it, so I knew that we had been well received by the quantity of saliva on my face as they spat out their appreciation.

But even with all this so-called excitement there was one day that was going to change the rest of my life. The daytime was spent in a girls' school with eleven- and twelve-year-olds who, due to the influx of British and American pop music, were able to join in with songs practically as soon as I sung them. That evening we were in the same town at a night club which was so filled with the scent of drugs that we had to keep popping our heads outside the door to stop getting high ourselves. It was in this evil, dark, dingy atmosphere, as my eyes tried to get accustomed to the lack of light and excess of smoke, that I saw and recognised some of the young girls that we had been singing to earlier that day. Now, with their pimps close by, they were being used as child prostitutes. This was the pits. There and then God spoke to me. Could this ever happen in Britain? Was it already happening in Britain?

What has the church to offer the children of our land? Like Mary in the Scriptures, I didn't forget these thoughts, but held them in my heart.

The tour ended with a visit to Hilversun radio, where we were to play live to millions of listeners. We were informed we would have to use their gear and there would not be time for a rehearsal. As our time came, a studio audience had to be draughted in who had as much life as a stuffed duvet. The presenter announced Rev Counta and the Speedoze, which were the only words that we understood, and off we went. To be more precise off the drummer and I went, as Laurie's lead was not working so there was no bass and Dave couldn't fathom out how to switch the keyboard on, so that too was rather silent. As Laurie's face grew redder trying to attract Pugwash's attention to bring him another lead, our overactive audience just watched in amazement as this strange English punk band, comprising four musicians, just chose to use two members, acoustic guitar and drums. By the end of the song a now scarlet Laurie, who had still not managed to capture Pugwash's attention, gave the song quite a unique ending by venting his fury and shouting at the top of his voice, 'Thank you Pugwash!' I'm sure the millions of listeners worldwide would have had great trouble trying to link up those two words with the lyrics of the song that had preceded it.

Little frustrations like this did not help our unity. We always had to find someone to blame, and instead of what at times should have been a simple rebuke and prayer together, it ended up in a battle, as on the rare occasion we would get rid of our aggression by physical combat in the back of the transit.

By April 1980 I wanted out. I'd had enough of the band, and I was sure that they had had enough of me. A special church meeting was held to discuss my future. From August I was going to be more available, so I was hoping that maybe the fellowship would see the need to use me more locally.

I gave them four options. One, to work full time for

them; two, to be employed by them two or three times a month; three, no change; and four, maybe it's not the right time for any of these. The unanimous decision came back, summarised as: 'The members present felt that no change was needed and that Ian should not be encouraged to spend more time in the fellowship, because his ministry would be rather wasted.'

This was not what I wanted to hear. I was already suffering from acute rejection; all I needed was to feel wanted somewhere. Due to the family feud heating up in the fellowship, I knew that even in band matters families were taking sides and I felt, rightly or wrongly, that I had opposition, as those who didn't want me around had made it abundantly clear. For the next few months I just smouldered, enduring severe migraine attacks sometimes up to three times a week. I was so wound up that many nights I couldn't sleep and would just walk around the streets. Irene was hurting as much as I was in all this. I kept asking God the same question, 'Why do we have to go through all this?' But I was just not in the right state of mind to hear his answer. Little did I know that within a few years I would be looking back at this time as one of the greatest training periods of my life.

In between these depressions we went to a tiny little studio in London and recorded what was advertised as my farewell album, but with the possibility of the three Speedoze staying together with a view to forming a new band. The album was called *Life Begins at Thirty*, (subtitled *Songs for Swinging Fatso's*) as both Laurie and I noticed that although our ministry did not seem to be expanding, certainly our waistlines were. Dave produced the album, and we were all pleased with the outcome. During the previous couple of years the Smale/Evans songwriting team had come a long way, and I was very proud of some of the songs that we had written together.

Again the Christian magazine reviewers gave us a mixed response, from 'Ahead of its time' to the classic comment that went, 'Its easy to point to this record's shortcomings, but after a while it gets to you. It's like being on a farm; three deep breaths and you don't notice the smell.'

By the time of our farewell concert the whole band had decided to go their separate ways, and no one at the time seemed to be too sad about it. Pugwash hired a gorilla suit and, keeping up his usual tradition of bad timing, chose to come bounding on stage in the one serious song in the set. Jimmy announced he was to be married, which we discovered afterwards was his joke, but then we never really understood Jimmy or his sense of humour.

But by this time I didn't care what stupid things anyone did. I was just glad it was all over.

17

Lord, I Want to Be a Glorie

Lord, I want to be a Glorie.
Lord, You know I really do.
I realise that You want all of me
And Lord, I just want You.

When heaviness looms over you like a large dark cloud, and due to your own insecurities you find it no longer possible to open up or receive counsel from anybody, the natural thing to do is to throw yourself into work, essential and not so essential, so that it leaves you no time to think and ponder over past events. This was the road that I chose to take. I put an advert in the Christian press that read, 'Ishmael available for solo ministry, for preaching, concerts, youth weekends, houseparties, etc, etc, etc.' In other words, I wasn't quite sure what I should be doing, but to occupy my time I was willing to try anything.

The only people I felt that I could trust were my immediate family. Irene was hurting as much as I was, so we would spend many hours discussing and praying about our hurts and pains. Joseph, Daniel and baby Suzy were too young to be affected by all this and proved to be a positive blessing to us. Of course my parents and sister and brother-in-law were always at hand, but I even felt that they hadn't backed me enough in their eldership capacity, due to the pressure of being part of the same family.

I was of course still smouldering about the fact that the fellowship had made it very clear I should be away more. This was also an incentive to make sure that I was away as many Sundays as possible, because I felt that our membership was full of people who had no respect for us as elders. Being in the vulnerable state I was, I just could not cope with any sort of criticism at this stage.

Even the desert times have their oases though, and one of the highlights at this time was when some friends of mine, from my much visited town of Petworth, gave me a Volvo Estate. This was the best car that I had ever had, and I was so thankful to the Lord and to them, for this was much more than a means of transport, this was a *luxurious* means of transport.

My first solo booking was in Manchester. I had managed to organise a northern tour, having made friends there from my past Elim days. I summed up this first evening in my diary by saying, 'I was pretty awful, too ambitious.' It was so hard to cope with the fact that just a couple of weeks ago I had been part of a solid wall of sound, but now it was just one man and his acoustic guitar. Not only could everybody hear every wrong note that I played, but I had still not mastered the art of how to tune up a guitar properly.

I always enjoyed preaching though, and some great opportunities opened up to get back into this. I am convinced that my preaching always did more for me than it did for my listeners. In the first place God spoke to me through it, and in the second it made me get down and study the Bible, which has never been a strong point with most musicians.

In Guildford there is a church known as the Millmead Centre, whose minister at that time, David Pawson, was quite famous. Now I must confess that due to my line of ministry and the circles I had moved in, I had never met David and knew very little about him. Millmead invited me to come and preach at a Sunday night Youth Service, and as I had heard of its reputation I felt thrilled and honoured by such an invite. Now apart from the Rev Counta era, humour had always played a large part in everything I had done, and I thanked God that I had the ability to relax people and make them laugh. While preaching, I found it a great medium to put across what God had to say clearly, yet without being heavy, and I'm sure that it was through this that I saw so many results in all the work I did – it certainly was not due to my Bible exposition. Bearing this in mind, I was somewhat apprehensive just before I started to speak. One of the leaders pointed to a very refined, rather serious-looking gentleman about six rows back, and informed me that I was now looking at one of the most gifted Bible teachers of our day. 'That's David Pawson,' he said simply. At this point I got the feeling that I would not be facing in that direction once I started speaking.

I found the folk very appreciative – they laughed in all the right places, which made it easier for me. Once I got going I really enjoyed myself. At the end of the meeting a rather stern-looking Bible teacher walked over to me and then suddenly broke out into one of the warmest smiles that I had ever seen. He thanked me for my talk and went on to say that it was just what he needed, he hadn't laughed so much for ages. From that time on, David and his wife Enid, Irene and I felt a real closeness for each other. From our first meeting I had a great respect for this man of God, but because I knew so little about him, I didn't treat him with great awe and reverence, I just talked to him as I would with a best mate and loved being in his company. He seemed to be a mastermind on so many subjects, not just the Bible. He contained a wealth of knowledge and, as the saying goes, opposites attract.

One concept that I had always been keen to hang onto was that of the Glories, although I knew I had to drop them with Rev Counta. I believed that I had been inspired by God when I was given this simple concept; there was a lot more milage in it yet.

One August I met up with Pete Banks and Andy, and, with the help of their genius, a portable studio and drum machine, I made a single of the Glorie Song and made the B side a song called 'The Return of The Magnificent Glories'. It was totally electronic and the only voices were my sister's children, our children and yours truly which we mixed in later.

I had a little brother called Tim. I hadn't known him for years, but he was now eighteen and set up for life working for Her Majesty's Government DHSS division. At the latter reign of Rev Counta he had come around with us and done a bit of roadying, and I knew that he had been having a few bass guitar lessons with Laurie, so on the odd evening I invited him to come around with me and play. Tim managed to take ten days' holiday in September, because I had a Dutch tour arranged, and although Holland was becoming like a second home, on this tour we were going to places that were not usually frequented by evangelising tourists. I was pleased we were able to take the Volvo with us – although even this one started to play up a bit.

The tour was packed with variety. We played at school after school, we played in a windmill and also a bakery.... Disasters plagued us: the PA system packed up, but even worse, we got stuck right next to a tulip field in the middle of nowhere with the Volvo suffering from an engine seizure. Frank the mad Dutchman, who was again our host, told us to take it to a garage and get them to put in a new engine. Then he contacted all his Christian friends who put their guilders together and paid for it. We praised God for this because we had no answers to the problem of being stuck in a strange country, with no car, no PA and, worst of all, no money. But God always has answers.

During this time all we did was very well received in most places, but I did get fed up with one particular Dutch tradition. Once we had finished the concert and seen people become Christians and get filled with the Spirit, we then had the special ordeal of another meeting, this one being with the committee of organisers. They would proceed to give us the third degree on why I said and did certain things. This was not helped by the fact that, due to the language barrier, neither of us seemed to understand what the other one was really trying to say.

A highlight for me was how well little brother and I

worked together. Tim was rather a quiet, moody, inhibited sort of person, who was a total perfectionist to the point of fussyness when it came to doing anything. I'm sure the Civil Service and Dad had taught him all these things. I was somewhat the opposite, so when we hit it off well together I knew that God must be in it.

The Lord was stretching me both in ministry and the gifts of the Spirit. We stayed with one lovely couple who had a little daughter. Every time she sat at the meal table she wheezed and could hardly breathe through chronic asthma. I went to bed and was disturbed all night by horrific dreams, and woke up soaking wet with sweat in the morning. When I went downstairs I mentioned my rough night to the lady of the house, trying to make light of it and blaming it on the cheese I had for supper, but as I was speaking she went a deathly white and proceeded to tell me that she and her husband had moved out of that bedroom for the very same reason. Every night they had experienced these dreams and got so exhausted they could think of no other action to take. When I asked why they didn't get counsel from their local church, she informed me that they had, and upon their recommendation they had brought in a water diviner. After his visit he had achieved nothing more than confusion.

That evening I prayed over the young couple and saw their lives wonderfully released in many areas. They were also both filled with the Spirit, although I had to keep asking them if they were praying in tongues or Dutch. We then went back into the bedroom and, having thrown out a few items that were not a particular blessing, we set to work praying and telling any demonic influences that happened to be present and listening in to leave this house in the name of Jesus. Again God was so good: not only did he do something very special in their lives, not only did he also heal the little one of asthma, but from that night on I slept like a log!

I needed my beauty sleep not only for the obvious reasons but also because I knew that once I got home life was going to be more hectic than when I was away. I wasn't wrong. As soon as we arrived on English turf Irene informed me that there was a three-bedroom house for sale in the next road to us, which just happened to be two doors away from my sister, and she had made an appointment to go and view it the following day. Now houses meant nothing to me, after all I really lived in a car, but even I was beginning to think that our cosy little two-up, two-down that we had loved living in was getting a bit overcrowded – not just because of the five of us, but because I had nowhere to work and store the ever increasing amount of equipment we were accumulating.

I love house-hunting because once you walk into a new house and feel that wonderful peace of mind that this is the one, the price and even the condition of it seems no problem. We instantly felt this way about this house, and sure enough within a very short time we had moved in and I actually had a room to work in – it made a change from cupboards and garden sheds.

While we were considering our move, the fellowship was sadly moving backwards. Even with my resignation from the eldership the division in our little group had not improved; it had in fact deteriorated.

In October the elders realised that it was a mockery to carry on calling our people a fellowship. That was the last thing it was, so they called together a church meeting and announced that the membership was to be dissolved. A paper was given to each person with three requirements that they had to agree with if they wanted to be members of the new fellowship. They were simply to affirm their commitment to Jesus, to the elders, and to their fellow members.

Out of the forty-one members at the beginning of the year, only twenty wished to continue. All the other members of Rev Counta had left, except Pugwash who moved back to his home in Surrey a few weeks later. I can't say that I was brokenhearted or even surprised by those that left. I may not have agreed with their viewpoints, but I respected the fact that they had their opinions and had stuck by their principles and convictions. My only sadness was for the one or two poor lambs who left because their friends did and seemed confused by the whole affair.

I couldn't see how any split could glorify God, but then the church didn't split when the people left, it had split months before. As with the band God didn't want a democratically run fellowship, nor did he want one run by a dictatorship, but the balance is hard to find when everyone is hurting and there is so little trust around . We had no foundations to rebuild a relationship, which could have been our only means of reconciliation, the main reason being in my opinion that none of us outside of our families had been taught what a real relationship involved anyway. Most of those who left us went back to the Baptist church that we had originally been sent out from, but with the small remnant left we were confident that we would learn from past mistakes. With our tiny nucleus, our hearts now being right with the Lord and each other, we could now move on to become a church that hopefully Jesus would be proud of.

On Thursday October 2nd 1980, amidst all this confusion, I shut myself in a room and again felt God inspiring me to start songwriting. I had five hours undisturbed, and by the time I emerged from that room I had the concept and the songs written out for a new album: *Land of Hope and Glories*.

For the first time since I had seen those child prostitutes in Holland I began to consider what our children really had to enjoy in their Christian lives, as it seemed to me that every good new thing that the Spirit of God was doing was either aimed at the teenagers or the older folk. I wanted this concept to be simple fun teaching for all ages to enjoy. Yet due to its inspiration and theme there was going to be a prophetic element that the children would not forget as they grew older. I didn't want the traditional child evangelist's approach of 'Come to Jesus and life will be one big sunshine smile', I wanted to put in the good times and the hard times that the Christian must encounter. At this stage I brought in the Miserie characters, dressed in black and always knocking the Spirit-filled praising

Glories. These were never the unsaved. No, they were the religious anti-charismatics, those who still lived under man-made laws and traditions, modern-day Pharisees who lived as though Christianity was only to be endured, certainly not enjoyed. Not only had I met plenty of these, but I had a shrewd feeling that once this album had come out I would come across many more.

I had got in touch with my Uncle Allan, with whom over the years I had lost contact. After I explained what a Glorie and a Miserie should look like, he put pen to paper and created the little cartoon characters. Then, as I explained how I saw the album cover – bold, loud and over the top, just like the little Glories – he again with a genius that was gifted by God managed to translate my ideas to paper.

I still needed credibility, so being a bit cheeky I approached my friend David Pawson who wrote a great intro for the album as only he could. I was so proud that he agreed to be associated with me and put his name and reputation alongside my work.

At this point I formed a business. I printed badges and teeshirts with pictures of the little Glories and Miseries on. These would not only be a good witness as people wore them, but also might bring in a little funding, as cash was still hard to come by. But then I noticed that the Miserie teeshirts were selling faster. Not really wanting to promote that sort of image (even though profits were good), I took them off the market. I named the little business the Glorie Company, which really meant a company of Glories, not some major business company.

From October to Christmas, apart from travelling around the country, my spare time was taken up with working on the new album. I really wanted this to be not only the best thing I had ever done, but significant for those who were to hear it. I approached Andy to see if he would come and produce it, but as ATF were doing so well he just couldn't spare the time. I rounded up some session musicians who in my opinion were the best. I had Les Moir on bass, Neil Costello on guitar, Dave Engels on drums, Chris Eaton on piano, and brought in Derek Moon and his daughter Hilary to do some synth overdubs. I also got my Glorie backing vocalists who comprised Becca age 9, Sarah age 8, Joseph and Anna age 6, Daniel age 5, and Johnny age 4, I thought Suzy age 1 was just a tiny bit too young to be included at this stage. The main reason that I chose only family was that these were the only ones I felt at liberty to ask to sacrifice their Christmas for the sake of rehearsals.

Dave Aston, the engineer, and I did what little production was necessary, but by the time the musicians had finished, they had already shaped what the album was going to sound like. By January 3rd the album was completed. I was so brainwashed by it that I couldn't work out what I thought of it, so I hid it away for a couple of weeks until I could make a proper assessment. Even then I knew that whatever I thought of it, 1981 was going to be a new era for me. From now on I was going to be entering the Land of Hope and Glories.

18

Land of Hope and Glories

Land of hope and Glories,
Land where Jesus is King.
Your Majesty, we are Your servants,
Please take these lives that we bring.
We dedicate ourselves to Your service,
And are willing to do all You say,
For You made us all into Glories
And Glories we're going to stay.

First came the advertising:

A letter from the Glories. Dear You, Ishmael's new album – or should we say our new album – takes you on a journey to Charismatic wood where you become one of us for at least forty minutes, hopefully longer. Through narration and song you learn what makes us Glories Glories, also the hard road we must travel along if we are to endure to the end. Of course the album is packed with fun, kids and good lively rock music, to keep us bouncing away for hours, etc, etc.

Then came the special offers:

We are putting a special giant-size poster of our adventures in with each album as a special treat, plus the first 2000 will be pressed on white vinyl.

Then followed the reviews:

From the headbanging folk of Ishmael and Andy to the headbanging punk of Rev Counta, Ish's exuberance, charm and outrageous sense of humour have been a source of blessing to thousands of people. Once described by Graham Kendrick as 'the only musical evangelist I know', Ishmael has been quite definitely used by God throughout Britain. This LP will be as well. Though the album is ostensibly for children, David Pawson's highly partisan sleeve notes give the game away. This is a record for the whole family, and Ish succeeds in the impossible task of making punk praise palatable for parents. The concept Glories versus Miseries which runs through the album seems ludicrously simplistic, yet Ishmael's tongue-in-cheek sense of humour, evident joy in the Lord and pungent lyrics all combine to teach the listener some important lessons. Not everyone will share the Smale theology and some will find difficulty in telling parody from intentional sincerity; however the burning question of the day is: Are you a Glorie or a Miserie? Buy this album and risk finding out.

I spent more time on preparation for this concept album than I had on any previous recording, and although no artist can live on reviews, it was just what I needed at the time; all of them were positive.

What thrilled me all the more was that the reviewers didn't just see it as an album for children; it was an album for all ages. I had never been motivated to be a children's worker, but on examining the first few verses of Matthew chapter 18, God had spoken to me very clearly and, instead of presuming that I had a wealth of knowledge to impart to them, I was more interested in watching their young lives and seeing what I could learn from them about humility, their simple faith and their uncomplicated relationship with the Lord. My idea was to use children on my albums not for sentimental reasons, but because I believed that grown-ups could learn a lot from the mouths of babes.

I was still very actively involved with British Youth for Christ, and an eight-day tour was arranged called 'The Loudest Whisper'. As well as myself, a band called Streetlevel and Clive Calver held it all together, and Clive also did a preach. It was a lot of fun and quite effective, but the night that stands out for me was the last night when we were playing in Surbiton. At the end of the evening my friend and fellow-musician, Noel Richards, introduced me to his friend Gerald Coates. Now, I had heard of Gerald but knew little about him except his reputation of being wayout, controversial and, as a pillar of the house church movement, involved in stirring up and splitting churches to add to his own ranks. Now, as I had been labelled with a similar reputation I was very interested to meet this man. As I looked at him and we exchanged a few sentences together, I saw a very different person. He didn't seem at all the overpowering empire-builder that I was expecting to see, but a gentle, caring man who undoubtedly had strong viewpoints but was a million miles away from the aggressive church-divider that certain of his enemies had tried to convince me that he was.

The next big venture I was to encounter was the ever-increasing Spring Harvest. Although I was to be available to go and sing to all ages my main brief was to oversee two of the fringe events. The first of these was a mid-day extravaganza called 'Lunchtime Funtime'. I never really enjoyed doing this much. It was a silly variety show to pass the time for the few campers who had not gone to eat their lunches, with such mindless trivia as silly games and shoving custard pies into people's faces. This did me more harm than good as I was dubbed 'Ishmael the custard-pie king', and for the next year or so many could not appreciate the serious points I was trying to put over because of my clown image.

I managed to regain a bit of my credibility in the evening however, when I was responsible for organising and compering the late-night concert which was known as the 'Pumpkin Club'. Although I enjoyed doing this, it was still a fearsome task as there was often an air of aggression in the audience. When the bands ran overtime the maddened crowd would often resort to booing and shouting, 'Get off!' when I had to go on and announce that the show, due to the lateness of the hour, had to end. I always found it hard to cope with these sort of reactions from Christians.

At the end of the week, at ten thirty p.m., I premiered the first stage version of 'Land of Hope and Glories'. The whole show was done by lighting and backing-tapes, and involved our six little Glories, plus me singing, leaping around the stage and each time a narration appeared, rushing behind the curtain to change our costumes. As David, my brother-in-law, sat in the audience with our little Suzy, operating a slide projector, my sister Heather and Irene were behind the curtains in the dark trying to see that we all managed to get into the right clothes in the seconds that we had available to us.

Needless to say, however serene it may have appeared in front of the curtain, it was absolute chaos behind. In the darkness I was accidently treading on and falling over the children, and even managed to put on Irene's white flowery sweatshirt instead of my own white one. Another added problem was that being an hour's production once it had started there was no way of stopping it. Consequently, one of the boys who had drunk too many cokes discovered he couldn't get to the loo and back, found a new use for a set of bongos. But amidst all the mayhem God was working, and by the time I walked on stage to pray at the end, dozens were getting their lives sorted out with the Lord. It was a great success, and even after the first performance it was starting to fulfil the dreams and expectations I had for it.

On returning home again, I became involved in what I called a 'Family Concert'. In some ways this was reminiscent of the early 'Ishmael United' days as it was a two-hour presentation involving a short piece from the Glorie Album, plenty of songs accompanied by my brother Tim on bass, a short talk, plus my latest acquisition which was a large glove-puppet resembling a monkey. Sadly, my poor little furry friend had a bit of an identity crisis as I would change his name at each venue to that of the organiser or minister. This, of course, went down a storm with everyone, except the organiser or minister.

During early June of 1981, disaster struck in the form of a terrible toothache. Having approached my dentist who could not seem to find the cause, I was prayed for by everybody and anybody who believed that the Lord had given them a healing ministry, but nothing seemed to happen. During this time I went to a Youth for Christ retreat and, feeling like a bear with a sore head, I was asked to lead the worship with Graham Kendrick. As you can imagine we made an interesting combination, as Graham was showing me guitar chords that I never knew existed, and I was showing him dance steps that he never believed possible. In the end we compromised our styles: I left all the slow songs to Graham and he left all the fast ones to me.

Nineteen days later my tooth was still raging and I was finding it harder and harder to concentrate on what I was doing. People knew that I was a person who loved smiling and fun, but this tooth was making me right fed-up. On the nineteenth day I was at a concert in Leeds, and although I tried to continue as though nothing was wrong, there came a point when I had to shout out that I had a lousy toothache. I actually felt a bit better after I had done that. When the concert finished a gentleman came up to me and informed me that he was an oral surgeon and if I came along to his surgery he would take a look at it for me. At two a.m. on Sunday morning I was in Leeds Hospital feeling great as the offending molar was going to offend me no longer as it sat in the palm of my hand. I learned a lesson through all this though, that as well as using the gifts of the Spirit, God still uses the talents and expertise he has given to his children. Paul always had his thorn in the flesh, I'm very thankful that I got rid of my pain in the mouth.

We had arranged a twelve-venue tour of 'Land of Hope and Glories' over the summer holidays. Apart from my sister's family and my own, we also took a friend, Roy Lowry, who had his own lighting rig. The tour started off rather badly as the mini-bus that we borrowed broke down halfway between Rustington and our first gig in Norwich, so although we had left home at two p.m. we didn't actually arrive in Norwich until five a.m. the following morning, and that was courtesy of the AA relay service. However, that didn't pour water on our fireworks. We knew that God was going to bless this tour and we were not going to let the odd breakdown ruin our fun. During the next two weeks we performed to more than 3,000 people, saw dozens become Christians, and for the first time in many churches saw all the members of the family attending the same meeting and having a really good evening out together.

I was being stirred up more and more by the feeling that the church had lost its way with families and could only cope with the different generations and age groups when they were split up and not when they were together. I tried to picture the Lord Jesus preaching the Sermon on the Mount and telling all the children to go onto another mountain where his disciples would run a crèche and a children's work so that the adults would not be disturbed by their presence. I even tried to picture 5,000 starving people who didn't get any fish and bread because the young lad who had them was told to clear off because the meeting was not suitable for him.

My mind started to work overtime as I wondered how we could bring Christian families back together again so they could worship, learn, laugh and have fellowship in the smaller units that God had placed them in. From that time on the diary was fuller than full – there was obviously a great need for this new family ministry. Roy of the lights joined me full time, and Tim joined us at weekends. I expected that we would get a mixed reaction and we certainly did. I had already faced the fact that I was not everyone's cup of tea, and most nights people would walk out after the first few songs. This, of course, was their privilege, but I couldn't understand why they didn't just leave quietly. Why did the ones who stormed out always wear the noisiest shoes and love banging the doors as they left?

During that autumn I returned to the recording studio twice. If I found that I had a couple of days free, I thought that it must be time for another album. I was honoured to be asked by the Bradford house church, who had brought over from America a children's album called *Supergang*, to be 'Preacher Pidgeon' on *Supergang 2*. The idea was to bring the backing-tracks over from the States and then to record all the vocals in England so that it wouldn't sound too American. Joff Day was in charge of their children's work at this time, and he was one of the most inventive children's workers that I had ever met.

The actual recording was not quite as easy as it sounds. I had to sing two songs sounding like a bird yet trying to keep in tune. Even after we had finished it, I wasn't convinced that I had managed to do either, but Joff was very encouraging and satisfied. In retrospect, the recording was secondary to what I was learning. I spent many hours talking to the children from this fellowship and they nearly blew my mind as they told me how God had filled them with his Spirit, how they spoke in tongues, and how God had used them in supernatural gifts. My mouth dropped wide open in amazement as I heard how these little ones were seeing more things happening than I was, and I pumped as much information out of them as I possibly could over those few days.

I also returned to the studio in my own right to record a low-budget cassette called *Songs for Bouncing Glories*. I was a little apprehensive about doing this recording as memories of the disastrous *Amazin' What Praisin' Can Do* cassette kept flooding back to mind. But I was convinced that because all the worship records being released sounded similar, and to my ears very laid back, gentle and effeminate, there was still a place for a good old rocky, bouncy, praise album. I decided not just to put on self-penned songs, but also some of my favourite choruses written by other people. I thought I would try to use adults singing backing on some tracks and children on others, then hopefully all ages would not only enjoy it but also buy it. We spent thirteen hours putting down twenty-one backing-tracks and within two and a half days we had completed the whole lot.

In November we embarked on the biggest tour that I had ever been involved in called 'Let God Speak'. We had twenty-two intensive dates and the line-up was David

Pawson, Clive Calver, Graham Kendrick, mime artist Geoffrey Stevenson, and poet Steve Turner. It only takes a glance at the names and talents above to see that we had enough potential material to fill up a week let alone a night. Once David made it clear that he was speaking on repentance, faith, baptism in water and baptism in the Spirit, we could see that there was no way he could give these major issues any sort of justice without at least an hour to do it, so that meant we all had to squeeze our contributions into the rest of the time provided.

The first couple of nights were quite shaky as we tried to work out the structure of the evening, but once we got that sorted out, I believe that it proved to be the most significant tour to hit the country. Each night David caused a stir as Anglicans and Church of Scotland folk had trouble accepting his preaching on water baptism, and many others had problems with his teaching on the importance of baptism in the Spirit and the joy of speaking in tongues.

Although my job in the evening was really just to get people relaxed and settled down so they would listen to what was to be said later, I wouldn't have minded not doing anything on stage. I just loved being with the team and fulfilling my counselling responsibility which was praying for people to be filled with the Spirit and to see them released in tongues.

Each evening I was given local counsellors to assist me. In one place none of my helpers actually spoke in tongues which was not a great boon, and in another place nobody wanted to work with me. As I saw dozens coming out to be prayed for, I got them to put their arms around each other in a massive circle and then I prayed with one of them. The Holy Spirit came down in power and they were filled one after the other just like a row of dominoes. I saw everyone from children to vicars in dog-collars walk in, be filled up and go dancing out for joy. Hundreds, probably thousands, were prayed for over those few weeks and had their lives changed as they let God speak and then acted on what he said.

As with every great blessing, the opposition always has

to get the boot in. An evangelist wrote an article in the *Evangelical Times* which had a go at all of us. He wrote me off as 'tasteless blasphemy', and again I just couldn't believe that a brother of mine in the Christian family, however much he may hate me, could be allowed to print such a thing without even doing things the biblical way and coming to talk things over with me first. I felt extremely exhausted after the tour and very hurt that after seeing God do so much these lies should come from our own people. I rang up the paper but they wouldn't listen to me, they just said that their reporters were allowed to write what they liked. I wondered if this would damage the ministry that God was giving me. Would gullible leaders listen to these untrue words and want to believe the worst of me? Would I for ever hold something against John, and if by chance I ever met him, would I feel like punching him on the nose or could I forgive him?

I need not have worried however, for that year the prophetic vision behind Land of Hope and Glories was actually coming true. If I was going to stick my neck out, I must expect a few bruises, if I really wanted to be used by God, then there were always going to be Miserie attacks. My only fear was that I would become hard and bitter, because I knew that the minute that happened my ministry would be over. Within a short while I was pleased to see that my fear was not realised. But I had learned an important lesson which was that when fighting the enemy I had to make sure that my armour covered my back and not just my front.

19

Supernaturally

I don't understand these Glories,
They're just the same as me.
They're naturally not super,
But they're supernaturally.

It's surprising how quickly time flies when you're enjoying yourself and kept very busy. Although life was a little easier financially as I had chosen to invest much of our income into various projects, at the end of the day we were not a lot better off. At this stage I still felt that I should not charge a fee and left it with the organisers to pray over what they should donate to my many hours of hard labour. My payment ranged from generous cash gifts to a set of old encyclopaedias, and as I had agreed to give Roy of the lights a percentage, the latter offering only left me with volumes 'Dacca' to 'Zurich'.

I still had great problems understanding the naïvety of Christians. I went to preach at a youth weekend, and after seeing where all the young people were going to sleep I was shown my single bed. This was not only in the same room as but parked right next to the pastor and his wife's double bed. I made some excuse that I needed my own room for preparation purposes and thankfully was moved elsewhere. This would have given a new meaning to the term 'close fellowship'.

I was also being invited to quite a few musicians' conferences, not necessarily to teach them about music, but more to teach them what they could do when they stopped hiding behind their instruments. I remember once at a conference centre called Pilgrim Hall in Sussex, Graham was speaking in the lounge and I was asked to set up the hall for a concert in the evening. I put the PA up with no problem, but as I set up the lighting rig I suddenly heard the fire alarm ringing all around the building. Suddenly there was panic as everyone tried to remember what to do and where they should go in an emergency. Eventually we all went into the owner's bungalow while the main building was searched to see where the fire was. Two fire-engines and a police car came racing up the drive, but no one could find the blaze. It was then that they discovered the cause of all the commotion – yes, you've guessed it, my lighting rig. I had set it up a few inches away from the heat sensitive alarm, and of course once the lights had warmed up off went the siren. The only good thing to come out of it was that it did wake up all those who were trying to catch forty winks during Graham's seminar.

Talking about strange things that lights can do, I should mention a friend of mine who always fascinated me. His name is Pete Gilbert. He is not the usual evangelist who always comes equipped with either a guitar or a Bible, or on the rare occasion both. No, Pete's props are handcuffs, strait-jackets and sometimes the odd hundred-foot crane. His medium for communication is escapology.

Pete and I decided to do a short tour together which we would call 'The Great Escape', as both of our fun ministries complemented each other. Now, using the word 'fun' was probably my big mistake because Pete took what he did very seriously and he would keep reminding me that it was skill not tricks. The tour was superb, many people who would never have entered a church building came along and a lot of them became Christians. I was thrilled to bits with this, but I felt that our performance, meaning Pete's performance, was becoming far too predictable. I always enjoyed watching Tommy Cooper who kept getting things wrong, but there was no way that this would ever happen with Pete as he was such a perfectionist; he would not just double-check, he would quadruple-check all his props.

On the last night of the tour I decided to assist him. During the evening he did an illusion with a banana, and as he spoke and peeled it back it was miraculously already cut in four pieces. I had observed Pete spending a long time prior to the show doctoring these bananas, so while we were praying beforehand I sneaked out and switched them. I waited patiently for the banana time to arrive and when it did I nearly died. Pete, as confidently as ever, did his little chat about them, then let people observe that they hadn't been tampered with, and then explained that as he unpeeled it, it would as though by magic be in four sections. Well, sure enough he started to unzip the banana, and he looked visibly shaken as he discovered that it was in one piece. At this point I had to exit stage left as I was rolling around the floor in uncontrollable laughter. Pete, meanwhile, was totally perplexed. It was impossible. How could it grow back together? After a few minutes though, being a professional, Pete laughed it off and continued with something else.

As soon as the show had finished he came up to me and tried to tell me that it must have been the heat from the lights that had sealed it up, which only set me off laughing again. He then guessed that I knew more than I was letting on so I explained what I had done. To say he was furious was an understatement. He blew his top and as he stormed off he told me that he would never work with me again. When he calmed down I apologised to him and even gave him a peace offering of my new cassette, whether he wanted it or not. In no time we were best mates again, but I knew it would take a few years before I would be able to mention the word 'banana' in his presence again.

The annual Spring Harvest was looming on the horizon, and as I didn't want to go back and just perform 'Land of Hope and Glories' again, I decided to go back into the studio and make up a new tape using a mixture of songs from the above album and the *Songs for Bouncing Glories* cassette. I thought I would call it *The Land of Bouncing Glories*, and by adding the praise songs it would be much more open for audience participation. Again I had to don my custard-pie king hat, but now the trend had caught on. Instead of using the proper foam, people were now walking up to me and pushing a plate full of shaving cream into my face which I was rapidly learning was rather painful on the eyes. But even with these minor drawbacks, I loved running the late-night concert slot and our new production went down as well, if not better, than the year before. But the highlight for me this year was the Praise Party on the last night where worship leaders like Dave Bilbrough, Rob White and anyone else who was around would just drop in and jam along. It was a great atmosphere with a couple of thousand people all enjoying praising God together.

Spring Harvest also provided great opportunities to meet people whom I had heard about but never met. I was very impressed with Floyd McClung, although it did look strange when he had meals with us and this giant of a man stood next to my four-foot ten-inch wife. Another time I had to interview Mary Whitehouse. As I was talking to her I mentioned how I resigned my membership from a video club because they had blue movies. I then threw in a little quip about how I lost a fiver in the deal. Poor Mary didn't understand my sense of humour and spent the next five minutes in front of 1,500 viewers giving me a sermon on how ashamed she was of me that I even considered the money. She was sweet though, and I have great respect for her.

After these so-called spiritual highs, it was always hard to adjust to reality when I got home. One reality that I did not like to acknowledge was that I was getting fat. My main problem was that Irene was an excellent cook and there was no way that I could leave anything she made. The other problem was that always being on the road, my favourite food in any transport café was two sausages, egg, chips, beans, plus of course two slices of bread and butter, which on no account could be called a low calorie meal. It's not that I felt unfit, in fact with all the bouncing about on stage I liked to think that I was very fit, but with the ever-expanding waistline I felt that I was going to end up looking more like Father Christmas than father Ishmael.

Mark, a member of our fellowship who was a long-distance runner, suggested that I joined him one evening for a gentle jog. As I am sure you have picked up from reading this far, I am an extremist and there is no way that I can do anything by halves. Mark, speaking with wisdom and experience, suggested just a slow mile-long jog, but desiring to lose at least two stones immediately I pressed him for a three-and-a-half mile race. The last thing I remember was staggering in through my front door, turning every shade between red, blue and purple, and announcing that there must be an easier way to keep fit.

Another one of my weaknesses was that I always went through fads and phases with things. One of these was citizen-band radio. My handle was Mr Bounce, and although I was very inhibited when talking to people on it, I was convinced that it could be used for the kingdom. My only real contact was some young lady I got talking to about the Lord, and she asked if I could call in and see her to continue the conversation. Could this be the start of a new ministry? No, sadly she wasn't really interested in God, she just needed some money. My CB was about to turn into an expensive phase, so in no time at all it was 'ten four, over and out'.

The time was approaching when I knew I needed a sequel to Land of Hope and Glories, so I sat down and started writing an album that would be a simple view of the work of the Holy Spirit. I decided to call it *The Power and the Glories*. I wanted to call my main character 'Y' as it seemed that whenever you talked to people about this great subject they would use the word 'why' more than any other. I wanted to hinge the story around this little character but cover such subjects as Pentecost, water baptism, freedom in worship, being filled with the Holy Spirit, the gifts and fruit of the Spirit, and even to go on to such issues as persecution and the second coming. Amidst all this I wanted my little Glorie to experience confusion, going overboard on tongues and even being hurt by other Christians, learning how he must forgive them. Although this sounds very ambitious and serious, I also had to put it over in a way that was fun even for children to listen to. It took ever such a lot of hard work to get it together. I even had some French lessons for one track where I sang deliberately in pidgin French to show people my linguistic abilities.

I was faced with one major problem: my six little Glories, although they loved the Lord Jesus, had not been baptised in the Holy Spirit, so I had a twinge of conscience about whether or not I should have them on the album. How I wished I could find a children's worker who agreed with this theology and would come in and pray for these children. I didn't particularly want to pray for them as I knew that they would do anything for me and I wanted them to do it for the Lord.

While in this dilemma, the Lord spoke to me and told me very clearly that instead of having the planned rehearsal on the following Monday night, he wanted me to pray for them to be filled with his power. On the Monday night all six of them came into my front room, the eldest being twelve and the youngest being six. I sat them down and explained to them that we were not going to rehearse that night, instead we were going to let God do to us what he had done to the little Glorie Y that we had been singing about. They were thrilled by this, but I'm not sure if that was because of the excitement of what was about to happen or the prospect of not having to suffer a boring rehearsal.

I continued to explain about the Holy Spirit and read them some verses from the Bible to explain what happened in the early church and that what God did then he still wants to do today. Then I got them to stand up and said that I would come round, put my hands on each of their heads individually and pray over them, then all I wanted them to do was to start praising God without using the English language. I was about to move over to the oldest one as somehow I felt that she might respond more quickly, but our little Daniel said, 'Do you mean like this Dad?' and started speaking in tongues. I told him to stop and wait because I hadn't even prayed for him yet. But just as I was about to pray for the oldest, Becca, they obviously couldn't contain themselves any longer and they all started praising God in new languages – and they were so loud.

I walked back to where I had been standing originally, feeling rather put out as I hadn't even had the chance to pray for them, but then as I looked around the room to my horror I saw nine-year-old Anna giggling and laughing. This is awful, I thought, just think if anyone was to walk into the room now and see this – it's absolutely irreverent. I was just about to walk across the room and rebuke her when I felt a sensation like someone grabbing me by the scruff of the neck and telling me not to move. The Lord then told me to leave these little ones alone and never to try and put my character in them. These are children, the Lord continued, and that little one is always giggling and laughing because it's the way I made her and want her to be. As I looked up, suitably rebuked, I saw her again only this time she had her hands raised in the air and her eyes closed, and was in a little world alone with her God, praising him with a radiant and beaming face. From that moment on, rehearsals took on a whole new meaning as we worshipped and learned together.

I gave Dave Bilbrough a phone call and asked him to write me a song to which he replied that he found it impossible to do songs to order but he would try. Within a few minutes he had rung back saying that he had written it. Pat, Dave's wife, came and helped me on the recording. She was a trained music teacher and had a great way with the children, bringing the best out of their voices. The preparation and making of *The Power and the Glories* took more out of me than anything I had ever done before. As well as the recording, I hadn't stopped travelling around doing live shows, and even during the recording week I had engagements to fulfil.

A couple of days after completing the album, Roy and I went over to the Isle of Wight to spend a few days at the Elim Youth Camp. As I lay in my tent on the first night I felt totally exhausted, and although I tried to sleep I just kept hearing the songs from the album. Try as I could, I could not clear my mind of them.

The following morning I felt terrible. As I walked to the washroom and smelled that smell of breakfast cooking, which I usually loved, I was violently sick. My back was killing me, so I went and saw the camp nurse who gave me a few aspirins which again I threw up. I was sweating and yet freezing, so I returned to the nurse and asked her to phone a doctor. A few minutes later she returned to tell me that there was no surgery until the day after tomorrow and could I hang on till then. That was it. I staggered to the car and got Roy to drive me to casualty as I'd never known pain like this and I still had those silly tunes whirling around my head.

On arrival I was put in a gown and told to lie on a bed in a little cubicle until the doctor came round. I jumped up and walked around the bed praying in tongues, which although helping to relieve the pain, did confuse the Indian Doctor who kept looking around the curtain thinking that I was talking to him. When he examined me I had first of all to convince him that I wasn't a drug addict who had come in for a quick shot, I really was in pain. As I described how I was feeling, he realised that I had a blocked kidney.

Having inserted a catheter in me, I was put into an ambulance and taken to the main hospital on the island. I felt every bump going along that road. I was then put in a ward, given a very strong pain-killer, and went to sleep. Meanwhile, back at casualty Roy was still waiting – nobody had informed him that I had been taken to another hospital. Irene had received a phone call from a doctor informing her that I had been rushed into hospital and they would keep her informed when they found out the diagnosis. This was on the Saturday. On the Sunday I still felt terrible, but I felt worse being stuck on the island in agony. I thought that I might as well go home and be in pain, so I discharged myself against the doctor's wishes and drove home with Roy.

Once in my own bed I was no better. Everyone came to pray for me, but somehow it didn't seem to help. For the next couple of weeks I could eat nothing, I couldn't sleep, and was continually passing blood. In addition to this, I would vary between hysterical bouts of laughing and crying – I had lost control of my emotions. Poor Irene, not only was she trying to nurse the worst patient that the world has ever known, but she was also frightened that I had finally cracked up. I had been told that some people were so against my ministry that they were actually praying that God would finish me off. If that was true, I bet they felt their prayers were being answered.

I had tests which not only confirmed my blocked kidney but also various stones that seemed to be rattling around inside me. Still people kept praying *for* me, mainly that I would be able to sleep and my mind would calm down. Within three weeks my kidneys were free, my stones had rolled away, and my mind was back to its usual state. I praise God for this experience; it taught me ever such a lot. Irene, the family, the fellowship and friends had really shown me how much they cared and appreciated me and I also saw how much I needed and appreciated them. It was the first real physical suffering that I had ever known, and I knew that as I met others who were in pain I would be much more sympathetic towards them rather than doing my usual and just telling them to cheer up and stop feeling sorry for themselves.

After a short holiday with Irene and the children, which I believe they needed more than me, I was raring to go again. God still had a lot for me to do and there was no way that I wanted to slow down or be left out of anything that he had in mind.

Around this time it was my privilege to see my grandfather, who was fast approaching the ripe old age of ninety, ask for baptism. He had given his life to the Lord at the age of eighty-six which was thrilling for us all, particularly for Mum and Dad with whom he was living. Dad had explained the procedure to him and although he was apprehensive about doing it due to Grandpa's age and physical well-being, Grandpa made it clear that this was what he wanted. So in October, a few days before his ninetieth birthday, he was baptised in a small portable pool in Mum and Dad's garden with the whole fellowship there to witness. I am sure there was not a dry eye, and it was the most thrilling baptism it has been my privilege to witness. Grandpa went to be with his Lord some four years later, and those last few years I know were of great intercession. You see, God can use you whatever your age.

I embarked on a new venture called 'Ishmael's Weekendaways'. For these weekends I would hire a conference centre and take a load of young people away to train them. On the first one they were so hungry to learn about the things of God that they wanted more and more seminars. It was as though they had the capacity to receive more than I could give. When I was their age I was more interested in members of the opposite sex and the social times, but these kids were of a different calibre – they seemed more open to God than any previous generation I had known or worked with.

By 1983 my home fellowship was going great guns. The love and warmth was growing weekly and the brand-new congregation that had emerged since the dissolution was a great bunch of people. About this time I was approached to rejoin the eldership, and as I felt that my previous hurts and insecurities were now a thing of the past, I believed that I would be able to have a positive input into our fellowship although I would be unable to be involved in all the local issues because of my national work.

Again we returned to Spring Harvest, but this time to perform *The Power and the Glories*. The aim of Spring Harvest at this stage was not to be classed as charismatic, or non-charismatic: they wanted to be somewhere in the middle so that they could relate to both opinions. Subtlety has never been my middle name, and with a production like *The Power and the Glories*, I knew that my position would be made very clear.

At its first performance all was going well until I gave an appeal at the end for anyone who wanted to be filled with the Holy Spirit to come forward. Now, I may have just got away with this at an adult meeting, but this was in fact for children. About a couple of hundred came rushing forwards and I simply told them to put their arms around each other and ask God to fill them. It was just like a multiplied version of my front room. They were off in tongues before you could say *glossolalia*. I saw no harm in that as I had not laid hands on anybody, I certainly hadn't worked them up – all I had done was to encourage the children to open themselves up to the Holy Spirit. But then the complaints came rolling in, not against God but against me. One of the organisers went mad at me and from that moment on I knew it was on the cards that this could be my last Spring Harvest.

As the Summer approached, Roy left me to go to university and I knew that I was in for a change. The Glories productions were great fun, but *The Power and the Glories* seemed way ahead of where most churches were at, especially in connection with their children's work. I felt I was encouraging them to dance before they had realised that they even had feet. I was going to have to do something to up the profile and the spiritual potential of the children, but in a way that would not just win over the children and their workers. Somehow I had to get to the leadership and the rest of the congregation because what I wanted to say would in time affect the whole structure of their church life. But I had to earn the right and their respect before I would be able to achieve this.

20

We Belong to an Army That Can Never Be Defeated

We are raising up our banner stating 'Jesus is victorious'.
Even though we're battle weary, we'll endure to the end.
Then King Jesus will return triumphant and glorious,
There'll be peace and joy for ever,
There'll be love and life for ever,
We'll praise His name for ever 'cause He's worthy to be praised.
There'll be no more wars and fighting,
No more demonic battles, no more tears and pain
Because Satan's been destroyed.

The family concerts had worked well, but I had to provide more than just a good fun evening out for the church. Up and down the country at this time there was an epidemic of celebrations. These meetings seemed to go on for hours, and divided up roughly fifty-fifty worship and preaching. Due to their sheer length and intensity they were certainly 18-rated and not a place to bring along your children.

At this point I thought of doing a special all-age celebration which I would continue to call a Praise Party. Although I was very keen to see God do things during the evening, I did not want it to become heavy, self-indulgent and boring. I knew that I would have to be careful to keep it well balanced or else it would just remain the same as the family concerts that I was trying to give up. I needed to make it a praise and teaching evening with a hint of fun, rather than a fun evening with a hint of praise and worship.

At this time I discovered that working with all ages in one meeting was going to be a real challenge and that it would take a lot of preparation. Working with just adults, teenagers or children was a doddle compared to this.

In a reasonably short period of time I recorded three *Praise Party* albums. The first was like a continuation of *Songs for Bouncing Glories*. I had used many songs that were not mine and that were already established favourites. With volumes two and three, however, I chose to be a little more adventurous and used 99% my own material, plus the odd song by Dave Bilbrough and by Mick Gisbey, one of our fellowship members.

I tried to observe what other children's organisations that had far more experience than me were up to. I suppose my biggest criticism of one or two was that their ideas were outdated and that they tended to treat the older children more as babies rather than young spiritual beings. It seemed to me that the renewal movement which had spread right across the country and denominational divides had touched every area of church life except the children's work. Yet I was convinced that the Holy Spirit had new and refreshing things to say to these younger ones as well.

Music had been my main means of communication for the past thirteen years; it was the first area I felt needed to be reformed. Having listened to such children's favourites of the day as the Wombles, the Smurfs and Animal Quackers, I saw that they were providing fun music that was rock based. This had been my style for years, but the time had now come to adapt my style of songwriting to help change the face of the old time children's choruses. The songs I wrote could actually be played in Sunday schools and family services and hopefully not only bring our children up to date, but also provide songs that were good Bible teaching and enjoyable for them to sing.

Now, to provide rock music it makes sense to have a good rock band. The last thing that Irene and I wanted though, was to go back to the Rev Counta days. Although

I knew that I had changed since then, it was still a case of once bitten twice shy. So I decided that in those early *Praise Party* days, brother Tim (who had now joined me full time) and I would have to suffice. But as time went on, Tim Jupp, who lived locally, joined us. Not only was he an excellent keyboard player, but he also helped to arrange and produce my songs. As well as these there was also a wealth of musicians who loved joining us whenever they could: people like lead guitarist Doug Horley, John Menlove, Sue Rinaldi and Clive Urquhart, who later joined the band 'Heartbeat', and even a drummer called Terl Bryant, who had not only toured with Sheila Walsh and Steve Taylor but also was involved with some secular bands. Great musicians enjoyed joining us, not just because I was very relaxed and told them to get on stage and enjoy themselves. No, even more important than that they wanted to learn as they watched how the music that they were playing brought God to the ears and hearts of their young audiences in a new dimension.

I recollected how, when I was a child all those many years ago, my favourite songs were those that required me to do some sort of silly actions. Nobody had been inspired or had the inclination to carry on writing these sort of songs as the children were still singing the same half dozen that I had enjoyed what seemed like centuries ago. So new action choruses were also to be part of the *Praise Party* menu, but I knew that it was not going to be an easy job to get my audience to participate in any of these as it seemed that both parents and children alike had somehow got used to being passive observers and I was going to risk looking a right head-case standing out the front doing silly actions all by myself.

To start with, I could get the children to participate after a while, but many grown-ups just sat watching them, which after a short while again proved to inhibit the younger ones. I then banned chairs from the Praise Parties, except for the OAPs or those suffering from bad legs, and this started to do the trick. It wasn't long before people got the idea that I wanted the whole family to have fun, learn and praise and worship together, and the more I saw them all becoming less inhibited, it seemed the more they found God doing things in their lives.

Touring enabled us to experience lots of Christian hospitality. The majority went overboard to be kind and generous to us, others had uncontrollable animals or worse still, uncontrollable children. Some gave up their own beds while others provided mattresses on the floor or beds with sheets that were so damp that you could wring them out and extract water from them. Some had enjoyed the Praise Parties and wanted to spend all night talking about what God was doing nationwide, others hated the Praise Parties and gave us a good grilling and no supper. It got to such a point that it wasn't worth the gamble, so to be sure of a good night's sleep we stayed with people who we knew or we would travel three hundred miles through the night home.

I felt very confident in teaching about tongues, interpretation and prophecy and encouraged others to be released in them as these were three gifts that the Lord had enabled me to use with no difficulty. God had spoken to me many times as I allowed children to pray over me. As well as being very accurate, this could be quite devastating as unlike adults they never held back from anything that God wanted to say or wrapped it up in softer language. Just like little Samuel having to prophesy such harsh things to old Eli.

Although music was to play the major part in the Praise Parties, I knew that I had to have more to give the people from God, but to do this I also knew that I had to receive more from him. Except for the odd occasion, like that in Holland, I had tried to avoid the ministries of deliverance and healing like the plague as I was convinced that these were not ways that God wanted to use me. I was sure that I had what was known as an anti-healing ministry: the sort where you pray for a cold and the person develops pneumonia.

Youth for Christ had arranged a small conference for some of their workers. It was to be led by an internationally famous preacher called Ian Andrews who had been incredibly gifted by God in the area of healing. My initial reaction was not to bother attending as I knew this was not what God had called me to, but then Irene and a couple of my friends who were also going persuaded me to go.

On arrival there were some wild stories going around about how Ian used a gift called the word of knowledge and that he was likely to point to you in front of everyone and then reveal all those nasty little faults and habits that you had that you would rather remained secret. I sat in the back row at the first seminar and as Ian spoke I was surprised how casual and relaxed he seemed. I was expecting some serious, high-pressured, shouting exhorter, not this fellow who kept making jokes. He didn't even look like a healer to me, he was very thin, very pale, wore spectacles and, to top it all, he spoke with a stammer. This put me at ease, because I now felt he didn't look as if he had all the answers. But then he started teaching, and he was profound. He started praying, and he was authoritative. Finally he started ministering into our lives, and he was devastatingly accurate.

By the time I left that conference I was a new man. I had learned more over those few days than I had over the past few years, and I was raring to go in my newly discovered healing and deliverance ministry. I'd made careful notes of how Ian did things, what he said, and how he prayed. In fact, I even took note of how he stood and what he wore, but on reflection I felt that the latter two were probably not vital to having this supernatural gift.

On returning home my faith level was as high as a kite, so I rushed around trying to find someone who was ill so that I could get some practice in. As it turned out everyone I went to seemed to be healthy, so remembering that my Dad had an old war wound in his arm I rushed around to pray for that. As we were in his front room and I was shouting and casting out everything that came to mind, I suddenly realised that nothing was happening except that I was losing my voice. Dad tried to encourage me by saying that he thought it felt a little better, but I knew that something had gone wrong. What else would Ian Andrews have done that I hadn't?

I was determined not to give up though, and the following day Tim and I were doing a Praise Party in a very large Pentecostal church and as we prayed beforehand I told Tim that I had the faith that God was going to heal five people that night. Not an enormous amount I hear you saying, but one has to start somewhere. I started the meeting by telling everyone that we were going to see people wonderfully healed that night and I could sense that people were getting quite excited by that prospect. Then came the first blow: we started praising God and as some of the visitors to the church got up and danced around the building a couple of the leaders walked out in disgust. But everyone was still excited and so was I.

After the praise I sat everyone down and told them that I was going to ask God whom he wanted to heal first, so as it all went quiet I started saying the first person that God wants to heal tonight is someone who has something wrong with their ... their ... and my mind went completely blank. I was sure that Ian had said that if you said this God would put something into your mind, but there was nothing coming to mine. I opened one eye and looked at the expectant congregation sitting in front of me and waiting with baited breath for my next sentence. In panic I knew I had to say something so I said, something wrong with their right foot. Now, this was quite a safe part of the body to mention. With a few hundred people sitting in front of me, by the law of averages there had to be dozens with right foot problems. I asked the person to put their hand up and respond. To my horror, no one did.

I kept repeating it a few times, hoping like mad that someone somewhere would help me out, but no one did. After a few minutes one lady, trying to be helpful, shouted out that she had something wrong with her left foot, did that count? I said that I was sorry it didn't as there was a difference between the right and left feet and with this I walked over to chat it over with brother Tim. Tim usually says very little, but he whispered in my ear with more confidence than I have ever heard him have before, you've got it wrong – it was the left foot. This didn't help me as it seemed worse to go back on what I had already said than to drop it and just get on and sing another song. Yet I knew what I had to do. I told everyone that I must have got it wrong, it was the left foot and perhaps the lady that had just told me she had a problem in that part of her anatomy would like to make her way to the front. As she proceeded to hobble down, she called out that it wasn't actually her left foot, but her left ankle. By now I was beyond caring if it was her left ankle or her left ear, obviously I was not managing to tune in to what God was saying. However, having said that I then mentioned four other illnesses I believed God wanted to heal, and thankfully they responded immediately.

Tim and I then walked down to our suffering five. I thought it would be safer to start at the opposite end from our lady with the ankle trouble, and as I closed my eyes and placed my hands on the head of the first, to my surprise as I started praying I suddenly couldn't find her head. I opened one eye and saw that she was now flat on the floor having narrowly missed taking Tim with her. This had never happened to me before and feeling quite embarrassed by it I hastily moved down the rest of the queue until I reached the infamous ankle job. Just before I prayed for her she told me that she wasn't a Christian and had broken her ankle in three places and the doctors couldn't get it to heal properly and that she wouldn't be able to walk properly again. Well, with all the little faith I could muster I prayed for this poor lady and then asked her how it felt. Her face suddenly lit up. 'It's healed!' she cried. Now, I wasn't so sure. I remembered reading about some healer who had not only told someone to get up out of their wheel-chair but also to jump up and down. I know this wasn't a wheel-chair, but for me it was the next best thing, so I told the lady to prove that she was healed by running around the church a couple of times. Off she went, the congregation clapped and cheered, a couple more of the leaders walked out as they didn't approve of people running around the church, and I nearly fainted.

From that moment on I started to expect to see healings. I could fill a whole book with the miraculous signs and wonders that it has been my privilege to see God perform. I had learned much from Ian, and Colin Urquhart, another man of God dynamic in this field, but God showed me that although it was vital to learn from these men, I must never try to copy them. They are unique and God wanted me to continue to move out in these areas in a way that would mean I would only be looking to him for the results and not to others for technique or profound words.

The more I saw God using me in these areas, the more I wanted to pass it on to my young protégés. I had been quite instrumental in the forming of a new fellowship in nearby Chichester, and although it was made up of young people, they were of a quality and depth that I had failed to see in the majority of established churches and fellowships with so- called mature leaderships. In no time at all this proved to be one of the fastest growing fellowships in the South of England. At the ripe old age of twenty-two, Roger Ellis, who led this wildly enthusiastic group, travelled around with us to gain some experience and also join us on some of our Weekendsaway. Roger was never an excellent children's worker, God had other things in store for him, but because of his incredible Bible knowledge he was invaluable to me as it saved me lugging around one of those enormous concordances.

As I began training up the little ones in words of knowledge and healing, it wasn't long before I realised that they were becoming more advanced in these gifts than I was. A ten-year-old girl was at one of our weekend camps. There were about a hundred children there. When I asked if anyone had heard God tell them anything specific about those he wanted to heal, she came rushing up on the stage to join me. In a loud voice she announced that God wanted to heal someone who had trouble with their back. After a short pause there was no response, so I asked her to ask the Lord when this person first felt the pain, and after a moment or two of prayer she said that it was in a physical education lesson in school. Again, a pause and no response. I never wanted to allow anyone to get discouraged, so I moved on explaining to the child that she may have made a mistake or else the person may have been too frightened to own up. This happened at the morning meeting.

The day passed by and when the evening meeting arrived, lo and behold, who was standing next to me on the stage but this same little girl. By now I was getting a bit embarrassed – after all, I had announced it twice, but she kept insisting that I ask again. I then realised that God was speaking to her very clearly, so I told her to walk off the stage, find the person, and bring them up to join us. As she left the platform, three children went straight up to her and said that they thought it was them but she replied that it wasn't. I knew that if I had been her I would have taken any one of these and been happy.

She walked right to the back of the hall and brought forward a lad who confessed that it was him, and with accuracy like that maybe it's not surprising that he was instantly healed as she prayed for him. It was a few months later that I met one of the leaders who explained to me the importance of this healing. The boy's parents had been going through a very hard time and were on the brink of separation, yet when they saw what God had done to their son, it not only brought them back to God, but also brought them closer together. God had used the persistence of a small Spirit-filled child.

At the other end of the country, a young eleven-year-old boy came up on stage and told me that God wanted to heal someone of asthma. When he said this about a dozen asthmatics put their hands up. I had listened carefully to what the boy had said, and he hadn't said twelve but one, so it was his job to find out which one God wanted to be healed through him. I asked if he knew who the person was to which he replied no. Then I asked if it was a boy or a girl, he said a boy. I then asked what age this boy was, and he replied ten. By now most had been eliminated, but there were still three left. I finally asked where this boy came from. Humanly speaking there was no way that he could have known, the children came from all over the country. He named a town. There was just one young lad out there from that town, and God instantly healed him. I am convinced that if I had asked the boy at the front to ask God for their telephone number he would have got it.

Only a couple of examples, but since that time we have seen thousands healed, ranging from dyslexia, deafness and heart disease to the common old veruccas, warts and ingrowing toenails. And these have happened as the children, not I, have prayed for people. Their potential in God has remained untapped for centuries by the church.

It was in January 1983 that I became part of Gerald Coates' Pioneer team. As I mentioned earlier, Gerald had a reputation for being a colourful and controversial character (still has), but both he and his wife, Anona, became very close to Irene and me. Gerald taught me such major things as what commitment means, what a real relationship is, and what it means to honour people and be submissive. When most people rang up to speak to me and found that I was not at home, they would promptly say they would ring back. But Gerald always saw Irene as being as important as me and would take time to ask how things were and to find out from her if everything was all right, which brought to my attention what an important part of my ministry Irene is and how much her wisdom has meant to me.

Touring nationally brings its own unique pressures and that is why it was so important to me to meet up with Gerald and my other good friends on the Pioneer team and allow them to have access into my life. I never felt vulnerable with them as I knew that whatever they felt that they needed to say, it was coming from hearts that wanted the best for me.

Our own fellowship grew very rapidly after the new start, and as well as having access into the other leaders' lives, our local leaders became true friends and, because the old hurts healed completely, I enjoyed great trust in their counsel and advice as well. A real friendship had also been struck up with the ex-members of Rev Counta, and after apologies and prayer we at last found a closeness that we had never experienced in the band days and respected each other in ways that we never had before.

As the Praise Parties grew and flourished, so I began to gain respect for my work with children. After missing only one year at Spring Harvest, I was interviewed by the Executive Committee to see whether I would be suitable to take on some of their children's work. I passed my audition and called our thing 'The Glorie Company'. In the first year we were given responsibility over a couple of hundred children, but as I had a very strong team of workers, plus a few brand-new ideas up my sleeve, this was very successful. From then onwards we were responsible for up to eight hundred children between the ages of nine to eleven each week.

The mornings were recreational and the evenings were praise and teaching put over in an exciting way with me leading a full-scale professional rock band to provide the music. One of my aims was to upgrade everything to do with children, from their hard-working, rarely encouraged leaders to the church budget allocated to children's work. For so long the work with this age group had been unrecognised, but now I wanted to bring it right up front and not give the children the adults' left-overs, but the very best that is available. At Spring Harvest I wanted this to be the highlight of their year. As we grew to know them, as with the adults we could see them developing spiritually and we could take them further into the exciting things of God.

I am still very careful over the speaking in tongues issue. The last thing I want to do is to teach a child the opposite of things his parents are teaching him, but neither do I want to restrict those children and workers who normally worship in this way. A little older, a little wiser? I hope so.

Along with this work, I also knew that God was using me to write worship songs that were going to be appreciated by all age groups. But I never imagined that after just sitting down for five minutes and writing what I thought was a fairly average song called 'Father God I Wonder' that God would use it to be a blessing to so many people. In fact, after I had first written it I played it through to Noel Richards who really liked it. If he hadn't, it may well have been filed away in my archives and never heard by anyone. Although I may write masses of songs, only the ones that I believe are the very best actually get air-play.

As time went on I was asked to lead the children's work at such events as Festival, Colin Urquhart's Kingdom Faith, Grapevine in Lincolnshire, plus numerous other large festivals and weekend camps. Apart from seeing many children become Christians and using spiritual gifts, one of the greatest thrills is watching them take over from my leaders and myself. I am now finding myself training up potential leaders from the age of eleven onwards.

There is no doubt about it, this generation of children is very different from any other, and at present it is taking me all my time and energy to see that the church wakes up to that fact and starts training up their little troops who are already involved in ferocious spiritual warfare every day at school and college.

An unfair criticism that I have often had levelled against me is that I am all froth and bubble and know little of the Bible. As I mentioned earlier, I will never be a theologian or master teacher, but I have always maintained that it is not only vital that children learn biblical truths but also that they discover the Bible. I am still a firm believer that there is power in Scripture, and as our Lord Jesus taught us, it is a great means of attacking the evil one as he seeks to attack us. With this in mind I went back into the studio and recorded an album made up of simple Scripture verses that the average person could learn off by heart in a very short time. I called it *Scripture Praise Party* as again, like the Praise Parties we were taking around the country, it still maintained that element of fun.

Apart from children, many leaders were starting to prophesy over me, and although none of them went against Scripture, weighing them up was never easy. One said that I would be performing to millions, which sounded great but rather unlikely. But when this same word came from a couple of other people I thought it was time to take this seriously. Coinciding with this, Geoff Booker from Kingsway introduced me to the producer and director of the religious department of our local ITV network, with the prospect of doing a series called 'The Glorie Train'.

I knew nothing about TV, but I knew a lot about the Glories and was beginnning to know a little bit about children. I saw this as being an action-packed fun show that would present Christian kids as being reasonably normal. When I arrived to be filmed at a station in Kent which has a little miniature railway, I couldn't believe my eyes when I saw three massive ITV lorries parked there plus a crew of over thirty people. As it is all still very hush-hush at the time of writing I can't let out any secrets, except to say if anything does come of this pilot, it will present a side of Christianity that has never been seen on the box before. Being so green when it came to standing in front of a camera, I was thrilled when I had the opportunity to be interviewed for another channel of ITV, as well as being part of the Spring Harvest *Songs of Praise* for the BBC. It was as if God was allowing me to have a bit of practice before the big one arrived.

So here I am, and as to what the future will hold, well only the Lord knows. Will I ever become a TV star? Will I still be bouncing around when I am sixty? Will I ever learn to tune up a guitar? Time will tell.

It's funny, but I don't seem to be controversial any more. Am I maturing or am I losing my edge? Am I giving people what they need or just giving them what they want? Have those who once opposed me changed their viewpoints and now agree with me, or have I changed mine and now agree with them? I'd like to think that we have all grown in our Christian faith – that we have all changed.

It is a few months since I began writing this autobiography, and it has been a strange experience having to relive all those years. I've laughed and wept as I've recalled them, but my aim in writing has not been self-indulgence. It has reminded me that through my successes and failures, through my joy and sadness, I'm still adamant about the fact that my life's aim is still to make Jesus happy and to be obedient to what he tells me to do. I know by doing this that I have got the most exciting, satisfying life that it is possible to have. It's time I wound Part One to a close, not because I've reached the end of the story, far from it. I still think that the best is yet to come. No, it's because I'm now up to date. I will leave you with the last chapter which shows something of what other people think of me. I told them not to be creepy but to be honest and truthful. You can judge for yourself whether you think that they have been.

It is hard for me to imagine that so much has happened over the past thirty-eight years, and it is so much easier to believe that much much more is going to happen within the next few. I'm obviously being trained up for something, but I still feel that I have a little way to go before I even start to achieve it. I wonder what it is. Maybe I'll be able to let you know in Part Two.

Keep on praising, and smiling.

Yours in his grip,

Ishmael.

21

Don't Be Afraid
(Ishmael by Others)

Don't be afraid – for those who are with us
Are more than those against us.

Ishmael is totally unlike any description you would give to 'a vicar' or 'servant of God' or 'a pastor'. He doesn't resemble anybody I've ever met in the church or any Christian circles. He doesn't have an outstandingly 'smart appearance' or 'a brilliant wit'; he is not the world's greatest musician.... In fact, when you think of it, he is probably very much like Jesus: real, down-to-earth, communicative, full of compassion, like a child – sensitive, honest and without pride, just himself. And God moves through him in amazing ways and in many places without Ishmael blinking an eyelid. Whether he is ministering or having a meal, or on the road, or spending the day with his family, or meeting the Queen or the Pope, Ishmael is just having a good time. Another day in the life of the Glorie Man. Good company he is!
BILL ANGEL *(Actor and Drama Teacher)*

Ishmael comes across as being enthusiastic in all that he does, allowing his enthusiasm to carry his imperfections.
DAVE ASTON *(Recording Engineer)*

Cheeky, impish (Puckish!), energetically relaxed, with eyes that suggest that, whatever anyone else is expecting, he expects to find pleasure. I first met Ishmael at a time when the 60s were handing over to the 70s. I met him in

company with Andy. They were a pair of likeable lads intent on communicating by entertainment. I had a sort of reunion with him in the mid-80s. I hadn't seen Ishmael for some years, and when I did the earth shook! More than two hundred young people were performing the 'life abundant bounce' in a large marquee in Staffordshire led by someone I first saw from the rear. He, too, seemed to have found means of suspending the law of gravity. Was it the untidy hair? The perspiration? The tatty jeans? The string vest? A combination of all this and more? I knew it was Ishmael. Two years later I worked with him at Spring Harvest, seeing the Pied-Piper of Prestatyn leading a roaring, excited, gymnastic gaggle of children around the camp in an almost spontaneous act of worship. Unpredictable? Indefinable? Uncategorisable? Indefatigable? Incomparable? Yes! And they love him.
GORDON BAILEY *(Schools Outreach)*

This man makes people laugh because he has learned to cry. Ishmael, above many others, has brought dignity back to children. The church often patronises them, but he honours them. I sometimes wonder if God has got Ish on a piece of elastic: how he bounces up and down and plays the guitar is a modern miracle. How often we have longed for heroes for our children – in Ish we have found one.
NORMAN BARNES *(Team Spirit)*

To know Ishmael is like waking up to a bright, warm, sunny day in the middle of winter.
DOUG BARNET *(Director, Saltmine Trust)*

To confine Ishmael's colourful character in the words of one sentence is like capturing a rainbow in a jar – impossible! What captures me is his insatiable appetite for life which is unspoiled by the cares and responsibilities of adulthood.
SUE BARNET *(Saltmine Trust)*

How does a television producer find his way to Glorieland? With difficulty, you might think, if Christian comment about the mass media is anything to go by. In fact, getting close to this jolly, energetic outpost of the Christian family is simple if you are a good map-reader and can intercept Ishmael and Irene as they career around the country energising and delighting a seemingly tireless young audience. The first time I saw Ishmael in action, the Miseries were definitely in retreat. In one of Surrey's more prosperous dormitory towns, we had to clamber over shopping trolleys and weekend shoppers to reach a much happier local centre of attraction. The Glories had stopped off on the way to set several hundred children singing and dancing, with a good deal of leaping and jumping thrown in. A normally staid community centre had become a Glorie grotto, their smiling faces peering down from the walls illuminated by multi-coloured disco lights. Some rather grown-up children were leaping about so much that it was essential to stand on a chair to see Ishmael in full cry. It was the most unlikely sermon you could ever have imagined, but the teaching and preaching was there among all the energetic cavorting.

The image of Jesus the clown has become a popular one in recent years, and even the most conservative believers have discovered that the sad and funny clown is a vivid gospel illustration. Ishmael seems to have more than a bit of a clown in him, and it's all too easy to see the Miseries with their mean plots singling him out.

Ishmael is, of course, much more than a performer. Go around with your map to one of the more obscure corners of the South coast of England and there in a quiet road is Glorieland, with the same smiling face last seen on stage to make even the latest and most lost television producer feel welcome. In the garden the neighbours' cats peer warily at a sort of extended potting shed where the Glorie operations are based. Ishmael is a performing delight; it seems that he will try anything once: I have seen him do it with hilarious results!) and yet clearly never compromise his very evident Christian commitment. It is a

shame that so few people are prepared to communicate a serious Christian faith through the gift of making the rest of us laugh. If you're looking for a man to tell a Bible story to a train full of children travelling on the world's smallest public railway while engulfed by a huge hairy dog ... Ishmael's your man.
ANDREW BARR *(Head of Religious Programmes, TVS)*

Ishmael may not be an Eric Clapton on the fretboard, or noted for his dexterity of voice, yet because he's never tried to be anybody except himself, an original, he's one of the most creative people I know.
DAVE BILBROUGH *(Musician)*

One of my first encounters with Ishmael was memorable for the fact that it was the only time I have performed on a football pitch. It was to enact the part of referee for the sleeve of his 'Ishmael United' album *If You Can't Shout Saved, You'll Have to Face the Penalty*. Working alongside him has made my knees a notable part of my anatomy around the world. It is impossible to be with Ishmael and not catch his boundless enthusiasm and energy, both of which bring an extra sparkle to life. He has a unique ministry and is one of God's special people.
GEOFF BOOKER *(Director, Kingsway Publications)*

Once met, Ishmael is never forgotten! This is not to say that we appreciate absolutely everything that he says and does, but as parents of young children we are thrilled to see how the next generation of boys and girls are being challenged and blessed by the Captain of the Glorie Company – and we thank God for him!
LYNDON AND CELIA BOWRING *(Care Trust)*

There is no doubt in my mind that through Ishmael's commitment and submission to God, we have all been rewarded with a wonderfully joyful, but gentle and con-

siderate man. His aim to reflect God is of immeasurable value.
TERL BRYANT *(Drummer)*

As someone who has memorised more Scripture verses from Ishmael's bounce-along songs than I ever did using those little memory cards that were always getting left in my shirt pocket and washed, I can vouch for the effective, fun way he uses his music to teach families about God! Colourful yes, controversial in people's eyes. But what impresses me so much is that it is clear that his whole aim is to do what he sees God calling him to.
ANDY BUTCHER *(Editor, Family Magazine)*

Ishmael has a kind of optimism that springs from an irrepressible faith in God's goodness. He seems uncomplicated but he is not superficial, and he has a rare ability to make the profound accessible. He has earned many friends, not least among children, whose love and trust is well placed in this warm-hearted 'bear' of a man.
NICK BUTTERWORTH *(Artist)*

Ishmael has good friends, new friends, and still one or two surviving old friends. As one who remembers him from hard-hitting, anti-charismatic, feet-on-the-ground, long-haired, folk-singing days, I think I come in the last category. Working with Ish over sixteen years has been a revelation. His capacity for loving people is something that I will always carry with me. When my eldest daughter Vicki, as a little four-year-old, was brought to trust Jesus for the first time by Ishmael, I never guessed how faithful he would be in his follow-up. Every few months a letter, tape or visit comes. She really looks forward to these times – and the seven years in which he has acted in this way have been a demonstration of what it means to be faithful in caring for our children in the gospel.

Ishmael is also delightfully funny. His humour and ingenuity have brought the word 'parable' into a twentieth-century context. Although likely to upset the apple-

cart and disturb the status quo, Ish has always tried to be completely consistent and faithful in his testimony to both his Lord and to Scripture. He has never maintained that his own position is one that all others should follow, but that God has given him something unique to share with children, and he has sought to be faithful to that calling in bringing to many children, and parents alike, the sense of the joy and the love which comes from Jesus alone. In his own family his children have a unique place in his ministry, and Irene is never far from his side in support. I hope this ministry will go on for many more years, but whether you can keep bouncing at forty is another matter entirely.
CLIVE CALVER *(General Secretary, Evangelical Alliance)*

Ishmael – the world's greatest example of a real-life walking, talking, leaping, laughing, dancing, bouncing Glorie. Not only does he sound and act like one, he even looks like one!
STEVE CHALKE *(Oasis)*

At the age of forty-five (Ishmael, in fact, claims to be thirty-eight – but none of us believe that) Ishmael is the only forty-plus juvenile delinquent that I know. 'Ishmael is my friend,' says my son. Ish has become the friend of thousands of children around this country. I can't think of a higher accolade than that.
STEVE CLIFFORD *(Cobham Christian Fellowship)*

Ish has been coming over here for years, even before Glorie days. From him I have learned that it is possible to know God and see him work mightily and also have fun (having fun is rarely associated with Northern Ireland).

I'm also indebted to Ish for bringing my kids on into the practical operation of God's gifts and not just a head-knowledge of such things.
RODNEY CORDNER *(Musician/Northern Ireland)*

Should I outlive my old mate Ishmael, I would like to inscribe upon his gravestone: 'He looked as though he

never knew what he was doing.' However, that is the art of a true master – making what he does look easy. Ishmael has made a relationship with Jesus, and the baptism in the Holy Spirit, as well as harmony and joy in families, look easy. That is why thousands upon thousands have been blessed through his ministry at events, through his albums, and now his book. I wish him and all his endeavours success in every sense of that word.
GERALD COATES *(Pioneer Team Leader)*

Ishmael and his wife, Irene, are good friends of ours and we've enjoyed happy fellowship as well as praying through times of difficulty and spiritual attack. I pray that his influence will continue to spread – for where Ishmael goes, that's where Jesus is.
ANONA COATES

One paragraph is not much space in which to describe any man, let alone someone as original as Ishmael. There is no doubt that original is exactly what the man is. The thing that impresses me about him more than anything else is that he is always himself. St Paul could write, 'I have become all things to all men that I might by all means win some.' If Ish was asked to paraphrase that I think he would have to say, 'I am always the same to everybody, it's simpler that way and more people come to Jesus by it. Anything else is too complicated.' There is a child-like simplicity about this which is reminiscent of Jesus himself. As far as I am concerned, no matter how I feel I am always glad to see Ish because he is always glad to see me. The man is one of the most loyal friends I have ever known. He has many gifts and many abilities, and in spite of the apparent simplicity of his approach to life and to evangelism, he is a person of deep feelings and profound insights. However, in the end I would have to say that his greatest gift is simply who he is. Ish is unrepeatable, inimitable, occasionally I am sure unbearable, often inexplicable, but always incomparably himself. That is his gift and it is one of the best gifts that God ever gave to the church in this country. He combines in one person all the pathos and all the fun of being a child of God in a fallen world and this is something which seems to be stronger as the years go by. In other words, like a fine wine or strong cheese, he is maturing with age.

God bless you, Ish. May there be many more like you.
ERIC DELVE *(Evangelist)*

Ishmael is a walking combination of a Rugby League football match, Billy Smart's Circus, and the American Marine Corps. In short (and he is fairly short), meeting him is a memorable experience! I first met Ish about ten years ago, and I must admit my first impression was 'This guy can't be serious'. But as with many of my first impressions, prejudice blocked the view. If you want to know the true measure of the man, then watch him with a room full of kids. Take a group of stroppy ten-year-old boys who have eaten a few Sunday school teachers for dinner, and let Ish loose with them for an hour. With warmth and sensitivity, humour and affection, profundity and simplicity he will tackle the priestly task of bringing people to God and God to people. He teaches children and adults alike that spirituality is meant to be utterly natural. I am no 'bouncing Glorie', but when it comes to a man like Ish I believe that every church should have one like him.
IAN COFFEY *(Director of Evangelism, Saltmine Trust)*

Both Tina and I have known Ish for many years. Perhaps the only Christian who could sell me a second-hand car! Perhaps described as the 'Atila the Hun' of praise. We should be OK at the end times, especially if he's leading some part of the praising! A man like myself, not afraid to be seen going into the local pub, even if the Pope was watching. One of the Guvner's Great Clowns.
DAVE COOKE AND TINA HEATH

Believe it or not, Ishmael was once a theological student. His ebullient personality shattered the solemn moments of lectures in Biblical Philosophy and Systema-

tic Theology. His tutors, without a word of knowledge, knew that he was not destined for a career in divinity. This hairy, rustic, rotund bundle of energy, who bounces like a rubber ball and exudes an uninhibited enthusiasm, deposits a Christian faith that is infectious. His gravelly voice and strident guitar chords reflect that determination of a Christian warrior who is both bold and strong because the Lord God is with him. Long live Ishmael, may God truly make of him, as his namesake, a great nation!
ELDIN R. CORSIE *(Principal, Elim Bible College)*

It's a good job I don't live too near to Ish. I could easily catch what he's got.
JOFF DAY *(Communications, Harvestime)*

We have known Ish from his earliest days with Andy. He has always been a pioneer and is not afraid to put his neck on the chopping-block. On one occasion he came to sing at one of our crusade services, in the tent. It was a youth night and he incurred the displeasure of many of the team by the way he was dressed, for in those days it was a radical thing to do. Today it is quite common at such events, thanks in no small part to Ish.
DON DOUBLE *(Good News Crusade)*

I believe Ishmael has exactly what so many pastors and parents and their children long for ... someone with some answers that are being explained in ways that kids can get hold of. Of the many answers I see Ish give the kids for the questions that they must ask, the most important is his example of being someone who has found his questions answered in the person of Jesus Christ. Ishmael expresses a relationship with Jesus that is uncomplicated, real and tangible. These qualities draw kids to a God whose love they can begin to understand through the ministry the Lord has given Ish.
WAYNE DRAIN *(Singer/Songwriter)*

Ishmael is: an embarrassing situation about to occur, a

word from the Lord just when you need it, a greasy joe, an early-morning alarm call, a fizzy Alka Seltzer, a packet of vitamin pills, a ganges revenge, a second-hand market stall, a kiddies' joke book, one long PACMAN, a gadget going wrong, a dating agency, a hammer with a liking for nails, God's loudhailer, a pint of Buddy, a summer breeze, the first person to visit when you're in hospital, not to be underestimated but always to be trusted.
ROGER ELLIS *(Revelation Christian Fellowship)*

Many are called to be prophets to their own generation, but relatively few have the privilege of prophesying to the next. Ishmael will be revered by thousands of adults in the significant years ahead as the prophet who pointed the way in their childhood.
ROGER & FAITH FORSTER *(Ichthus Christian Fellowship)*

Everyone knows what an amazing singing voice Ishmael possesses (!). Not many people realise that he is the finest Japanese Sumo wrestler that England has ever produced.
GARY GIBBS *(Evangelist)*

Like most of life's natural clowns, there's a serious, feeling and thinking bloke behind the smile. But the beauty of Ishmael is that *both* sides are real and open – he's a constant source of consistent encouragement and energy, uncompromisingly blunt, generous but canny (any Scots blood there, Ish?), prophetic in much he does and says (usually spot on, but watch out for those things that are just good ideas), and all mixed up with a lot of fun. And yes, I *have* forgiven you the banana trick, Ishmael!
PETE GILBERT *(Escapologist and evangelist)*

Ishmael is fun, He has the gift of laughter, he makes you relax, trust and let go of the junk you're carrying. We go back a long way to the Ish and Andy days, but even in the dim and distant Ish was always positive and gave people a sense of their own worth and value. He never

strokes his audience, he is never smooth or cheap. He has a genuine, earthy, rustic honesty of approach and a passionate concern that folk should know who Jesus is and what they are leaving out of their lives if they choose to ignore his love gift for them. Ishmael is a mover and shaker – watch out!
NIGEL GOODWIN *(Genesis Arts)*

I can remember quite clearly the first time I met Ishmael. It was in 1979 at a gospel presentation held in Norwich. I was playing drums for a Christian singer and 'Ishmael United' were appearing on the same programme. I had previously heard of this so-called 'Christian punk' band, and had already formed an opinion of what they would be like. When I walked into the theatre and saw them on stage rehearsing, I thought my worst fears had been confirmed!

Later on that day, everybody who was taking part met for prayer. I wasn't quite ready for what happened next. Instead of the usual 'formal' and 'nice' prayer meetings I had been used to, this one was noisy, lively and exciting, and I found myself almost hanging on to my seat as the whole place took off. Here was this 'Christian punk' band praying and calling on God with a depth and reality I hadn't known before. For me it was a bit like Pentecost all over again. So much for my preconceived ideas. It proved to be a real provocation in my own life as I sought God for this kind of reality.

Since that time I've come to regard Ish as not only a really good friend but also someone I respect for his honesty and openness to God and others.
RAY GOUDIE *(Heartbeat)*

Ishmael is a man with his feet on the ground and his heart in the heavenlies. Through all the years I have never known anyone who can so motivate children in worship or lead them so securely into the things of the Spirit of God. I thank God for this gift to the body of Christ.
JIM GRAHAM *(Gold Hill Baptist Church)*

In my work in the streets and prisons in this country, many youngsters believe that being a Christian means 'giving up – being miserable', even worshipping a Jesus who is dead. Ishmael continually shows the joy one gets when they come to Christ – shows it, lives it, loves it, and this he passes on to his youngsters.
BRIAN GREENAWAY *(Prison Evangelist)*

I first met Ishmael in Newcastle-on-Tyne Cathedral. I'd been sent there to view the concert by 'Parchment' who were all the rage. Ishmael and Andy were a supporting item. The 1,000 plus kids seemed to go with the supporting item. As I was there to interview the group on behalf of BBC Radio Teesside for the religious slot, and as the group didn't seem overkeen to talk to me, I ended up talking to Ishmael. He generously gave me my first interview.

My second meeting with Ish was two or three years later in 1974 when I had agreed to take charge of two Elim churches in North London. To run two churches by yourself seemed quite a full-time task, so I wrote to Elim Bible College and asked if there was a student who would like to help me for a year. Mr Ian Smale volunteered. Almost immediately, Ian and I moved to North London and got stuck in. During that year I was due to go to South Africa to preach. I remember that I needed a few hundred pounds to pay the ticket. Ish, in a totally genuine way, came to me and said, 'Here's your ticket money.' He presented me with his whole year's grant to pay my ticket. This man, I realised, is the genuine article.
ADRIAN HAWKES *(Minister, New Living Ministries)*

A DEFINITIVE WORK

ISHMAEL: noun. a glowing, hairy person who even when standing still gives the impression of upward propulsion.

Verb. to express the glorious attributes of the divine with homage and thanksgiving.

Adj. jumping about till you're sick (see also 'vertical take-off' and 'trampoline', although both of these states

are mechanically assisted and thus cannot be counted as genuine Ishmaeling).
STEWART HENDERSON *(Poet)*

I have called him a modern-day Peter: mighty in the Spirit and stubborn in the flesh. He leaves most of us behind because he is willing to take incredible risks, not caring whether he looks stupid or not. He is pioneering, whereas most of us are pottering about – and I love him dearly for it.
ALFIE

I always remember doing a concert in Dover with 'Ishmael and Andy' just as I was going full time in music in 1973. We sat in a café together and they gave me advice, as they were retiring at that time. I think Ishmael's significant role has been to put some guts into the charismatic style of worship choruses. The wimpishness of some of the music was giving a less than full-blooded view of God. Ish is more than full-blooded – in fact, he is thoroughly out of control. He has knocked away some of the pietism and given people more of a sense of enjoying God.

I think I look back with most fondness to the 'Rev Counta and the Speedoze' period, which I thought was very relevant to what was happening at the time culturally. A man of sledge-hammer subtlety and manic energy – you always seem to smile when he's around – that's a gift!
GARTH HEWITT *(Recording Artist)*

I've enjoyed singing along with thousands of others 'Father God I Wonder'.
BRYN HOWARTH *(Singer)*

Ishmael: unreligious, a nutcase, generally a good bloke who loves Jesus – my sort!
MARTYN JOSEPH *(Recording Artist)*

Ishmael is by any standard a breath of fresh air, and I for one consider it a privilege to know him. He is sweet

and sincere, though a bit impetuous. He has a unique ministry, especially among children, that most parents would be grateful for.
R T KENDALL *(Westminster Chapel)*

When Ian Smale invited me to stay in his parents' house in Littlehampton, he never warned me that the house was immediately adjacent to the railway line. Lying in bed the first evening, the peace was suddenly shattered as an express train thundered with apocalyptic violence past the other side of the bedroom wall.

I took part in an evangelistic coffee bar called the 'Soul Clinic', and remember having discussions there about Christ with some French teenagers on holiday, giving me the chance to practise my 'Franglais'. I think it was there that I met a Christian band under the fascinating name of 'Something Else Entirely'. I recall there were three guys and they each displayed a word of their band's name proudly on three specially printed T-shirts as they performed in line. Needless to say, the middle band member was dubbed 'Elsie'.

My first encounter with the enigma of Ishmael was at an MGO-sponsored gospel music event in Portsmouth where we were both on the programme. At this time I was performing serious, lyrical, poetical, contemporary folk songs with more than a touch of melancholia and pathos and much intricate guitar picking. I remember being just a little peeved when on bounced this character Ishmael who proceeded with about as much subtlety as a small bomb in a public library to get a more enthusiastic response from the crowd than I had evoked. His 'secret' then, as it still is, was sheer joy and contagious enthusiasm bubbling out of a total commitment to following Jesus whatever the cost and whatever others might think or say.

One of God's eccentrics, Ishmael has a habit of breaking the rules and getting away with it through sheer enthusiasm. Purists of all kinds, singers, guitarists, preachers, evangelists and dancers will no doubt continue to flinch not a little as he leads worship or ministers, but most of them will have achieved far less in terms of bringing in the kingdom of God, especially to children.

A stranger to subtlety, Ishmael has been a kick in the rear end to the complacent, an offence to the religious, and a shot of heaven's vigorous joy to a beleaguered generation of young people into whose consciousness he has implanted the truth that following Jesus is an energetic all-or-nothing commitment.

GRAHAM KENDRICK *(Singer/Songwriter/Worship Leader)*

Ishmael is one of those people that it's easy to make an assessment of and even more easy to make the wrong assessment. Usually the wrong assessment is that there is not very much depth or understanding attached to him. Ishmael is a fun person, but he is also a very sensitive individual. He loves kids and has a great heart to see the church of God as a family and not fragmented into sections. He is extrovert and up front, he clowns around, he laughs a lot. But underneath is a deep relationship with God and a deep understanding of the needs in people's lives. He does not suffer fools gladly, and in no way could be counted a fool himself. To borrow a cliché, Ishmael to me summarises an individual who is spiritually natural and naturally spiritual. However, just in case this sounds as if he has no faults, I suppose Ishmael is essentially a pragmatic person and therefore perhaps his area of weakness lies in the realm of theology and doctrine of those things which are not the fundamentals of the faith. To sum up, I believe that he is one of God's eccentric one-offs, who I am glad to count as my friend.

RODNEY KINGSTONE *(Broadwater Christian Fellowship)*

My wife and I first heard Ishmael when he took part in our daughter Ruth's wedding to Clive Calver over fifteen years ago – an unforgettable experience! Now we hear him when our grandchildren play his tapes which they love.

GILBERT KIRBY *(Evangelical statesman ...)*

Ishmael is a strong, brave, individual character. He is caring, kind and totally dedicated to his calling.
ANDREW LEES *(Spring Harvest Administrator)*

I had heard of Ishmael's legendary bounce. What I saw gave a rubber ball, by comparison, the bounce of a dollop of custard. This nuclear bounce is harnessed to great effect in his Christian ministry. Children are so often told to shut up and be quiet, so it's refreshing to see them, with Ishmael, expressing their joy and energy to the full. Bible stories and the teaching of Christ are seen to be a path to happiness and fulfilment rather than austere restrictions.

Children find Ishmael an irresistible 'pied piper' who leads them not only round the houses but also into quiet moments of prayer and tranquillity.

The live *Songs of Praise* from Spring Harvest, Skegness, was a great success – but I was always a little worried about the stability of the stage. I remember watching the monitors as Ishmael launched himself into the chorus of 'Father God', hoping that he wouldn't out-bounce himself and suddenly disappear into a splintery hole! All held firm and the song, I'm sure, set the nation alight.
CHRIS MANN *(Producer,* Songs of Praise, *BBC)*

I wish I had his energy!
DAVE MARKEE *(Musician)*

I first met Ishmael at Spring Harvest in 1983. I was a bewildered speaker trying to find my way around this massive conference, and Ishmael and family saw my need for hospitality and fellowship and took me under their wing. They invited me into their bungalow at Spring Harvest and shared some fine fare. Although we have not had opportunity to spend a lot of time together, I have come to appreciate the serious side of Ishmael, knowing that he has a great longing to bring people into a full release of the Holy Spirit in their walk with the Lord.

I've also seen the fruit of Ishmael's ministry in several fellowships that I've had contact with around Great

Britain. He has helped people to grow in freedom and worship and to experience the reality of spiritual gifts. I consider him to be one of those of God's servants who has really discovered what humility means, for anyone who knows how to minister to children has discovered humility.

Of course, Ishmael is not all seriousness. He is also a man who knows how to laugh, both with others and at himself, and I find that a rare and wonderful combination. Far too many of us take ourselves too seriously and can't have a good laugh – not so for Ishmael. He is a man who loves life, and what better testimony could there be for a Christian?

FLOYD McCLUNG *(Youth With A Mission)*

Ishmael is a cork bursting out of a champagne bottle, a spring that has been sprung, a caged animal set free – all at once. Just reading his name makes me feel tired!

PETE MEADOWS *(Consultant)*

I got to know Ian really well during our time together in 'Ishmael United', latterly 'Rev Counta and the Speedoze'. Although with two strong personalities it was inevitable that we had our ups and downs, they were times that, looking back, I wouldn't have missed. Ian is someone who has always followed his own convictions and underneath all the clowning and lunacy there is a man who is committed to seeing God's kingdom extended. It is a mistake to think that his ministry is only for kids, and increasingly in the future I believe God will use him mightily in other ways. I learned so much from my years in the band with Ian, not least that humour is a very effective way of getting things across. Ian possesses this quality in great abundance and I hope his book sells millions of copies! [So do I – Ish.]

LAURIE MELLOR *Consultant/Author)*

Ishmael! Probably the best laughter in the world. With love, appreciation and gratitude.

MIKE & KATEY MORRIS *(Evangelical Alliance/Authors)*

Ish is your typical thirty-eight-year-old teenager – always on the move. His neck would probably break out in a rash if called upon to wear a tie, and his feet also if told they couldn't dance. His brand of 'glory' is not for adults, whatever their age, but for the young in heart, whatever *their* age!
CHRISTINE NOBLE *(Team Spirit)*

As his name suggests, Ishmael is one of God's glorious enigmas. He combines an incredible lack of subtlety and finesse with the ability to write lyrics that, in the main, make adults want to scream with pain. The only problem is that the Lord has seen fit to give him a heavy anointing and a complete acceptance by 98% of all children under ninety-five. I have a question, Father – 'Is this really fair?'
JOHN NOBLE *(Team Leader, Team Spirit)*

Ishmael is one of God's clowns. Heaven needs its court jesters, but it is a costly calling. Many are called but few are chosen. They will be nobodies in the public eye. The sophisticated will think them simple. They will be laughed at even when their hearts are breaking. Adults can be very childish.

Yet the childlike will understand. Laughter and tears will jostle as the comedies and tragedies of life are enacted. For this is no caricature. This is the real stuff of life. Misery and glory are the warp and woof of human experience.

Some will object to this basic division of people into two categories. They object to black-and-white contrasts, believing that most of us are shades of grey. Life is more complicated than that. We are a mixture, alternating between depression and elation.

'Land of Hope and Glories' is prophetic, which means that the present is seen in the light of the future. And at the end of the day there are only two places because there will be only two sorts of people. The Glories will be in heaven and the Miseries will be in hell.

Ishmael knows that there are only two roads along

which we may walk. Baptism in water and baptism in the Holy Spirit have been for him and countless others vital steps on the one that leads to glory. He is unashamed to urge them on to others. The onus is on those who object, to prove from Scripture that they may be bypassed.

This fool for Christ's sake is really asking, 'Whose fool are you?' Pride and prejudice could resent the question – and the questioner. Or you could become as a little child for half an hour and may even hear the chuckle of a heavenly Father? For he will be listening with you. After all, Ishmael means 'God hears'.

DAVID PAWSON

It is a pleasure to be a friend of this prehistoric man turned glorie.

PHIL AND JOHN *(Recording Artists)*

How can I write about you? It would be different if you'd died, then I could say what I liked! You're my brother, and I don't mean just in the Christian sense. You're more a part of my life than you'll probably ever know. I'm proud to be your brother, and anybody who wants to get at you had better be willing to answer to me!

ANDY PIERCY

Ishmael is a spiritual Alka Seltzer. He infuses energy and bubbly enthusiasm and is committed to getting things moving.

DAVE POPE *(Worship Leader, Saltmine Trust)*

Ishmael is someone I think of as a man free in the Holy Spirit, expressing the joy of the Lord in the ways we would all (secretly) like to. He is a 'one off', someone I would affectionately refer to as 'one of God's eccentrics' – even if he is still under forty.

MIKE PUSEY *(Leader, The King's Church)*

Ishmael is, to quote one of his songs, 'naturally supernatural'. His life and his ministry show people, particu-

larly youngsters, that they can follow Jesus and be wonderfully normal at the same time.
MICK RAY *(Songwriter)*

Ishmael is one of the few Christian leaders in Britain who is actually saying and doing anything of significance. He is a major influence on this generation and a hero to the kids!

The pompous and religious have tried to knock him down, but he always bounces back. Thankfully, he will be around long after they have fallen from their pedestals into the sea of irrelevance.
NOEL RICHARDS *(Singer/Songwriter, Pioneer Team)*

He is always good for a laugh and a Chinese meal, and he has the ability to say deep things simply. Great sense of humour.
JOHN RITTER *(Keep in Step)*

Anyone who holds their wallpaper up with gaffa tape is all right by me! Ish has been a very encouraging bloke over the enormous amount of years I have known him.
SUE RITTER *(Keep in Step)*

Don't be fooled by his jovial exterior. Underneath there is a serious, thoughtful pastor trying to get out.
DAVE ROBERTS *(Youth With A Mission)*

Of all the people I've had the privilege to work with and for, Ishmael is, to use a well-worn phrase, the most supernaturally natural and naturally supernatural. My wife loves him. And I hate consistently having to tune his guitar for him. Praise the Lord for electronic guitar tuners.
CHRIS ROLINSON *(Worship Leader/Recording Artist)*

My first picture of Ish remains strongest: a crazy hippy sitting on the floor playing a guitar brightly painted with a map of the world on the front.
BEV SAGE *(The Technos)*

It would be impossible to be around Ishmael for long and not be affected by his real and uncomplicated expression of the joy of knowing Jesus. The lives of thousands of children have been changed through contact with Ishmael's ministry, but he will always be special to Pauline and me because he took time out with our kids and made a difference.
PETER SANDERSON *(Minister/Author)*

Ishmael is a man who enjoys his food – my first meal with him was a fourteen-course Javanese meal, and since that time I always seem to meet him either in the Spring Harvest Big Top Restaurant or the Chinese take-away in Minehead.
COLIN B SAUNDERS *(Chairman, Joint Projects Executive, Spring Harvest)*

Ishmael is somebody who has a great vision for reaching people for Christ and is determined to 'go for it' without being distracted by other soft options.
GEOFF SHEARN *(Just Music)*

Ish and his ministry are quite unique. Some may say that is a good thing, but really we need more of his sold-out, on fire, get 'em moving, 100% dedicated *sacrificial* praise. Let's face it, nobody feels like praising the Lord all the time, not even St Ishmael, but when we make a sacrifice of our 'feelings' God is honoured and pleased and lifts us up into the heavenly places. As an American, I appreciate Ish's style, which breaks down the barrier of your 'English reserve' in a way which imports cannot do. The Glorie Company refreshes the hearts other bands cannot reach!
GEOFFREY STEVENSON *(Mime Artist)*

Ishmael is to music as Genghis Khan is to etiquette.
STEVE STICKLEY *(Director, Footprints Theatre Company)*

I first knew Ishmael as a pre-teenager in the days of

'Turn to Christ' in Worthing, then as part of the 'Ishmael and Andy' duo. I have followed the growth of his ministry into BYFC and eventually the Glorie Company, alongside his pastoring in Elim churches. I have watched with great interest the development of one of the finest communicators to children today. At no stage of his development did I envisage such an outcome, but whatever the 'in-thing' in British churches, Ishmael has always been one step ahead, often causing great criticism of himself and misunderstanding of his ministry, but going on anyway. His ability to lead children into forms of worship that many adults have not grasped yet never ceases to amaze me.
TONY STONE

I recognise in Ishmael a great man of God, even if he is almost forty. The problem with men of God who are filled with the Spirit is that they are sometimes difficult to be with. I make the same distinction with Smith Wigglesworth, who also served the Lord.
KEN TAYLOR *(Justice of the Peace)*

During my time as the National Youth Director of the Elim Churches, Ishmael was stepping out into his unique ministry. He was often misunderstood by many of his contemporaries and by those of an older generation, but those who had a discerning spirit could see that this young man had a view to win the unchurched for Christ. His sincerity has been without question ever since I have known him, and although his methods may not have been of a traditional nature, there is no doubt that he has contacted hundreds and hundreds of people whom some other evangelists would never have contacted with the gospel. Only eternity will reveal what Ishmael's ministry has accomplished. There are names which have been written in the Lamb's book of life because this man dared to step out and face the current of criticism which was fierce on many occasions. His heart was right and at the end of the day man looks on the outward appearance but God looks

on the heart.
PASTOR ALEXANDER TEE *(Minister of the City Temple, Cardiff)*

Travelling twenty-one gruelling days, eating and drinking in many restaurants and pubs, setting up and tearing down a sound system and musical instruments in twenty-two venues, gave me some insight into the powerful ministry in the humour of Ishmael. Sometimes hilarious, sometimes painfully honest, but always seasoned with the ministry of Jesus.
DONN C THOMAS *(Recording Artist/Pastor, Abundant Life Church, Georgia)*

In the ever growing world of Christian arts, many performers try to develop a style that is different from their contemporaries. Ishmael, however, is quite unique. Sometimes he's outrageous, sometimes he's just plain funny, but no matter where he is or who he's with, you can rest assured that he'll have something to say that will challenge the very roots of your Christianity. On a personal note, I find him refreshingly different and wish him a long and happy Christ-centred life.
LYNN S TODD *(Researcher, Central TV)*

Ishmael is a 'one off', a unique character. The anointing on his life makes him a great communicator of the truth and power of the gospel to young people.
COLIN URQUHART *(Director, Bethany Fellowship)*

Although Ishmael is renowned for his infectious joy and praising heart, his wholehearted commitment to winning the lost and blessing the saved (especially our children) is a wonderful blessing to the body of Christ. The church is so much richer because of his presence.
TERRY VIRGO *(Leader, New Frontiers)*

I confess, 'twas I that first attached the name Ishmael to young Ian when he was nine years old. Was it because here was a person whom 'God would hear' as the name means, or was it that I foresaw that he would become a 'wild ass of a man'? Well, neither actually, 'Ian Smale', 'Ishmael', it just seemed the thing to do at the time. Little did I know the name would stick and become Ian's professional handle. Our paths have continued to cross since those early days. Later, as the then director of British Youth for Christ, I was approached by this hairy-bearded youth – 'Do I still have to call you Uncle Phil?' – who was hoping to go into full-time Christian work. I listened to a tape of Ian singing and playing, formed an opinion, unchanged since, that he couldn't sing or play that well, but took him and Andy on as associate evangelists.

So what has been the secret of Ishmael's success? Undoubtedly, he is a born communicator, a great enthusiast, but above all he is a man who has a heart for God, which is what really matters.
PHILIP VOGEL *(Team Spirit)*

Ishmael is himself, trying to be no one else, succeeding in being what God wants him to be, telling, singing, communicating the full gospel as only he knows how, contemporary but founded on the age-old truths.
TOM WALKER *(Elim Executive)*

In the company of those who play it safe, Ishmael is a dreamer who goes for it with all his heart. I love him!
SHEILA WALSH

I am very thankful to God that he created an individual like Ishmael, even if he is bordering on the lunatic! Jo, Debbie and Naomi, our three daughters, have each been helped and encouraged to know God more through Ishmael and so use their own creativity for the Lord. Knowing him has been a very important part of their childhood and their formative years.
MARION WHITE

Probably quite unique in the history of Christian supertwits! But you can't help liking him, especially when you

know that all he does is motivated by one thing: an insatiable desire to see other people filled to overflowing with the joy of Jesus Christ.
ROB WHITE *(National Director, British Youth for Christ)*

At Pip'n'Jay we classify people like Ish as 'sane saints'. By that we mean, they keep their feet on the ground although their hearts are in heaven, they actively enjoy their faith and warmly share it and they even dare to laugh in church. Of them all, Ish is the sanest.
MALCOLM WIDDECOMBE *(Vicar, Pip'n'Jay, Bristol)*

Would you have him on your leadership team?

Could you easily distinguish between a wild idea and a special revelation from God which is seeking to break through your own natural reserve and caution?

Would you attempt to curb his extremes?

Would you seek to advise and guide him?

What is his ministry anyway – an evangelist, a prophet, a musician, a worship leader, a children's worker?

I would say he is basically a stirrer – a good stirrer used by God to challenge, encourage and motivate, and he can do that for any age group. Ian, you have stirred me, you have challenged, encouraged and taught me much. You have helped me find greater freedom and closeness with God. You have blessed our children and family in countless ways. You have tried my patience and borrowed my car.

But my life has been so enriched by having you as a brother-in-law. I believe the Fellowship here has been so enriched by your input, which is very great.

There are thousands of people who have been converted, healed, refreshed and blessed in so many ways by your ministry.

Thank you, we love and appreciate you very much.
DAVID THATCHER *(Fellow leader of Rustington Christian Fellowship and Brother-in-law)*

Ishmael and the Glorie Company can be contacted at
PO Box 828
Rustington
Littlehampton
West Sussex
BN16 3NS
For details on Glorie Company products, please enclose sae.

Ishmael's Photo Album

Ishmael the Young Worshipper

Lucky Heather

The Quiet Time

Old Rectory

Dad, Mum and Me all ready for church

Flower Power Fred, Alfie and The Handsome Beasts

The Psychedelic Car

Uncle Allan versus my long hair

Ish and Andy

Here comes the Groom

The Pastor's Flock

Ishmael United

Rev Counta and The Speedoze

Little Suzy

The Glorie Road Show

God's Clown

Glorie Company Band

A little older, a little wiser

Angels With Dirty Faces

by Ishmael

Ishmael loves children. Here's how—and why.

'Through all the years I've never known anyone who can so motivate children in worship, or lead them so securely into the things of the Spirit of God.'

—Jim Graham, Pastor, Goldhill Baptist Church.

Children Of The Voice

by Ishmael

He was Little Trouble by name, because the grown-ups who ruled Oldchurch thought he must be that by nature. Keep the Littlehorrors out of Real Church, and, when they show signs of growing up, leave them to the Bigwideworld.

But Little Trouble wants to hear the Voice—the One everyone says they go to church for. Fed up with Oldchurch, he sets off on his quest, passing on his way through Crosscountry, Wastetime University and the alluring Securicity.

He has a lot to learn, some new friends to make, and some surprising enemies. And at the end of it all, he has to go back to Oldchurch...

This is Ishmael's first work of fiction, blending the mood of *Pilgrim's Progress* and *Animal Farm*. Fun for any age, it speaks volumes about the divisions we so often try to maintain between God's older children and his younger ones.

Also by Ishmael in Kingsway paperback: *The History of Ishmael Part One* and *Angels with Dirty Faces*.

Children Of The Voice 2

by Ishmael

Children of the Voice 2...the story continues.

Little Christian, Buddy, Harmony and Angela are settling in at Newchurch, but the Enemy Superpower's won't leave them alone for long. Evil Professor Mindwarpt and scheming Greedy Gutrot send in an invasion of robot Littlekids to trick the Children of the Voice. With the Voice and the Manual to guide them, the Newchurch Littlekids enter a new battle.

Heavy Shepherd, Dodgy Prophet, Lucy Morals and Percy Cutor all sneak in to do their worst. Will their wicked plans succeed?

Sometimes gripping, sometimes hilarious, this little book cuts right to the heart of the problems and joys facing the church of 2000 AD.

Another page-turner for Littlekids and kids at heart. Fiction that's taken from fact, and a warning to all future Newchurch leaders.

Also by Ishmael in Kingsway paperback: *Children of the Voice, The History of Ishmael Part One*, and *Angels With Dirty Faces*.